# COST-EFFECTIVE TECHNICAL SERVICES

## HOW TO TRACK, MANAGE, AND JUSTIFY INTERNAL OPERATIONS

edited by

## GARY M. PITKIN

NEAL-SCHUMAN PUBLISHERS, INC.

NEW YORK            LONDON

Published by Neal-Schuman Publishers, Inc.
23 Leonard Street
New York, NY 10013

Copyright © by Neal-Schuman Publishers

Printed and bound in the United States of America

*Library of Congress Cataloging-in-Publication Data*

Cost-effective technical services.

  Bibliography: p.
  Includes index.
  1. Processing (Libraries)—Cost effectiveness.
I. Pitkin, Gary M., 1947–
Z688.5.C66   1989        025.02        89-12229
ISBN 1-55570-041-1

# Contents

iii

# Introduction

In today's climate of tight money combined with spiraling costs, library managers are being held to increasingly stringent standards of accountability for the costs of internal operations. A primary target for cost measurement and containment is technical services. Managers must justify expenses for production—ordering, receiving, check-in, claiming, and cataloging. To make matters worse, these are areas often considered likely candidates for automation in order to effect long-term savings in both time and money. But if automation is proposed, with its attendant initial costs, justifying these costs becomes even more urgent.

*Cost-Effective Technical Services* is a response to the pressing need to solve the complex problems of achieving and maintaining cost-effective technical services. Based on the proceedings of an American Library Association Technical Services Costs Preconference (held in New York in June 1986), it has been substantially updated and edited to incorporate the latest developments in cost analysis.

Sponsored by the Resources and Technical Services Division's Technical Services Costs Committee, the preconference addressed questions such as: How can a manager best utilize cost-effectiveness studies? How is cost-effectiveness determined? How is proper methodology applied, and why is it necessary? What have other libraries done to monitor and contain costs? Should standards be developed?

This book is organized in three sections. The first, "The Need for Costing: A Necessity or Superficiality?" begins with a discussion of costing methodologies and applications appropriate for all types of libraries, as well as a debate over the necessity for vs. the superficiality of costing. Five reaction papers, of agreement, disagreement, and amplification, conclude this section.

Eight case studies are detailed in the second section, two each in acquisitions, cataloging, serials, and technical services. They represent exercises in accountability and cost-effectiveness conducted in academic, public, and medical libraries in a variety of areas, including cataloging and serials.

The last section explores the issues of standardizing operational costs for the purposes of uniform study and application—an approach being attempted in Great Britain. A recent study of cataloging costs in selected Association of Research Libraries member libraries is considered as a possible precursor to standardization.

An exhaustive annotated bibliography on technical services costs includes over 300 citations covering studies published through 1988. We hope that *Cost-Effective Technical Services* will provide solid information and valuable guidance for decision making to directors, deputy and assistant directors, department heads, and business managers in all types of libraries who are faced with determining and justifying operational costs.

*Gary Pitkin*

# 1
# The Need for Costing: A Necessity or Superficiality?

# Introduction

## Kenneth J. Bierman

Session One of the ALA Preconference consisted of three papers dealing with the issues of costing library processes and services. Gordon Shillinglaw's "keynote" paper presents a wealth of factual information about costing, which he likens to a quick trip through Accounting 101. He covers both responsibility accounting and activity costing and emphasizes the use of cost-based estimates in decision-oriented management systems. A careful reading (or perhaps two careful readings) of this presentation will greatly enrich the novice's understanding of vocabulary and concepts in the discipline of cost accounting.

In the next paper, Malcolm Getz explains and defends the usefulness and importance of cost information in making management decisions about the future. At the Preconference, Getz was speaking to the already-converted—otherwise, why would participants have paid to attend a conference on costing? To illustrate the usefulness of cost data for decision making, he presents three ways that library managers might use cost analysis.

In his paper, Del Williams plays the cynic (or devil's advocate) in arguing that cost studies in libraries are a waste of time because they are not accurate and they are not useful (or at least are not used) in making management decisions in libraries. The paper is an interesting contrast to the first two. As you might expect, his position was vehemently attacked by the conference participants, but I believe there is much truth in what he says in terms of *current* practice in library management and decision making. The future may prove that the profession is moving toward Getz's view of library management and is leaving behind William's view. Clearly this was what the majority in attendance hoped.

The first section of *Technical Services Costs* presents five reaction papers following the first three papers. The reaction papers were not presented but were solicited from attendees after the conference. Denise Bedford responds to Getz and Williams by first identifying and then both supporting and challenging their underlying assumptions.

Kenneth J. Bierman is Assistant Director of the Tucson Public Library, Tucson, Arizona.

Robert Miller provides a manager's perspective on the real costs of doing accurate and useful cost studies as well as the costliness of ignorance! He concludes that managers must have a sound understanding of the uses, abuses, and pitfalls of cost accounting and then decide in each instance whether the potential benefit of knowing the cost is worth the cost of the study.

Joe Hewitt eloquently defends the usefulness, indeed the necessity, of cost information about technical processes in libraries. He methodically challenges a number of Williams's fundamental points.

The reaction papers are rounded out by Jennifer Younger and Pamela Brown. Younger provides an interesting and intertwined analysis of all three presentations but, like Hewitt, pays particular attention to the antagonist Williams. Brown questions the usefulness of cost information for the typical (that is, small) public library. She concludes that being knowledgeable and realistic about costs is vital if we are to serve the public's needs as effectively and efficiently as possible.

# Costing Methods and Applications

## Gordon Shillinglaw

What does "cost accounting" mean? And how is it useful to libraries? Cost accounting consists of two main parts. The first, *responsibility accounting,* is designed to identify the costs each manager is responsible for. The second, *activity costing,* attempts to identify or estimate the amount of resources each activity, product, or service requires. Each library has to decide for itself whether to develop either, both, or none of these types of cost data. Because each library's situation is unique, what's right for one system may be totally wrong for another.

## RESPONSIBILITY ACCOUNTING

For responsibility accounting purposes, accountants view the organization—in this case, the library—as a set of *responsibility centers,* each the province of a manager who has an obligation to use the center's resources effectively. The accountants then identify the resources each manager has used and the benefits each has generated. At the end of each accounting period, they prepare reports, comparing these results with target performance standards—goals the center should have achieved during the period. Differences between actual results and the performance standards are known as *variances.* The managers, usually with the accountants' help, analyze these variances and try to decide what responses are appropriate.

The three most important facets of responsibility accounting are: the cost performance standards management may choose; the cost account structure for responsibility centers; and the role of allocations in responsibility accounting.

Gordon Shillinglaw is Professor of Accounting at the Graduate School of Business, Columbia University, New York.

Cost Performance Standards

A cost performance standard should identify the amount of cost appropriate to the level of output the responsibility center has achieved. In service organizations such as libraries, output is determined in large measure by the demands placed on individual responsibility centers—books to be purchased and processed, inquiries to be answered, and so on. Given current facilities and staffing levels, the manager can do little to alter these demands.

Cost performance standards in these situations must be sensitive to the amount of cost variability in the responsibility center. If all of its costs are *fixed*—that is, if they aren't expected to change in response to variations in service demand once the cost budget has been set—the amount of budgeted cost is the appropriate cost performance standard. If any costs are *variable,* however—that is, if they are expected to change in response to output variations—the performance standard should be adjusted to the center's actual output level. In a very simple situation, you might calculate the performance standard from a formula such as:

$$\begin{array}{c} \text{Budgeted} \\ \text{cost} \end{array} = \begin{array}{c} \text{Fixed cost} \\ \text{per period} \end{array} + \begin{array}{c} \text{Variable cost} \\ \text{per output unit} \end{array} \times \begin{array}{c} \text{No. of output} \\ \text{units achieved} \end{array}$$

This kind of performance standard is called a *flexible budget.* The standard and its accompanying performance comparisons have a very short-term focus. Costs may equal the budgeted amounts even though current staffing levels are wrong for the long term. We generally try to get at that by calculating unit cost ratios—for example, $23 a book or $1.10 per item circulated. A high cost ratio may signal the need for a staff reduction; a low cost ratio may point to a need for more staff.

Responsibility Center Costs

Costs for responsibility accounting have two basic dimensions: the responsibility center in which they occur and the kinds of resources they represent. For example, the salary of the reference librarian in the fine arts library might be coded 24–01, where 24 is the identification code for the fine arts library and 01 is the code for professional salaries.

A typical two-dimensional coding structure is shown in Exhibit 1. This is only a partial listing, of course. Technical Services, for example, encompasses major subareas, including acquisitions, cataloging, catalog maintenance, and preservation. The code number for catalog maintenence might be 339, and additional digits could be added to identify even finer organizational subdivisions.

EXHIBIT 1.   Responsibility Center Cost Codes.

| | Responsibility Center | | | | |
|---|---|---|---|---|---|
| | *01* . . | *11* . . | *24* . . | *31* . . | *33* |
| | *University Librarian* | *Social Sciences Library* | *Fine Arts Library* | *Special Collections* | *Technical Services* |
| 01 Professional salaries | 01.01 | 11.01 | 24.01 | 31.01 | 33.01 |
| 02 Wages | 01.02 | 11.02 | 24.02 | 31.02 | 33.02 |
| 03 Benefits | 01.03 | 11.03 | 24.03 | 31.03 | 33.03 |
| 04 Supplies | 01.04 | 11.04 | 24.04 | 31.04 | 33.04 |
| . . | . | . | . | . | . |
| 39 Sundry | 01.39 | 11.39 | 24.39 | 31.39 | 33.39 |

To use this kind of system, a data-entry clerk who is responsible for recording a particular expenditure for resources (for example, a purchase of operating supplies) simply searches the list of descriptive codes until he or she finds the one that fits best. Use the same process to identify the responsibility center in which the costs are incurred. In the initial recording of costs, these code assignments reflect the concept of *traceability*—that is, when a cost is incurred, a document identifies the responsibility center using the resources.

## Cost Allocations in Responsibility Accounting

Responsibility centers are of two main types: mission centers and service (or support) centers. Mission centers produce the goods or provide the services that constitute the organization's purpose(s) with respect to the outside world; service centers provide services or support to mission centers and to each other. In a multi-branch library system with centralized technical processing, for example, each branch library is a mission center; the central processing department is a service center.

All the costs traceable to a given mission or service center are the center's *direct costs*. In some cases, these are the only costs the responsibility center manager can influence or control. Some managers, however, can exert indirect control over costs incurred directly in other responsibility centers. They can do this because they use the services the other responsibility centers provide, and they can control the amount of services they use. When this is the case, the manager's periodic control reports should include a charge for the services actually used that period. We call this an *allocation* of service center costs, and any cost so allocated becomes an *indirect cost* of the responsibility center to which the allocations are made. In the multi-branch library, each branch library has its direct costs plus the indirect costs charged to it for the services it uses from the central processing department.

The main principle underlying allocations for control reporting is very simple: No allocation should lead to a difference between the amount allocated and the performance standard, unless this difference arises from causes the manager can influence. This has two corollaries:

1) If the manager can't control the amount of service the responsibility center receives, either no allocation should be made or the amount allocated should equal the amount budgeted for the period.

2) If the manager can control the amount of service used, the allocation should be made at a predetermined rate or *transfer price,* which is then multiplied by the number of service units (for instance, hours) used.

A charge to a branch library for services provided by a data processing center in the library system's central office probably will be made by means of a transfer price. Transfer prices may also be used to charge library responsibility centers for services provided by service centers that are outside the library but are part of its parent organization, such as facilities maintenance, printing, and payroll preparation.

The predetermined transfer price should be set before the managers using the service decide the amount of service they will use. If the same transfer price is used to calculate both the budgeted charge for service and the actual charge for the period, any difference between these two charges will reflect a difference in the physical quantity of service used, as shown in Exhibit 2.

These variances can be controlled by the managers, who decide the amount of service they will use.

EXHIBIT 2.   Actual Versus Budgeted Charges.

| ACTUAL | BUDGET |
|---|---|
| Actual quantity used | Quantity budgeted |
| × | × |
| Predetermined price | Predetermined price |
| per unit of service | per unit of service |

DIFFERENCE ("VARIANCE")

(Actual quantity − budgeted quantity)
×
Predetermined price per unit of service

When managers follow these allocation rules, the total of the amounts charged to other responsibility centers will differ from the total cost of operating the service center. This is of no concern, however, because the purpose of the allocation is to provide control information, not to distribute costs. If some other purpose requires complete distribution of service center costs, the accountants can do this; however, they should not use those allocations for control reporting.

## ACTIVITY COSTING

Control reporting is important, but it is not the usual focus of cost accounting in libraries and other not-for-profit organizations. The usual focus is on the other main branch of cost accounting—activity costing. In activity costing one measures or estimates the costs of providing specific services or of carrying out specific activities within the organization.

Library staff, for example, usually perform both public services (for outside clientele) and technical services (for others within the library system). Examples of public service activities are reference, circulation, and data retrieval. In a multi-branch system each branch is likely to perform a set of activities much like those of other branches, so an individual activity may be either branch-specific (reference at the main library) or system-wide (all reference services at all branches). The costs of carrying out each activity will include the costs of that activity's share of staff time, supplies and materials, data processing services, and so on.

Activity costing in a library system is divided into six areas, which will be described in the sections that follow:

1. The purposes of activity costing
2. Kinds of activities
3. Traditional methods of activity costing
4. Decision applications
5. Reimbursement and external funding applications
6. A costing methodology for library services

### The Purposes of Activity Costing

Activity cost information is used in five ways. First, manufacturers use activity costing to determine the amount of manufacturing costs to be assigned to goods still in inventory at the end of the period for public financial reporting. Since librarians don't face this problem, I will not discuss it here.

Second, organizations can and should use estimates of activity costs in deciding how to utilize their resources. Some activities will be continued only if they bring in enough revenue to cover their costs; others will be continued only if the perceived nonmonetary benefits are great enough to justify their costs.

Third, activity cost information can be used in some instances for reimbursement calculations. Some funding agencies agree to reimburse other organizations for the costs of activities they are willing to sponsor.

Fourth, organizations may use cost information to establish the prices they charge either inside or outside users of their services. A reference department, for example, may wish to establish fees for search and retrieval services. For services provided to the organization's researchers and faculty (inside users), the fee or transfer price may be set equal to some measure of the cost; for similar services provided to outside users, cost data may establish a pricing floor or point of departure. This use may tie into the reimbursement purpose if a funding agency allows service costs—say, for computer use or library search and retrieval—to be treated as direct costs of the activity the agency is sponsoring.

Finally, organizations can use estimates of activity costs for external funding solicitations. A library could bolster a funding proposal by documenting the estimated costs of services for which funding is being sought.

## Kinds of Activities

There are many ways to classify a library's activities, but from a costing point of view, a simple two-category classification is enough: service and support activities, and mission activities. The library itself consumes the outputs of service and support activities; the library's users consume the outputs of mission activities. Book acquisition is one of the former; reference service is one of the latter.

By and large, organizations can use the same costing methods for service and support activities as for mission activities. However, the distinction is important for two reasons. First, library management may need to decide whether specific service and support activities produce benefits worth their costs. Second, the service and support activities are often necessary to support the mission activities, and a portion of their cost, therefore, is part of the cost of the mission activities. In making decisions regarding mission activities, we must consider their effects on the costs of service and support activities.

Traditional Methods of Activity Costing

All methods of activity costing are essentially variants of one of two basic methods: process costing and job order costing. We need to review these before deciding how to measure or estimate the costs of library activities.

*Process Costing.* Process costing is by far the simpler of the two. Costs are assembled by responsibility centers. The costs of each center are then assigned to each of its activities on the basis of a simple average—for example, average cost per hour of service performed by the center.

The denominator of the average must be a quantity that you can measure for each of the responsibility center's activities. The average cost of each activity can then be expressed as a proportion of the total. For instance, if an activity uses 1,000 hours of service each month out of 4,000 service-hours devoted to all activities, you would assign it one-fourth of the responsibility center's costs for the month.

You can calculate separate averages for different cost elements, if different unit cost divisors are appropriate. For example, hours of equipment use may be an appropriate divisor for depreciation, electricity, and equipment maintenance costs, while hours of staff time may be a better divisor for wages, salaries, and fringe benefits.

The cost of a given activity is the sum of the costs assigned to it in all the responsibility centers contributing to it. A given activity may absorb 10 percent of the costs of one responsibility center, 20 percent of the costs of another, and none of the costs of a third. These costs are likely to include the costs of service centers allocated to the responsibility centers in which the activities take place. I'll come back later to the question of how much allocated cost you should include in activity cost.

*Job-Order Costing.* In job-order costing, the costing focus is the individual job order, contract, or project, rather than the output of a responsibility center during a period of time. Costs are assigned to jobs in two ways:

• Those that can be traced readily to individual jobs are assigned in their entirety to those jobs. These are the jobs' *direct costs.* They are measured on the basis of detailed records of time spent, materials used, and so on.
• All other costs are referred to as *indirect costs* or *overhead costs.* They are assembled in pools before being assigned to jobs. The average cost of each overhead cost pool is then used to assign the costs in that pool to individual jobs. This average is called an *overhead rate* or *burden rate.* Again, the denominator of the average is some measurable characteristic of each job, such as the amount of staff time directly traceable to the job.

For example, many large libraries receive requests to microfilm materials in their collections. Such a library might used job-order costing to measure the cost of filling each of these requests. The library would determine the direct costs of staff time by recording the amount of time employees spent searching and retrieving the material, preparing it for microfilming, operating the microfilm equipment, and so on. The library would obtain direct materials costs by identifying the order numbers on the requisitions for microfilm stock and other materials. Other costs, such as supervisory salaries and depreciation on microfilm equipment, could be assigned to the orders by means of an overhead rate.

In some systems, each responsibility center working directly on individual jobs has its own pool of overhead or indirect costs; in others, the pools combine the indirect costs of several responsibility centers. Occasionally, two or more pools are created for a single responsibility center. The principle is always the same, however: Find a denominator for the overhead rate that is measurable for all jobs and is a reasonable indicator of the factors that cause short or long-term cost increases or decreases as the volume of activity goes up or down.

## Decision Applications

Before we can decide which costing method is appropriate for library services, we have to go back to the more fundamental question we started with: What are we going to do with activity cost data when we get them?

From a costing viewpoint, the first two groups of purposes are resource allocation and service pricing—that is, *decision applications.* The requirements of these applications have a great deal to do with how the costs of individual activities are to be measured.

*Measuring costs and benefits.* The guiding principle for decision applications is the *incremental principle,* which holds that decisions are choices among perceived alternative actions and that these choices should be based on estimated differences among these alternatives. In a profit-seeking organization, both costs and benefits can be measured in the same manner, by the inflows and outflows of cash anticipated for each alternative. This permits a simple calculation of estimated net benefit, as shown in Exhibit 3.

Although alternative A has lower cash receipts than alternative B, its net benefit—measured by net cash receipts—is $40 greater than that for alternative B.

Both costs and benefits in this comparison are measured by cash flows because cash is the only uncommitted resource. A decision that commits the library to spend cash reduces the amount of cash available for other purposes; a decision that increases the net cash flow adds to the

Exhibit 3.   Deciding Between Alternatives.

|  | Alternative A | Alternative B | Difference (A − B) |
|---|---|---|---|
| Cash receipts | $100 | $180 | $− 80 |
| Cash outlays | 40 | 160 | −120 |
| Net cash receipts | $ 60 | $ 20 | $+ 40 |

library's (or university's) ability to fund other projects or cover its deficit.

In a not-for-profit organization benefits are seldom measured by cash flows. Service to the organization's constituents is its own benefit, because that's why the organization exists. The problem is that service output is neither precisely measurable nor comparable from activity to activity.

How do we resolve this? First, if only a fixed total amount of cash is available, the task is to choose the set of actions that will maximize the total estimated benefit from this outlay of cash. Second, if the amount of cash available for spending can be increased or decreased, the task of management or its funding agencies is to decide whether the qualitative benefits of the least desirable proposed activity are worth its cost.

In either case, the decision process involves a technique known as *zero-base budgeting*, which has been applied in both the private and public sectors.[1] Stripped to its essentials, zero-base budgeting is a procedure by which each activity is subdivided into level-of-service segments, starting with a segment that would provide a minimum level of activity service and progressing to a proposal for expanding the scope of the activity. Each segment of each activity is ranked ordinally, according to its perceived benefit, with the minimum-level segment assigned the highest rank and the most expendable segment assigned the lowest. In principle, management (or its funding agencies) can then fund the highest-ranked segments first, moving down the ladder until the funds run out or the cost exceeds the perceived benefits, whichever comes first.

This process is illustrated in Exhibit 4. The ratings, ranging from a high of 6 to a low of 1, are shown at the right of each box representing a segment. If $50,000 (the total cost of all segments) is available and if segment X3 (the lowest-ranked of all segments) is beneficial enough to justify spending $2,600, the organization would fund all segments. If only $39,200 is available, then the organization would fund only service-level segments with ratings of 4 or higher (X1, Y1, Y2, Y3, Z1, and Z2).

This isn't the time or place to prescribe a detailed system for

EXHIBIT 4.   Activity Ranking for Zero-Base Budgeting.

| Activity X | Rating | Activity Y | Rating | Activity Z | Rating |
|---|---|---|---|---|---|
| Segment X1 | | Segment Y1 | | Segment Z1 | |
| $6,000 | 6 | $11,000 | 6 | $8,500 | 6 |
| Segment X2 | | Segment Y2 | | Segment Z2 | |
| $4,200 | 3 | $6,200 | 5 | $5,500 | 4 |
| Segment X3 | | Segment Y3 | | | |
| $2,600 | 1 | $2,000 | 4 | | |
| | | Segment Y4 | | | |
| | | $4,000 | 3 | | |

implementing zero-base budgeting, or even to suggest its adoption in a formal sense. The basic concept is universal, however: each expenditure should produce enough benefit to justify its cost and, in the usual case of limited resources, expenditures with the lowest perceived benefit per dollar should be the first to feel the ax.

*Measuring incremental cost.* The organization should measure the expenditures in this analysis by the incremental cost of the activity segment in question. The incremental cost of any segment is the difference in the total cost of operating the organization with and without that segment.

Ideally, incremental cost should be estimated by means of an ad hoc estimate of the increment in each cost element each time the organization has to make a decision. This is costly and time-consuming, however. For most studies, we have to start with data on activity costs that have either been prepared before the organization realized its need for the specific decision or are derived by approximate formulas rather than by a detailed analysis of each and every cost element.

In designing these approximate formulas, we need to study carefully the distinction between fixed and variable costs. The horizontal line in the left-hand diagram in Exhibit 5 represents total fixed cost, the cost of providing the capacity to carry out the activity; the variable costs are the additional costs necessary to use this capacity to provide service. The slope of the curved line in the upper portion of the diagram at the left indicates the rate of cost increase for a one-unit increase in the volume of activity—it is steep at low volume levels, then flattens out, then becomes steeper again. This pattern of variability translates into the average variable cost per unit pictured in the right-hand diagram.

One danger is that an analyst may conclude that only short-term variable costs are incremental in most situations. Nothing is further from the truth, particularly in the library. The fact is that few decisions affect only a single unit of volume. For example, the incremental cost of

Exhibit 5.    Fixed and Variable Costs.

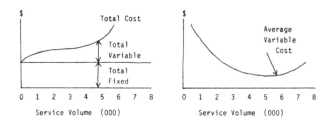

charging out a single book to a client or student is virtually zero, but no library is likely to use the cost of a single charge-out in decision making. Most decisions of this sort are class decisions, dealing with alternatives that differ substantially in total volume or in method of operation.

These questions call for a much more inclusive definition of incremental cost. For example, a big problem in libraries is the cost of providing and maintaining the amount of space required by steadily expanding collections. The costs of new space must be included in acquisition decisions because they are incremental with respect to these decisions, taken as a class.

One library, incidentally, has taken a different approach to controlling space costs. This library is a research library in a commercial firm. It never acquires a book unless a researcher requests it. All books are ordered by telephone, shipped by an overnight courier service, and cataloged the day they are received. The delivered cost of each book is quite high, but the total cost of operating the library is lower than it would be if the library bought a larger number of books and stored them for possible future use.

Recognizing the limitations of short-term variable cost in incremental analysis, some authorities recommend going to the other extreme by using the *full cost* of an activity to approximate its incremental cost. Full costing is the most widely used concept underlying service costing systems, but it is often used uncritically, unquestioningly, with no consideration of the relevance of its output to the costing purpose at hand. For example, Philip Rosenberg's manual on library costing doesn't even hint at the existence of any concept other than full costing. His presentation is a good one, but it focuses on the mechanics of data accumulation and allocation for cost accounting or cost-finding purposes, leaving discussion of the conceptual foundation of his system for another day.[2]

The main problem with using full cost in incremental analysis is that it leads to cost estimates that almost always overstate the incremental costs of managerial actions. A better alternative is what I call *attributable cost*—the effect on total cost of a substantial change in the volume of activity, expressed as an average (dollars per hour of staff time, for instance). The purpose of the concept of attributable cost is to provide a rough answer to the question full costing is intended to answer: How much cost does the presence of this activity actually *cause?* A method that presumes that *every* cost has to be allocated to *some* activity departs from that simple notion. Estimates of attributable cost per unit of service can be used to approximate the incremental effect of a decision on many cost elements, to save analytical time without materially weakening the relevance of the analysis.

*Budget justification.* Budget justification is another decision application of activity cost data, this time from the advocate's point of view. Department heads and program directors may use activity cost data to persuade management to improve their funding requests. Again, the data for this purpose should reflect the costs attributable to each activity, without arbitrary allocations of nonattributable support costs. Department heads and directors should present the latter for what they are, necessary functional support for all activities combined. Using the attributable cost concept will keep this amount to a minimum, however.

*Service pricing.* The third decision application of activity cost data is in pricing services. This has two dimensions: transfer pricing within the organization and pricing to external patrons or users. Two examples of the effects of transfer pricing—one from the private sector, one from a government agency—show how internal transfer prices can influence behavior. Many years ago a company decided to charge each of its operating divisions market-based rental rates for the space they occupied in the company's headquarters building in Boston. Within six months the divisions had vacated three floors of the 14 stories the company had been using, making them available for rental to outsiders.

Similarly, a Canadian government bureau[3] responsible for translating documents from one language to another began to charge other departments for discretionary translations; mandatory translations of official documents were exempt. Within a very brief period, the number of translation requests dropped significantly.

The point of internal transfer pricing is to encourage users to apply cost-benefit tests to their requests for service. As long as a service is free, employees will overuse it. The organization has to decide whether it wants its managers to apply cost-benefit tests or whether it wants to encourage unlimited internal use of its services.

The guiding rule for internal transfer pricing is to set the price at the market price of the service or at attributable costs, whichever is lower. Since market prices are likely to be unavailable for most library services, the organization should set the price at attributable cost. This will neither encourage excessive use nor discourage uses that justify the cost of the service. Attributable cost is better than either average full cost or short-run variable cost for the reasons I cited earlier.

Management needn't apply attributable cost blindly, however. It is an average, and management may choose to install either a two-part tariff or peak/offpeak pricing schedules. A two-part tariff consists of a fixed monthly charge—that is, a form of "retainer" to reserve a budgeted amount of service—and a unit charge for each service unit used. The retainer is intended to cover the fixed costs of providing service capacity; the unit charge is to cover the variable costs. The idea is that as long as the capacity is available, it might as well be used, whereas decisions to ask for more capacity will be reflected in increases in the monthly retainer.

Peak/offpeak pricing takes a different tack. Higher prices are charged for use during peak hours than during offpeak hours. This is the kind of pricing formula OCLC and other online bibliographic utilities use as a means of evening out demand for their resources. The differential should be adjusted to shift enough of the demand to the off-peak hours to match the resources available. Cost data may not be very helpful in finding the proper differential, although a starting point might be to assign all the fixed costs of providing capacity to the peak hours.

External pricing of services is more complicated. Here the main role of cost is to establish a floor below which regular prices won't be set, and again attributable cost is the appropriate cost concept. In pricing microfilming services, for example, the library needs to know what it costs to provide its microfilming capacity as well as what the direct costs are of using that capacity for individual microfilming jobs. Even here, however, the organization may wish to set two types of prices—equal to or higher than attributable cost for routine services and below attributable cost for service provided on a when-available basis. Cost data are of only marginal usefulness in this context.

## Reimbursement and External Funding Applications

When the library has activities some external funding agency is willing to support or for which the library is seeking support, attributable cost is too narrow a costing concept. The reason is that general administrative support activities seldom draw specific support from funding agencies, but they are essential to the organization's operations. The sum of all attributable costs is likely to be smaller than the sum of all operating costs. If all funding is limited to the attributable cost of supportable activities, therefore, the organization won't be able to operate.

In this situation a full-cost concept *is* applicable. The library should assign each activity a proportionate share of central administrative support costs. For this purpose the denominator for average administrative support cost has to be some activity-traceable measure of the factors requiring administrative support. The Cost Accounting Standards Board has provided that this denominator be the sum of all other costs assigned to contracts.[4] This is known as a "total cost input" costing base. Other systems use such variables as total staff time or total cost minus materials and supplies cost.

## A Costing Methodology for Library Services

To summarize:

1. Activity cost data can serve two broad classes of purposes: decision making and reimbursement or funding.
2. Cost data for managerial decisions should approximate incremental cost, defined to fit the particular resource allocation or pricing problem management is concentrating on.
3. Measures of attributable cost are a reasonable approximation to incremental cost for most decisions, but the library may have to modify this in some situations.
4. For reimbursement and funding purposes, full-cost data are generally more appropriate than attributable cost data.

That said, what should a system of activity costing in a library system look like? To begin with, activity cost data should reflect estimates made from time to time (once a year or even less frequently) on the basis of sample data or judgmental estimates unless a cost reimbursement arrangement requires routine ex post facto assignments of costs to activities. There are two reasons for this:

1. The routine accumulation of costs by activity would be far too expensive and burdensome.
2. Resource allocation decisions are typically made once a year, at budget time, and must be based on estimates of what costs will be, not on records of what costs have been.

But what method should be used to assemble costs of library activities? Neither process costing nor job-order costing is likely to be a satisfactory method of measuring the costs of library services. Process costing seldom works because most library responsibility centers engage in such diverse activities that no single measure of output can serve as the denominator of the costing rate. Job-order costing can't be used because the clerical cost of keeping track of the direct costs of individual activities would be prohibitive. It should be used in the library only for one-of-a-kind activities, such as special exhibits and internal study projects.

Instead, accountants have devised systems of *administrative costing* that combine elements of both process and job-order costing. In administrative costing, the accountants first identify any major cost elements that can be traced in their entirety to specific mission activities. The remaining costs, and that includes most of them, are accumulated by responsibility centers, as in process costing. The accountants then assign these costs to the responsibility center's activities or "functions" on the basis of estimates of the percentages of the total that are applicable to the various functions.

Sometimes this will be enough. That is, the activity we're interested in is carried out in its entirety in a single responsibility center. The function and the activity therefore are one and the same. In other cases, however, each function supports a number of activities, and a further step is required. Exhibit 6 illustrates this sequence. Two responsibility centers perform two functions each. These support three activities, each of which requires support from two of the four functions. The total cost of activity X, for example, is $12,800, consisting of the entire $8,000 cost of function A1 and 40 percent of the $12,000 cost of function A2. Activity Y requires support from both responsibility centers, for a total cost of $28,200.

In carrying out this analysis, the accountants should classify the costs that aren't traceable in their entirety to any one function as either divisible or indivisible. Divisible costs are those that can be reduced more or less proportionally, in time, if one of the responsibility center's functions is removed while all other functions remain intact. Clerical salaries, computer time, and office supplies are likely to fit this defini-

EXHIBIT 6.   Allocating Responsibility Center Costs.

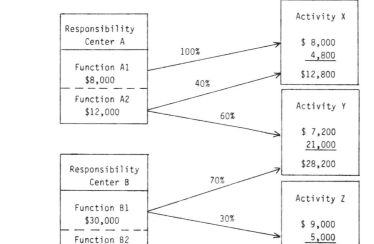

tion. Indivisible costs may include items such as the salary of the department head.

The reason for this classification is that indivisible costs shouldn't be allocated at all. Instead, they should be classified with costs of a general administrative support function. Estimated divisible costs, on the other hand, should be allocated to functions on the basis of estimates of functional use of these resources.

In some cases judgmental estimates may be good enough—for example, the department head may estimate that clerical personnel spend 40 percent of their time on one function, 35 percent on a second function, and 25 percent on a third. When more accuracy is required, management can take a sample to estimate the amount of resources associated with each function. Personnel time can be monitored during a short test period; so can supplies or telephone usage, if they are significant. Other divisible costs can then be allocated in proportion to some functional characteristic, such as employee time.

In some budgeting situations, functional cost estimates may be enough. If functions serve two or more activities, however, and activity cost data are deemed necessary, some additional steps are necessary. First, if a function serves one activity exclusively, assign its costs to that activity in full. Next, for all other functions, identify one or more governing factors or work units and estimate how many of these are associated with each activity. Then calculate the average of all divisible functional costs—the indivisible costs then remain as general functional support. Next, multiply average divisible functional cost by the number of work units associated with each activity. The resulting activity cost totals are estimates of the costs attributable to each activity.

The final step in the analysis is to allocate all the general support costs to activities, but libraries should do this only if they need the activity cost data for funding or reimbursement purposes.

This may seem like a highly onerous procedure, but in practice it's likely to be less formidable than it sounds. First, it doesn't have to be done very often, certainly not more than once a year and probably even less frequently. Second, you can take many short cuts in practice, mainly by limiting the detailed analysis to the biggest cost elements—salaries and wages, for the most part. Third, crude percentage estimates are adequate for most purposes. So, if you decide activity cost estimates are likely to be useful, they can be developed at a reasonable cost.

I have taken you on a very rapid trip through the mine fields of cost accounting. Remember this key point: Costing is more an art than a science, and many variations on the basic method are available. You should choose a method for any specific case only after carefully identifying the purposes the measurements are to serve, the time available for the analysis, and the incremental benefits additional analytical complexity will likely provide.

## Notes

1. For example, see Peter A. Pyhrr, "Zero-Base Budgeting," *Harvard Business Review* 48, no. 6 (November–December 1970): 111–121 and Arthur F. Brueningsen, "SCAT: A Process of Alternatives," *Management Accounting* 58, no. 5 (November 1976): 55–60, 66 and "SCAT II: A Process for Planning," *Management Accounting* 59, no. 6 (December 1977): 57–61.
2. Philip Rosenberg, *Cost Finding for Public Libraries* (Chicago: American Library Association, 1985).
3. Arva R. Clark and Regina E. Herzlinger, "Transfer Pricing in a Nonprofit Organization: Chargeback and the Translation Services," Case Study Collection, Harvard Graduate School of Business Administration (Boston: Harvard College, 1976).
4. United States Cost Accounting Standards Board, Standard 410, "Allocation of Business Unit General and Administrative Expenses to Final Cost Objectives," in *Standards, Rules and Regulations* by the Cost Accounting Standards Board (Washington, D.C.: U.S. Government Printing Office, 1976), 205–224.

I am indebted to Heike Kordish, Assistant University Librarian of Columbia University, for some of the illustrations and references in this paper.

# Cost Analysis and Library Services in the Electronic Age

## Malcolm Getz

Understanding costs is essential for good management. Costs are simply measures of the resources, human and otherwise, devoted to a particular activity. If a manager is to achieve as much as possible with a given budget, he or she must be conscious of striking balances among competing claims for resources. A manager will find opportunities to begin new programs, and challenges to cut back old ones. In each case, a good sense of where resources are going is important.

Just as there are various reasons for measuring resource flows, different analytic tools are appropriate for different purposes. *Cost accounting techniques* can gauge the resource flows within current operations. *Statistical comparisons* among organizations can show how costs will vary in different settings. *Monitoring past changes* in the costs of new technologies may point to new opportunities. A good manager calls on a variety of analytic tools when choosing new directions for his or her organization.

Costs are not the whole story. Budgets derive from a broader base, from the development of programs focused on the fundamental missions of an organization. Managers are interested in the value of a particular activity. Activities that cost more than they are worth are good candidates for cutbacks. Activities that are worth more than they cost are likely to be sustained. Knowledge about what it would cost to expand Program B is often the basis for judging willingness to pay to expand Program A. For example, knowing that original cataloging may cost $45 per title will influence our willingness to pay for copy cataloging. Of course, measuring willingness to pay is often difficult.

Analysis is costly, and so the amount of investment a library manager makes in analysis will reflect a balance between the usefulness of an

Malcolm Getz is Director of Libraries at Vanderbilt University, Nashville, Tennessee. He is also a professor of economics and has published extensively in the field of cost accounting.

investigation and its cost. In the long run, I believe the performance of libraries will be improved if managers make greater use of analytic techniques.

There are three ways in which analysis of costs is essential to understanding libraries. The first is simply how comparative cost information helps managers judge their own performance and that of their organization. Second, knowledge of how costs vary among different organizations might yield insight into whether a given library should be larger or smaller. Third, information about costs helps in making decisions about electronic systems. This last issue is of growing importance for libraries and represents high stakes for managers.

## USING COSTS TO ANALYZE MANAGERIAL EFFICIENCY

We expect the quality of management to make a difference in the performance of a library. Managers should define work flows and levels of responsibility for employees. The same people may be more productive when better organized. A manager influences the morale of workers by defining the terms and expectations of work—for example, through compensation schemes. A manager is often responsible for recruiting, promoting, and dismissing workers. How can the quality of management be improved? Formal measurement of managerial efficiency—including analysis of costs—may enhance managerial performance.

The measurement of managerial efficiency involves the simplest application of cost concepts. Let's define managerial efficiency as the difference between an ideal level of output achievable with a given set of resources and the level of output actually produced with the resources. If an ideal were well defined and credibly measured, one might expect institutions to reward managers who achieve higher efficiencies, much as managers in the for-profit sector receive profit sharing. Even if bonuses are impractical, knowledge of the efficiency achieved by a particular manager might lead to more rapid career advance. One would also expect the methods of those library managers with high efficiency scores to be mimicked by others. In this way, the quality of management would improve over time.

One method for measuring managerial efficiency identifies the cost of an operation for a random sample of libraries with similar outputs—for example, comparing public libraries serving comparable communities. The sample size should be large enough to permit generalizing from the statistics. The sampling could be stratified by type and size of library, so comparisons could be made within homogeneous groups. The investigation might simply define the least cost library as the ideal. The difference between the least cost and the cost at each other library is then attributed to differences in managerial efficiency.

There are a number of difficulties in using cost measurement as a basis for measuring managerial efficiency. The central difficulty is controlling for the level of output. If the unit being examined is an entire library system, the task is formidable because there may be a number of different outputs that are difficult to add. For example, a library might treat circulation and reference questions as different outputs. Measuring managerial efficiency is easier for a department where there is a simpler objective, a single output. The problem of measuring outputs is complicated by the difficulty of measuring differences in the *quality* of output. Circulation of more expensive books may in fact reflect a greater value and represent more output than circulation of inexpensive books.

A second difficulty comes from factors that are beyond a manager's control. For example, wage levels differ from place to place. We must control for price level differences to isolate the manager's effect. Other factors may include union shop work rules, space limitations, and policies on equipment replacement. Even when such constraints can't be measured in a formal way, they should be recognized in drawing conclusions.

An investigation of managerial efficiency need not be concerned with measuring or allocating overhead costs. Overhead costs that are beyond the immediate control of a manager are irrelevant in thinking about managerial efficiency.

The measures of labor costs in technical processing done by Kantor[1] and by Getz and Phelps[2] go some distance toward providing plausible measures of managerial efficiency. Of course, it is important to measure outputs consistently and to recognize quality differentials. For example, not all libraries catalog serials. Among those that do, not all maintain the cataloging on a current basis.

As mentioned previously, a large sample size is important. In the studies cited the sample size was under ten. With a larger sample size, more sophisticated statistical methods could be applied for estimating cost relationships. For example, a method might recognize that different managers may appropriately choose different combinations of inputs when the inputs have different relative prices. In a large city where wage rates are high relative to other inputs, one might expect to find a less labor-intensive operation. One might then want to employ a more sophisticated description of the ideal cost level for a given set of input prices. If multiple outputs can be measured, as with circulation, reference questions, and attendance, a method might be employed to define the ideal cost level in terms of the various outputs. Larger sample sizes allow managerial efficiency to be defined in a more subtle and realistic way. The ideal is then defined as the least cost operation for producing given levels of outputs when a particular set of input prices prevail.

## USING COSTS TO DETERMINE SCALE

A second reason to explore the cost of library operations is to investigate the consequences of having libraries of different sizes. Let's think of the problem in terms of a university library although similar issues arise for other types of libraries. Is a university better off with one large edifice or is it better served with a number of smaller library locations? If the latter, should many small libraries serve a campus as opposed to a smaller number of large libraries? I call the effect on unit costs of the locational pattern the plant effects.

A related but different question is whether the libraries will operate at lower cost under a centralized, hierarchical administration (the larger scale administration) or under a decentralized administration of independent units (the small scale administration). I call the effect on unit costs of the administrative pattern the administration effects. Administration and plant represent two different dimensions of scale.

The effect of scale is defined in terms of unit cost—that is, the cost per unit of output as size changes. When unit costs fall, say cost per circulation, then we say there are economies of scale. When unit costs rise, we say there are diseconomies of scale.

Let's look further at costs as related to scale. On the one hand, we sense that the single structure need have fewer service points, for example, a single circulation area, a single photocopy service, a single security system, and so on. We'd also expect less redundancy in collections with the single facility—fewer dictionaries, encyclopedias, and other standard works, and fewer claims for duplicates of material than in a conglomeration of smaller libraries. We can think of the cost of the small number of service points being spread over many more users in the single entity case, and so expect to see the unit cost be lower in the single facility library than in the multiple library system.

On the other hand, users will have to travel greater distances, on average, to get to the single location than if the libraries were smaller and spread around. The more libraries there are, the lower the cost of travel by users to get to them. We assume that the libraries are each well located.

Assessing the advantages and disadvantages of scale should balance these two effects. Because the travel time cost of users is typically not in the library's budget, an assessment of scale effects that excludes such costs would not seem to be incomplete. Nevertheless, decisions to consolidate library operations should be based on recognition of both on-budget and off-budget costs.

The make-up of the administrative entity may also influence cost and performance. Smaller, decentralized administrative units may be more personal, have higher morale, and so yield better service per dollar of expenditure than larger ones. On the other hand, a larger, centralized administration may capture more advantages from the specialization of labor. If small administrative units did prove superior, one might change the administration of a single location into quasi-autonomous administrative units, much as some department stores are a collection of boutiques. Or if specialization of labor has a big payoff but one wanted many locations, one might administer multiple locations centrally.

The estimate of scale effects poses significant methodological challenge. To define unit costs one must define a unit of output. Some investigations use circulation as the output; some use the bookstock. One might think of some composite of these elements as the *output*. One might then compute the cost per unit of output at a number of libraries of different size, and look for a pattern.

To take separate account of scale advantages in location and scale advantages in administration, it is necessary to observe a number of libraries that differ in these two dimensions and to measure separately the locational pattern and the administrative pattern. It will be especially important to observe examples of "boutique management" in a single facility and central management of dispersed locations.

The efforts to measure scale generally have not distinguished administrative from locational scale. Cooper,[3] for example, regresses operating expenditures on six measures of activity including circulation and hours for academic libraries. He does not distinguish libraries organized in branches from those without branches.

As with managerial efficiency, it is necessary to adjust differences in general price level from one place to another. If big libraries are in big cities with high wage rates, then the big libraries are more costly per unit. This conclusion, however, would have little or nothing to do with economies of scale.

In judging economy of scale, think about overhead. Comparing libraries of different sizes, account for the resources spent on overhead and coordination. Indeed, the relative advantage of one big collection versus many small collections may well be the difference in the cost of coordination.

This thought model makes clear that the size of the book collection a university may choose is separate from the presence of economies of scale. The issue is whether to locate a book collection of a given size in a single facility or spread it among smaller facilities.

The collection size a university chooses for itself reflects a balance of costs against willingness to pay. The willingness to pay for a larger collection depends on the programs and missions of the university. For example, a university that aims to achieve international prominence in the humanities will want to pay for a very large library even though the cost per unit of output (whatever measure of output you choose) may rise the larger the library becomes. On the other hand, a university whose mission is to train many engineers at modest cost may elect to have a small collection even though a larger collection would lower its cost per unit of output. Willingness to pay, shaped by the institution's fundamental mission, matters as much as cost.

## USING COSTS IN SELECTING ELECTRONIC SYSTEMS

A third arena for applying cost concepts is electronic services. As electronic systems become more important, they will change the pattern of costs of many library functions. They may lower the cost of decentralized operation for some functions and may raise it for others. Let's look at some general emerging cost patterns for electronic systems.

First, the cost of computing is falling at about 20 percent per year, encouraging more and more use of electronic systems. For example, more people will be managing personal bibliographies electronically. Library applications for microcomputers are growing.

Second, the cost of storing information digitally is falling at about 20 percent per year. Magnetic media have become less expensive, and optically-based systems may cause costs to fall by an order of magnitude. Compact disks containing bibliographic and full text information are now being marketed aggressively.

Third, telecommunication costs are falling. The shift from analog to digital communications is a significant reason for these declines. Digital telephone switching gear is replacing analog switches on most university campuses and in many telephone companies. Satellite and optical fiber transmission media are a second reason. Campuswide communication systems using coaxial cables and fiber optical links are being installed on a number of campuses. Satellite transmission of data is becoming common. The development of packet-switched digital systems will make OCLC remarkably less expensive than its present private line system.

Major shifts in telecommunication costs have led to changes in the regulation of the communications industry. As firms operating in locations across the country began to develop private communications systems they bypassed the telephone companies. Deregulation of long-distance telephone service was necessary to allow the common carriers to compete with private communication services. The changes in the regulatory environment have caused prices for some specific telecommunications services to increase. Nevertheless, the trend in the cost per unit of telecommunication is downward.

Fourth, we expect software costs to fall as well. The development of fourth generation programming languages gives less sophisticated users access to computers without intermediation by programmers. As more software is written in portable languages, it will move easily from one piece of hardware to another. The Unix operating system offers portability as a main feature. Portability means that software need not be reinvented for each different machine, so the market for software will become more competitive.

As electronic information systems become less costly, we can expect libraries to use them more aggressively. At first, the systems will take over and improve on tasks previously done manually. The organization will change little. Once the new systems are mastered and accepted, however, organizational changes will result. For one, the skill mix required in technical services may change. For another, some of the advantages of the large library may diminish, prompting universities to choose more decentralized patterns. The functions of computer centers and libraries may also change. A library manager faces the problem of deciding when, how, and how much to invest in new systems. A sensitivity to changing patterns of costs and of willingness to pay is essential in such a rapidly evolving environment.

One such choice is the make-or-buy decision. At one time, quality software was not available for purchase, so a library had to develop software to automate a particular function. In recent years, however, an active market has developed in library software. Separate circulation and catalog systems are now giving way to integrated systems. For larger libraries, software packages priced in the $50,000–$100,000 range provide functions that might cost from $1 million to $2 million to develop and test. Note also that inhouse development involves much more risk than buying. Some universities have invested millions of dollars in developing software systems that never worked.

Moreover, software has a continuing maintenance cost of 10 to 25 percent of the development cost. With purchased software, the annual maintenance cost will be about 10 percent of the cost of maintaining homemade software. A library might sensibly decide to develop and maintain its own software when the same functions are not available commercially. In such a case, some of the development costs may be recovered through resale to others with similar needs. For example, Harvard University developed an enhanced acquisition system for the NOTIS environment that handles its elaborate fund accounting structure, and will market its package through Northwestern. Vanderbilt is developing software in the NOTIS environment to control library access using bar codes on identification cards. Once homemade software is in place the decision to maintain it or abandon it in favor of a purchased system will depend on cost.

Similarly, in developing a complete system, one faces a make-or-buy choice: whether to buy a turnkey system or be one's own system integrator. Turnkey vendors sell a complete package of hardware, software, training, and systems support. Alternatively, a library can buy hardware, software, and other system components and services separately. The library must then integrate the various system elements itself. A library implementing its own system, picking and choosing among components, will require a more skilled staff than a library that selects a turnkey system. For most libraries, this is prohibitively expensive, because skills are needed episodicly.

Cataloging also poses make-or-buy choices. Most libraries now buy all the cataloging they can from bibliographic utilities, the Library of Congress, and other services. Homemade cataloging is five to ten times as expensive as purchased cataloging, so the choice should be easy. Some libraries have not moved to minimize their homemade cataloging and they doubtless bear significantly higher costs. With pressure for managerial efficiency, such practices are likely to change.

Cataloging is commonly bought online from remote bibliographic utilities. The transaction involves the use of long-distance telecommunication and remote computers. As computing and electronic storage costs fall more rapidly than telecommunication costs, catalog information will probably be distributed on optical disks and libraries will be able to retrieve cataloging information locally. Such source material would provide a new search service for library users, with subject and keyword searching of citations to materials at other libraries. It would also avoid the diseconomies of scale inherent in large interactive computing systems.

In cataloging, as with software, a corollary to the "don't make what you can buy" dictum is—"what you do make, sell." When a library creates cataloging locally, it should be offered for sale to other libraries. Bibliographic utilities give credits to libraries creating or enhancing cataloging on their systems. They are likely to continue performing as brokers between buyers and sellers, event as new mechanisms for trade develop. For example, utilities may license the use of optical disks containing subsets of their databases for use with local systems.

By the same logic, we can expect other electronic information sources that are now accessed via long-distance communication to change. Lockheed's Dialog service, for example, is a wholesaler of database service. Owners of databases, however, may find it worthwhile to make their databases available via license for use on campus-based systems. The databases might be distributed on optical disks for local mounting and searching. Such an approach will substitute smaller local computers for large, remote computers accessed by long-distance telecommunications systems. The databases will be maintained by their creators, and the distribution service will include appropriate updates. A local library will license the information, and most of the storage and computer search expense will occur locally.

With optical storage systems, local mounting and searching will occur at significantly lower cost than remote mounting and searching. With low-cost local searching of, say, article index files, the amount of searching should increase significantly. Online searching that once was limited to funded research projects could reach undergraduates and other large populations at very modest rates.

Changing costs may also influence personal libraries. Most university faculty members subscribe to some journals and collect books. As the cost of electronic media falls, electronic materials will find their way into personal libraries. Personally tailored libraries may be distributed electronically; working papers and work in progress in industry and the academic setting are likely to be shared electronically. The willingness of a university to pay for certain library services may well be shaped by what faculty members can do for themselves.

A major issue in the growth of local systems is the willingness of universities and other institutions to bear the costs. They must consider whether students would be willing to pay more for schooling that offers the richer, deeper learning that automated systems sustain. Students do appear willing to pay more for quality, although there are limits. Would the expense of automated systems offset other costs in the university? Perhaps student/teacher ratios would rise when student learning is enhanced with electronic tools. If substitution for other costs is difficult or impossible, then universities will not be able to invest heavily in automated information systems.

Expenditure on electronic systems will also depend on the quality of service. Information online can be delivered into faculty offices, student dorm rooms, and homes. Services can be offered for more hours than libraries are generally open. Electronic searching can be easy to learn and when appropriately designed, can compensate somewhat for user error. Convenience and usefulness are worth paying for. Analysis of costs, and of alternative ways to achieve a particular end, will significantly shape new services.

Formal analysis of costs is helpful in designing an overall strategy for developing electronic systems, selecting vendors, and evaluating results. New systems are likely to be most successful when they take advantage of technologies with falling costs, or provide very significant advances in levels of service. A library will benefit from comparison shopping. Expected cost will influence an institution's willingness to pay for a particular electronic service, and monitoring costs vs. perform-ance will enable managers to make informed decisions about current and future generations of technology.

## ANALYSIS, CONFLICT, AND TRUST

A solid understanding of costs will help library managers improve the quality of services in all three arenas described here. It will also help build trust and gain political support for new projects from administra-tors. Sound analysis builds on a recognition of the fundamental mis-sions, the nature of the finances, and the historic character of an institution The analytic point of view need not be in opposition to other points of view. Indeed, careful analysis rather than unsupported advo-cacy is a more certain path to building personal confidence and political capital.

Analysis does not promise to eliminate conflict. Reasonable people may disagree about results as they disagree about political or other values. In particular, willingness to pay will depend on who pays. The choice of values may lead to conflict, but an analytic point of view will help managers understand the position of other parties. With a sound analytic base, parties to a decision may quickly recognize an impasse, and so move smoothly to seek arbitration, saving political capital for circumstances when persuasion has a better chance of carrying the day.

As library managers confront the challenges of electronic systems, they have an opportunity to look ahead, to analyze the currents of change, and plot a course to a new location. Those equipped with an understanding of cost analysis will have a distinct advantage as this revolution continues.

## Notes

1. Paul B. Kantor, "Relations Between Consortia, On-Line Services, and the Cost of Processing Monographs at Eight University Libraries" (Unpublished paper prepared for the Council on Library Resources, 1984).
2. Malcolm Getz and Doug Phelps, "Labor Costs in the Technical Operations of Three Research Libraries," *Journal of Academic Librarianship* 10, no. 4 (September 1984): 209–219.
3. Michael D. Cooper, "Economies of Scale in Academic Libraries," *Library and Information Science Research* 5, no. 2 (Summer 1983): 207–219 and 6, no. 3 (July–September 1984): 321–333.

# Beware the Superficialities of Cost Analysis

## Delmus E. Williams

Most advocates of cost studies urge you to enthusiastically embrace cost-benefit analysis for your organization. It is my role to put something of a damper on that enthusiasm, but not to denigrate the potential of either cost studies or other management techniques across the board. Modern management theory offers library managers a great deal, and its prudent use can do much to made operations more effective. I am not a Luddite; nor do I hold that management is an art acquired only at birth. Managers are made, not born. Good decisions are based on good information, and the capacity to use information is an acquired skill.

It is also not my aim to substitute other management techniques for cost/benefit analysis. I believe that the value of management tools is situational, so it is difficult to say that one tool is more useful than another without understanding the specific circumstances of its application.

What I hope to do in this chapter is bring the expectations of those who invest in cost studies in line with the capabilities of this technique. I view cost studies as evaluations of organizations, and my comments are biased by my belief that an evaluation should be judged by both its capacity to solve an immediate problem and its capacity to increase the flexibility of the library organization. Stated simply, *a good evaluation is one that provides the manager with the kind of information that contributes to the capacity of the organization to adapt to its surroundings.* I see two sets of limitations on the capacity of cost studies to serve this purpose. The first limitation is a technical one centered on the difficulty of securing adequate costing data about library operations. The second is a more fundamental concern about how advocates of cost study techniques expect their data to be used and how this related to decision making by library managers.

Delmus E. Williams is Library Director of the University of Alabama in Huntsville.

## ASSUMPTIONS UNDERLYING COST STUDIES

With these comments in mind, what are the assumptions underlying cost studies? Cost studies are based on the idea that organizations operate to produce the maximum amount of goods for the minimum amount of effort, and that there is a direct quantifiable relationship between the resources invested in a process and the results achieved.[1] In a rational world, according to this model, the manager is expected to seek optimum efficiency in reaching the stated goal of the organization. That person's ability to manage is measured best by comparing the cost of producing a unit of worth in his or her area with the cost of producing comparable units supervised by other managers. The key to management is making sure that resources are used to best advantage and that this can be measured.

When a manager is dealing with impersonal items, costing presents no real problem. The chicken farmer knows that when chickens reach a certain age, the number of eggs they lay will decline in relation to the feed they are given and that, once the decline begins, it will not reverse. When chickens pass their peak, it is time to feed new chickens and use the old ones for stew. Farmers merely chart productivity, and, when it dips, they start over. The decision to kill off the chickens is a relatively easy one. No one is hurt (except the chickens), and the relative productivity of new and old chickens can mean the difference between the survival of the farm and bankruptcy.

But in human enterprises the decision is more difficult, and in not-for-profit organizations, it becomes even *more* complex. Labor is always difficult to relate directly to output. When one removes the profit motive from an organization, the relationship becomes even more tenuous. In libraries, 60 percent of total expenditures and 85 percent of the cost of servicing our materials relate directly to labor.

But why is this is a problem? Advocates of cost study methods will tell you that labor is a variable cost that can be regulated like any other commodity in the production process. When General Motors cannot sell cars, the production line stops, the workers are laid off, and costs are curtailed. In the end, an automobile contains x tons of steel and y hours of labor.

But even in the context of the production line, manufacturers are finding that the dislocations caused by layoffs are not helpful to the enterprise and that more continuity is required. The prospect of a layoff does not encourage productivity. For service agencies like libraries, the reasons for hiring and retaining staff do not always correlate directly with the needs of production, and in many instances layoff is not an option. People are hired and retained for many reasons, and although it is true that people contribute to accomplishing the goals of the organization, they serve a variety of other functions. People signify power and prestige, and in most libraries it is far easier to give up a personnel slot than it is to regain one.

In an enterprise that is seeking to make a profit, the relative success of an organization is measured by the amount of money it makes. This can be recognized directly in the form of payments to those who work for the company. In business, incentives are in place for optimizing production. In a not-for-profit setting, this kind of reward system is not possible. The measures of success in the organization tend to be growth in the size of the organization, the degree to which the organization upholds real or imagined professional standards, or the budget the organization can command. Although these may well be useful measures, the relationship between them and the stated goals of the organization is far more difficult to gauge.

Too frequently an organization's primary operating goals shift from service to constituencies to security for the staff. Anthony Downs described the growth of organizations as a process that adds procedures and complexity to the operation as a security against possible cutbacks in the resources that are available to the manager.[2] As organizations grow, people become comfortable in what they are doing. They can lose the objectivity needed to judge their contribution to the library's mission: serving its clientele. Personal goals preempt organizational goals. As a result, the capacity of the library to adapt is severely reduced.

A HYPOTHETICAL MODEL

In a library setting, an example of the results of this process might go as follows. The library of the University of Northern South Dakota was, until the 1960s, a tiny operation that supported the curriculum of a normal school by adding only a few thousand books a year to its collections. Beginning around 1965, the student population began to grow, placing new demands on the college. As the curriculum expanded to that of a regional university with graduate programs, the collection expanded quickly. Staff was added to keep up with the flow of materials. By the late 1970s, money became tighter, inflation took its toll, and fewer volumes were added. Technology offered opportunities for streamlining operations with the addition of an automated acquisitions system and OCLC. But the size of the cataloging staff was not decreased until 1983 when funding cuts in the university resulting from problems related to reduction in farm incomes forced the library to let people go. As a result, the cost of cataloging the average book increased dramatically during this period.

Why would this happen?

1. Librarians were long-standing employees of the university with all of the prerogatives of that position. Although it might have been possible to transfer these people to other parts of the library, many did not have the skills needed to make that transition. And, besides, no one wanted to tell them that the tasks they were performing were no longer needed. Other staff might have been transferred, but these people were retained in cataloging because they were useful and/or well liked, and they carried the basic load for the operation. Therefore, the library was forced to choose between efficiency and inertia, and, in these cases, inertia often wins out.
2. Librarians have long been exemplars of Parkinson's Law (work expands to fill the time available).[3] Any organization can find jobs that are not being done as well as they might be if more time were available. As a result, when tasks are removed or streamlined, refinements can be made so that we are doing "better" searching, "better" authority work, or "better" almost anything. Although there is a case for adjusting workload downward in over-worked organizations or for adding routines to refine activities as time permits, difficulty arises when no real judgment is ever made as to how much more useful it is to do a specific task "better." Productivity is reduced, without considerating what benefits might be produced.
3. Librarianship as a profession places great value on the performance of complex tasks and relatively little value on productivity. As a result, the more time that is available to a library staff, the more likely it is that relatively simple procedures will be replaced by more complex ones, and more time and energy will be devoted to the maintenance of standards. In a one-person operation, cataloging tends to be streamlined. In practice, the cataloger often finds that many of the niceties taught in library school cannot be applied because neither the time nor the resources are available.

   As more time is available, however, the complexity of cataloging increases. Some of this is a function of the need to create tools that make a larger catalog more usable. But there is no question that the individual cataloger benefits from this change of orientation. A capacity to handle complex problems gives an individual prestige among peers in the profession and increases the intellectual challenge of the job. These added procedures also add requirements for more management, since a larger staff requires more coordination. That means promotions and salary increases. The rate of production decreases in relation to the number of people involved as newer, higher standards are established for minimum cataloging. When cutbacks occur, staff is reluctant to sacrifice these newly found standards, titles, and salaries. As a result, personnel cutbacks more often lead to backlogs than to a more efficient cataloging operation until the organization makes a conscious decision to adjust to its new situation.
4. The primary goal of libraries (and other not-for-profit organizations) is survival rather than efficiency.[4]

   This means that the manager competes for resources with other agencies. That person views any decline in the resources available as a loss of power and prestige and as a threat to the organizations's well-being. No library is willing to go to its administration with a request that it be allowed to give up 10 percent of its staff with the argument that it can get along just as well without them. Nor is the head of a serials section of a library going to halve its staff willingly for reasons of efficiency. There are always areas where those staff members can be used without transfers of this sort. Questions of efficiency seldom enter into the discussion.

5. The staff members in a unit spend only a portion of their time carrying out the specific functions they were hired to do. Committee work, social interaction, and other activities for the good of the library, its clientele, and its workers consume much of the time that is available in the normal workday. These activities are valued by the work force, and some of this kind of slippage helps improve staff morale. But the addition of these values to economic ones relating to productivity means that the cost study can only show superficially what it costs to perform a specific function. A cost benefit analysis can show what the University of Northern South Dakota spends in its cataloging unit. To be effective, it must also discriminate between the costs of cataloging a book and the costs associated with maintaining the organization (for example, the cost of "gossip" or informal communication).

6. There are rigidities in structures that are highly resistant to change. Some staff members prefer to do something in a specific way and simply refuse to adjust to new routines. When the staff member is tenured or protected by a civil service personnel system, it is frequently viewed as being less costly to let the person be and tolerate the inefficiency rather than remove that person or force him or her into another mold. Sometimes this resistance erodes over time. Sometimes the person leaves, and change is introduced with a new person. But sometimes the library just accepts the inefficiency with the rationale that it is a fact of life and includes it as a cost of doing business.

The result of all this is that the data produced in a cost study analysis of the cataloging unit of the University of Northern South Dakota are likely to provide only a fuzzy snapshot of the operation at a particular point. It is a description of the organization that has been forcibly quantified rather than a truly substantive analysis of its operations. Cost analysis deals easily with the cost of supplies used in an operation, the cost of computer time for OCLC or serials check-in or an acquisitions system, and even with the cost of the facilities used to house the operation. But it cannot reasonably be expected to account for the cost of personnel as long as the library is expected to deal with people as individuals.

As a result, costing is only useful to the manager as a beginning step in an analysis of the underlying values operating within a cataloging unit. It is unlikely that knowing how much a subroutine costs will force the cataloging staff to alter it. If they value the procedure or if some matter of principle can be invoked to justify its continuation, it is likely to be retained. One can never assume that the people who work in an organization really want to change what they do, even if they honestly want the organization as a whole to alter its course.

This brings me to the second major reservation I have about the value of a cost analysis: the decision making role actually played by the data generated. The world of the chicken farmer is one that conforms relatively easily to what Herbert A. Simon referred to as the rational theory of organizations.[5] In this model, the manager (or chicken farmer) gets all of the information that might relate to a specific problem and then uses that information to select the "one best way" to meet the demands of the situation. On the farm, one can watch the productivity level of the chickens, and when the number of eggs produced drops, you get new chickens. Decision making based on hard data is very attractive to those who are charged with operating in a complex world with few certainties. For the past two decades much effort has been invested in getting enough information to make the kind of informed decisions that are seen as ideal in this system. New budgeting techniques, management information systems, and a variety of organizational models have become important parts of the manager's arsenal as a result. Computers have made increasingly sophisticated data available to managers. The emergence of cost studies is clearly a part of that trend. However, it has not yet been established that all the data that have been generated are being used by managers, or even that the use of that data in not-for-profit enterprises has led to an overall improvement in the management of those organizations.

## LIBRARY MANAGEMENT—ORGANIZED ANARCHY?

By their nature, libraries are a combination of several kinds of management structures. Most are basically bureaucratic[6] with elements of collegial and political decision making superimposed by conventions within the profession and situations in their environment. If one must choose among decision-making models in describing libraries, I would suggest that, at least for academic libraries, the model that works best is what Cohen and March call "organized anarchy."[7] Organizations fitting this model are marked by an ambiguity of purpose and problematic goals, unclear technology, a limited capacity to learn from experience, and a limited understanding of what constitutes success for their operations. This kind of organization lacks the cohesiveness that allows a manager to move quickly to implement rational decisions. Simon's model envisions an organization that clearly understands its purpose, an organization where all the workers are directing their efforts to meet its goals. If everyone agrees with the stated goals of the organization, the best managers should try to get all the information available, use it to make good decisions, and then implement them quickly. Cohen and

March see none of the certainties that lead to this kind of reasonableness. What is the result?

Successful library managers tend to operate less reasonably than Simon would like. Henry Mintzberg found in a survey that leaders of organizations have little time to concentrate on one activity, instead giving small amounts of attention to a variety of tasks.[8] They strongly prefer verbal (meetings or phone calls) to written communication as a means of getting the information that they require, and they put great stock in organizational gossip (informal communication) for much of what they know about the organization. According to Mintzberg, managers tend to make highly subjective judgments on most issues, relying on what they know rather than on quantified data. They are primarily involved with linking the organization to its constituents rather than handling day-to-day operations. The most common element in their personalities is a bias toward action rather than the research orientation preferred by Simon. Mintzberg concludes that much of what is currently being offered as management theory runs counter to management practice.

## A MORE ORDERLY IDEAL

One might say that just because this is the way things are does not mean this is the way they should be. It is not unreasonable to seek a more orderly ideal. But I would suggest that most organizations are not rational in the strict sense of using all the data available to them to make the best decisions and that, in fact, they should not be. I would also suggest that good managers more often than not use less sophisticated decision-making strategies such as "muddling through" and "brushfire management," and that these methods are successful at least as often as rational decision making. I would suggest further that seldom is there actually one best solution to a problem, and seldom are the available data the prevailing factor in the decision. As a result, I propose, as does J. Victor Baldridge,[9] that decision making is driven more often by a consideration of the composite values of those working in an organization than by objective facts.

This kind of political decision making differs in several ways from Simon's model. Where Simon says that the optimum way to manage is to seek the "one best way" to do something and urges the manager to use quantitative analysis to determine what that one best solution is, Baldridge says that there are several reasonable solutions for any problem. The task of the manager is to decide which fits best in his or her organization and then choose that solution. Mistakes made in the process are corrected during implementation. Where Simon emphasizes a font of authority in the organization, Baldridge speaks of the obligation of the manager to form and maintain coalitions to support the course of action selected. This is not to say that one advocates an autocratic style, while the other is more democratic. Rather, it is a distinction between the need to "sell" policy to the staff and the users of the library as opposed to a reliance on the "rightness" of a position to carry it through. Finally, Simon sees the organization as a monolith, focusing on its goals with a common set of values, while Baldridge views it as a collection of people who have come into the organization for a number of reasons and who have brought with them a variety of value sets. To function in Baldridge's model the manager must come to understand the values of those who work in the library and use that knowledge along with more objective data to plot the course of its operation.

In this context, the manager's role in the organization changes dramatically. Instead of being a data gatherer, the manager becomes the keeper of the organizational objectives and the person who is charged with bargaining among those who work in the library on behalf of the stated goals of the organization. To accomplish this task, that person must provide persuasive arguments to the various groups working in the library. Hard data are useful, but they are not the only (or even the most important) kind of information used in making decisions. It is at least as important for the manager to understand the values operating within the organization to be successful and to speak to those interests as it is for the manager to collect and apply statistical data about the cost of operations. The main reason for developing cost data in Baldridge's model is to sell a point after the decision has been made rather than to assist in the making of decisions.

The political model for decision making is difficult to accept at face value. It provides far less in the way of concrete methods for improving the quality of management than does the rational model. Its substitution of coalition building for data gathering is difficult for those who work in the information industry. But, as Jeffrey A. Raffel points out, it does solve some problems for the library manager.[10] It allows for ambiguity of purpose in a way that economic decision making cannot. It also allows the organization to use bias and conflict for its benefit rather than try to avoid them. Conflict management includes the views of both the people working in the organization and those it serves. But, perhaps most important, it provides a far better description of the way in which most not-for-profit organizations (and a good many for-profit enterprises) actually operate than that provided us in the rational decision making model.

## LIMITS OF QUANTIFICATION

What are the implications of all this for cost analyses? Without condemning all modern management techniques or cost studies in particular, it nevertheless seems clear that the trend to quantification and economic decision making is too often applied beyond its usefulness. Certainly arguments made with numbers (and particularly those that relate costs to activities) help sell ideas. This is true particularly when the user has a limited understanding of actual operations—as in a library. This benefit alone is enough to make cost studies useful to the manager under certain circumstances. However, the individual manager should not assume that the data being gathered accurately define the cost of doing business or that quantitative data are critically important to decisions about the future of the organization. Data of this sort are, in my opinion, not accurate enough to be used in this way, and it is unlikely that quantitative data can be produced fast enough to be used for anything other than justifying decisions already made. The "facts" used to make the decisions are more likely to be based on judgement, intuition, and less formal data-gathering techniques.

In the final analysis, the value of cost studies is limited to justifying a manager's prejudices about his operation. The cost of doing business is important, but even if hard data can be obtained on how much any activity costs, those data are likely to be less important to the organization than the values of those working in it, the biases of the manager, questions related to personal prestige, or even the inertia of the existing situation. No decision-making process can reasonably hide behind the rationality of quantitative judgment and hope to respond to the needs of a dynamic library organization.

Notes

1. Murray S. Martin, "Cost-Benefit Analysis for Austerity," in *Austerity Management in Academic Libraries,* ed. John F. Harvey and Peter Spyers-Duran (Metuchen, N.J.: Scarecrow, 1984), 236–254.
2. Anthony Downs, *Inside Bureaucracy* (Boston: Little, Brown, 1967).
3. Cyril Northcote Parkinson, *Parkinson's Law and other Studies in Administration* (Boston: Houghton Mifflin, 1957).
4. Downs, *Inside Bureaucracy.*
5. Herbert A. Simon, *Administrative Behavior: A Study of Decision-Making*

*Processes in Administrative Organization,* 3rd ed. (New York: Free Press, 1976).

6. Beverly P. Lynch, Libraries as Bureaucracies," *Library Trends* 7, no. 3 (Winter 1979): 259–267.
7. Michael D. Cohen and James G. March, *Leadership and Ambiguity: The American College President* (New York: McGraw-Hill, 1974).
8. Henry Mintzberg, "The Manager's Job: Folklore and Fact," *Harvard Business Review* 53, no. 4 (July–August 1975): 49–61.
9. J. Victor Baldridge, "Introduction: Models of University Governance— Bureaucratic, Collegial, and Political," in *Academic Governance: Research on Institutional Politics and Decision Making* ed. J. Victor Baldridge (Berkeley, Calif.: McCutchan, 1971), 1–19.
10. Jeffrey A. Raffel, "From Economic to Political Analysis of Library Decision Making," *College and Research Libraries* 36, no. 6 (November 1974): 412–423.

# Reaction 1:
# Cost Studies Pro and Con

## Denise Bedford

The essence of the management process in any organization is decision making—choosing among alternate courses of action to achieve some objective. Every manager has a decision model—a conceptual representation for determining the effects of alternative actions. A model may be informal (based on hunch) or elaborate (well-defined mathematical models arrived at by linear programming). All decision models, regardless of their complexity or simplicity, require information. Managers select for input the type of information they believe most relevant to the decision at hand.

Different managers have different needs and preferences for cost models, information, and types of cost data. Some managers need cost information as input for a highly structured mathematical model, and some need it for a simpler comparison of alternative programs. In both cases the managers believe that the value of the cost information is greater than the resources they must spend to obtain it. They believe that the decisions based on cost information will result in a more efficient or effective allocation of resources.

Different managers have different information needs, depending on their level. The information needed to manage a few tasks or activities at the operating level differs greatly from the information needed to manage the entire library, both in degree of detail and comprehensiveness. To manage a unit requires detailed information about daily activities; to manage a library requires succinct summary information about the total library environment. As information needs move from the unit-head level to the executive level, they become increasingly concise yet comprehensive. Decision making at the top management level requires relatively small amounts of information, summarizing a very broad spectrum defined and gathered by operating and middle managers.

Library managers use many types of cost data. Unit or division managers require information on the resources needed to produce

Denise Bedford is a Library and Information Center consultant, Silver Spring, Maryland. She was the 1983 Lazerow Fellow and her project was "Technical Services Costs in Large Academic Research Libraries." She is a Ph.D. candidate in library science at the University of California, Berkeley.

different levels of outputs, on the unit costs resulting from a variety of processing methods, on the performance levels of individual staff members, and on the effect of those levels on the unit's or division's budget and productivity. Middle managers, or department managers, require cost information on broader work load trends to make decisions on the effective and efficient use of resources.

Data on expenditures and output/activity levels form the basis of any broader economic analysis or decision. Although middle managers might be expected to be aware of these dollar costs per output or activity, cost benefit and cost-effectiveness analyses would be more relevant to their management responsibilities. Library directors or university managers would be more likely to use more sophisticated forms of cost data.

The basic question: What type of information is needed to manage libraries and information centers? How you answer depends on your management style.

## ECONOMIC COST INFORMATION

Gene H. Fisher suggests, "All costs are relevant to some decision or other, past or future, for otherwise they would not be costs."[1] In running a library, it is the manager's responsibility to distinguish relevant from irrelevant costs. For example, in a large academic research library, expenditures such as those for facilities may be irrelevant to the library's decision-making process. This is not likely to be true for all types of libraries, corporate libraries in particular. Decisions related to corporate space (its dollar cost and value) may well be among the most important to a corporate library manager.

In my experience as a practicing librarian and as a consultant to libraries and information centers, I have come to regard economic cost information as an indispensable input to any decision model. Costs in our profession are generally thought of as what is paid in dollars to provide a service or piece of information. Costs in our professional literature are frequently measured in terms of materials purchased or labor used. An economic cost, however, measures both the actual expenditure and those costs associated with *not* using the resources in another effort. It assesses the actual dollar cost of a particular decision and the opportunity losses associated with not having made a different decision.

Examples of decisions that might require economic cost information include the following: whether to apply for and accept a federally funded grant project or to recatalog some materials that are not easily accessible; whether to accept and process gift items or to catalog backlogged materials; whether to allocate funds to develop an expert system to handle cataloging functions for a particular subject area or to develop an online catalog; whether to acquire WLN (Washington Library Network) or RLIN (Research Libraries Information Network). In each of these cases, I have a personal preference as a manager, but my personal preference might not result in the greatest possible long- or short-term benefits for my library users.

In my experience, management decisions are often based on personal preference and are supported with cursory descriptions of expenditures required to complete a project or achieve a particular objective. The decision thus becomes one of "Do we have the dollars?" or "How can we get the dollars?" If the dollars are not readily available, the cost data is used to sell the administration on allocating the funds.

Mr. Williams suggests that the value of dollar cost data lies in its ability to support or sell decisions arrived at by library managers. This assumes that the manager knows or can derive the best decision based solely on his or her experience. I agree with Mr. William's characterizations of how we use data, but I do not accept them as justification for dismissing cost information as a primary source of information for decision making. Information on economic costs should form the basis of any decision model used to allocate scarce resources among alternative products, programs, or services. If we take the approach Mr. Williams advocates, we really have no way of knowing what opportunities have been lost to our users. The difficulty results from not identifying the full range of alternatives, which in turn depend on understanding the goals and objectives for which alternatives are sought.


## PROBLEMS IN DERIVING UNIT COST DATA

Although it is easy to advocate using cost information in managing libraries and information centers, it is not so easy to obtain it. The nature of our work and work flow makes application of standard economic and accounting tools more difficult than in a factory. It is difficult to consistently define units produced, to control for the many task variations associated with a particular process, to allocate expended resources to multiple rather than single outputs, and to predict future demands for our products and services.

There are great variations in derived unit costs for the same expenditure and production data, depending on the nature of the base measure chosen. In technical services, we find that some functional categories are more complex for costing purposes than others; to collect expenditure data and derive unit costs for catalog record production and maintenance are more complex than for serial control activities. Even for a well-defined function, where expenditure data and base measures are readily and consistently available, the interaction of factors may require considerable research before variations in unit cost levels can confidently be explained.

## PROBLEMS IN USING ECONOMIC COST DATA

Still other problems arise in using the cost information, once you've derived it. Managers and cost accountants in manufacturing firms have greater planning control over the level and nature of their work flows because their actions are guided by the market for their products. Our work flows, at the present time, are largely determined by budgetary constraints and the publishing industry's output.

Yet another stumbling block to using cost data is that we're not sure how reliable such data are for budgeting and planning purposes. Although we have a profound procedural understanding of our work flows, we don't have a thorough understanding of the causes of variability in work flow for all functions. We can't use the cost information we derive to manage libraries unless we can also predict future variations.

One of the greatest obstacles to using economic cost information in libraries and information centers rests on our assumption that professional skills are not transportable from one function to another. Consequently, alternative products and services will always seem to require new or additional resources. I don't believe this assumption is true. If our professional skills have grown in only one particular functional area over many years, it is because there have not been opportunities to cross over to other functions. This belief justifies reexamining the principles that underly our professional education rather than dismissing the value of cost information to the management function.

Librarians must do more before we can use cost information as easily as do manufacturing firms. But solutions can be found. The greatest obstacle to using cost information lies in our failure to identify alternatives to existing processes, products, and services. We must ask whether what we are doing is in the public's best interest, and whether it is the best we can do with the resources available to us.

One more question we need to ask is: "What are the long-term costs of managing without economic cost information?" Mr. Williams assumes that the personal and political preferences of our managers will dominate our future, that University presidents will continue to make decisions regarding the library's technological orientation on the basis of academic political sense rather than on the carefully considered costs and benefits associated with alternative courses of action.

Professionals in other academic areas such as engineering, computer and mathematical sciences, and economics are learning to manage and value information resources. They will be prepared to assume management responsibilities for an institution's or the country's information resources if library professionals fail to manage these resources in the most effective manner. Today's students are learning to consider information as a commodity. They are taught to determine their information needs and how to satisfy them, and to estimate the price at which they can obtain information, as elementary tasks of any decision-making process. This is a positive development, and one that we should seize upon to further the interests of both our users and nonusers.

The implications of Dr. Getz's arguments are that library managers will take a more sophisticated and productive role, becoming managers of information resources, rather than of physical materials. The information-poor about whom we are so vocal will suffer the most if we do not realize that access means more than physical availability, and that information resources are not ours, but belong to both users and nonusers.

The question is not whether we need cost data, but whether we are willing to consider the opportunity costs of doing business. Will we create and consider alternatives, or will we continue to look for methods or machines that allow us to simply do faster what we have always done? Deriving and using information on costs are the first steps we must take.

Notes

1. Gene H. Fisher, *Cost Considerations in Systems Analysis* (New York: American Elsevier, 1971), 35.

# Reaction 2:
# Ignorance Is Not Bliss

## Robert C. Miller

Cost studies are of critical importance to the successful management of libraries. As one who has confronted frightening results of both local and comparative cost studies. I can say that there are times when ignorance is bliss. Since I had to pay for those studies, I know that knowledge costs, in both human and dollar terms. But having learned, too late, the real costs of some operations, I can also vouch for the costliness of ignorance. The following thoughts are a reaction to the first three papers in this book by an administrator who sympathizes with all three perspectives.

The first presentation by Gordon Shillinglaw gives a clear introduction to some important ideas in the field of cost accounting, centering on responsibility accounting and activity costing. The material is complex and detailed, at least for the uninitiated, and requires a careful reading. Greater attention might profitably have been given to the important distinction between activity and function. My experience suggests that these definitional problems tend to be a real stumbling block in the implementation of budgeting and costing programs.

Malcolm Getz's viewpoint as an executive responsible for a major research library—Vanderbilt University Library—lends weight to his cogent remarks. At times, I sensed he was too optimistic about the possibilities for useful comparative cost data. The difficulty the Association of Research Libraries has had in putting together relatively simple annual statistics highlights the problems of comparative data. Moreover, I have some concern that short-run emphasis on cost data in evaluating managerial performance may lead to long-run inefficiency and ineffectiveness. On the other hand, his discussion of off-budget costs is very important. This is a concept that needs to be explored, not just in libraries but in institutions everywhere.

I would question Getz's assessment of the costs of optical disk technology. At this time the total cost of utilizing this approach to

Robert C. Miller is Director of Libraries at the University of Notre Dame, Notre Dame, Indiana.

database searching is lower than online service only if the volume of searching at the outset is very high. There are significant fixed costs for optical disks that can be recovered only through high volume. This high volume may develop later, but probably only after eliminating individual search charges.

Getz deals very well with the alleged conflict between political and rational approaches to decision making. As he emphasizes, they can be and frequently are complementary. Perhaps the most intriguing part of his presentation dealt with the concept of "willingness to pay," not unexpected from an economist. His statement on the impact on individuals of electronic media and lowering costs is potentially frightening and needs careful consideration by the research library community as it considers its mission: "The willingness of a university to pay for certain library services may well be shaped by what faculty members can do for themselves."

Delmus Williams presents the view of the line administrator, and it is an interesting and useful example of the kind of thinking that pervades the library profession: We are different, unique, and what works for others won't necessarily work for us. In fact many librarians, even managers, don't like to think about costs, and when the subject is raised, their response is frequently couched in terms of top management's insensitivity to user needs, or quality cataloging, or worker satisfaction in doing the best job possible. He gives what may well be a reasonably accurate description of the way many librarians approach decision making, but it is hardly universal, and even less a role model for sound management. Moreover, I believe the situation in the profession is changing rapidly, or at least I hope it is.

Williams's cynicism about the role of rationality in organizational decision making is unjustified. Organizations, including libraries, do take costs into account in making decisions. Indeed, failure to do so could prove fatal to the future of libraries as effective information centers. Moreover, coalition building, which Williams sees as the operating mode in many libraries, does not obviate the need for data gathering both before and during the consensus-building process. His conclusion may be cute, but it is plain wrong: "In the final analysis, the value of cost studies is limited to justifying a manager's prejudices about his operations."

## COSTS OF COST STUDIES

Though cumulatively the three papers bring out many of the problems inherent in cost studies, there are several areas that do not get sufficient attention. Most important, perhaps, is the cost of cost studies;

both to develop them and to collect the necessary data. Fortunately, as library operations are automated, and library managers become more sophisticated about electronic data collection, problems in this area should be reduced, though they will never be eliminated. Second, study design and particularly data collection methodology can be critical: By varying the data collected, the results can be manipulated to serve specific ends. Often this is unintentional, and it may require careful analysis and understanding of the specific operations to reveal what has happened. There have also been cases where the data collection has been deliberately falsified. Sometimes this can be detected only through replication of the data collection, a time-consuming and expensive process. Sometimes, the deception is never revealed. Finally, such studies, if presented to external agencies may unintentionally raise questions that are embarrassing or difficult do deal with. This possibility must always be kept in mind in developing studies and preparing their presentation.

As I read these three papers, I initially found myself agreeing with almost everything said, even when it was contradictory. As I reflected on my reactions, it occurred to me that this was one of those "dammed if you do, dammed if you don't" situations. So very often, library managers feel that they can't afford to do cost studies because the data gathering will be too difficult and expensive; on the other hand, they have that lingering sense that they can't afford not to do them, because the cost of a mistake would be too great. (Perhaps the dilemma would be partially resolved if there were more accountability for mistakes.) This is where, perhaps, an old-fashioned virtue, prudence, comes in. Though not widely discussed these days, prudence—judgment based on experience and understanding—is critical to effectiveness in this as in many other areas. Neither textbooks nor the seat of the pants make for good decisions. Administrators must develop a sound understanding of the tools and techniques of managerial accounting, their potential uses, abuses, and pitfalls and then decide in each instance whether the cure is worth the cost.

# Reaction 3:
# Using Cost Data Judiciously

## Joe A. Hewitt

Del Williams played the role of the debunker at the preconference, a role that, although assigned, he played with obvious enthusiasm and conviction. I happen to fall into the category that Williams suspected made up the majority of his audience—one who sees considerable potential for cost analysis as a management tool in libraries. For that reason, my reaction will be stated mainly in terms of a response to Williams, although I will refer to both Shillinglaw and Getz from time to time to support my own observations.

Williams's paper is the perfect stimulus for evoking a reaction from an advocate of cost analysis. The paper expresses the traditional, shopworn objections to the application of cost analysis methodologies to library operations. His method, invariably applied to every point, is to set up as straw men the most rigid, simpleminded, and unenlightened approaches to cost analysis, thereby associating current methods with primitive, production-oriented industrial models generally regarded as both counterproductive and obsolete in human organizations. If, indeed, the advocates of cost studies in libraries are of the "chicken farmer" mentality, conducting what Williams calls "forcibly quantified" studies resulting in insensitive, one-dimensional decisions that ignore human and political realities, then Williams's paper makes sense. But that is not, in fact, the case—a point I believe was illustrated by most of the cost studies presented at the preconference.

## COST STUDIES AS MANAGEMENT TOOLS

The image of the current status of cost analysis in libraries, which seems to me to emerge from the papers as a group, might be described as follows. Cost studies are a useful, at times necessary, tool of manage-

Joe A. Hewitt is Associate University Librarian for Technical Services at the University of North Carolina, Chapel Hill. He has published extensively in the field of technical services.

ment in libraries. They tend to be used selectively for specific purposes. In decision making, they are used with sensitivity as data illuminating a single (albeit important) factor involved in complex decisions. Although methods are being progressively refined to account for organizational and procedural complexity, cost studies are not perfect—they can be applied injudiciously and inexpertly in libraries. On the whole, librarians using cost studies are aware of their limitations and dangers and are attempting to make use of cost studies as tools of rational, humane management. This is not the picture that Williams presents as the counterpoint to his own case.

I do agree with Williams that cost study data generally are not the determining factors in major decisions in libraries, nor should they be in most cases. They are, however, a significant step in the direction of making certain types of decisions more objective, or at least demonstrably conscious. Librarians in most institutions no longer find it possible, or at least advisable, to rely exclusively on the more subjective and intuitive elements of their professional judgment in decision making. Many have done so in the past, and may continue to do so, by appealing to the impenetrable complexities of organizational relationships, personal values and sensibilities, goals and objectives, unquantifiable standards, politics, institutional climate, and so on, as if the total situation were so densely and inextricably interwoven, not to mention interactive, that it cannot be treated objectively. Williams's solution, it appears, is to turn this situation over to the manager/guru. The cost study advocate, on the other hand, while also recognizing that decision situations always represent a composite of factors, would be inclined to objectify as many factors as possible, quantify when possible and appropriate, and exercise his or her practiced judgment on a composite body of data and information rather than on one of impressions and hunches.

Either approach may, by the way, be combined with an action orientation and a variety of charismatic leadership styles. A peripheral but particularly disturbing aspect of Williams's paper is the implicit position throughout that a preference for cost quantification precludes the qualities of breadth of vision, value sensitivity, political and organizational savvy, and dynamic leadership, as if these are exclusive attributes of the nonquantifier.

Two key misconceptions in Williams's paper need to be set straight. First, he contends specifically that costing methodologies cannot discriminate the "costs associated with maintaining the organization" and appears generally to doubt the adequacy of costing to assess resource expenditure for activities that do not result in measurable output. This simply is not the case, as suggested by a number of points in the Shillinglaw and Getz papers, and it reflects Williams's persistent inclination to base his opinions of cost analysis on its most primitive forms. In fact, as librarians move into a period of organizational experimentation to capitalize on the effects of computing and telecommunications, the examination of the costs of maintaining organizations of various types may well be a most fruitful area of application.

Second, Williams seems to assume that because library policy and practice often reflect institutional politics and history, the personal capabilities and preferences of staff, and any number of nonquantitative factors, cost data is of little or no value. In other words, because cost data is rarely a controlling factor in decisions, it is not worth having—an attitude that is about as reasonable as that which discounts the usefulness of seismic studies because we cannot control earthquakes.

## NON-COST CONSIDERATIONS

Most administrators in technical services tolerate and at times actively encourage programs, services, procedures, and organizational structures that are known to be less than cost-effective. We do so for many reasons—to meet the requirements of other administrative units of the university, to stay in good standing with an influential school or academic department, to meet special user needs or standards of excellence to which the institution is committed, to meet network standards, to keep the staff happy, or for any number of reasons falling generally under the rubric of keeping peace in the library and institutional family. Rather than diminishing the value of cost data, these situations actually serve to magnify its usefulness. Cost data measure the value of our favors and serve as one of the coins of the realm in which our political capital is stored.

Let us consider an obvious but not exaggerated example. The Acquisitions Department of a medium-sized ARL Library operates a sizeable OP (out-of-print) search program, occupying about one-third of the time of a professional supervisor, one full-time Library Technical Assistant, a graduate assistant, and 30 hours per week of student staff. The fruits of the OP section's labors tend to result in additional costs for other sections of acquisitions as exceptions and special-handling requests reverberate throughout the processing cycle. It is an expensive operation by any measure. The OP program is blatantly out of scale with other acquisitions activities for the size of library; it has been suggested by some staff (most notably those in the Reference Department struggling to keep up with a burgeoning demand for information retrieval searches and end user training) that the concentration on OP acquisitions is in conflict with newly adopted service concepts of access to rather than ownership of materials and that the OP staff might be more usefully deployed to other functions. Yet the OP Search Section continues in all its glory. It does so because it serves the special interests of the history, English, and classics departments, traditionally powerful forces on the Faculty Council and the Library Committee. In this particular institution, Chancellors and Provosts tend to be drawn from the ranks of the history department, a trend illustrated by the incumbents in both positions.

The intelligent library manager is likely to retain the OP search program in this situation but make a point of knowing exactly how much it is costing the library. This information is brought into service, for example, when the History Department representative to the Library Committee objects to the library's funding of the Chemistry Department's subscription to CAS online or to the purchase of machine-readable datafiles. It serves as a telling and effective example of the library's struggle to maintain expected, traditional services while attempting to provide new services based on contemporary technologies. In other words, when technical services librarians trade off cost-effectiveness for political or other reasons, as they often must, they should know the value of these trade-offs, both to make the best decision in the first place and to ensure that gains, in whatever coin, justify the cost. Williams is correct in pointing out that cost data are rarely a determining factor in decision making, but in the political arena that he postulates as preeminent, cost data are rapidly becoming one of the library manager's most effective tools.

Obviously, the Williams paper has served its purpose of eliciting a reaction, but it is time to move ahead. Several important uses of cost studies received little attention at the preconference or were not mentioned at all. These uses are worth mentioning to round out the perspective provided by the conference as a whole.

## COST STUDIES AND PAYBACKS

The first of these might be called "payback" studies. Payback in terms of compensating Technical Services for services rendered was mentioned prominently in connection with the Vanderbilt and Cornell studies, but another type of payback is becoming increasingly common—the case in which the library is given a "loan" from the institution to capitalize its automation efforts with the understanding that the funds will be paid back (only partially, one would hope) through savings in other areas over a period of time. This is a complex type of study, but it is necessary if the library is to make a reasonable deal with the institution. One possible outcome of such a study may be that it is not reasonable to expect the library to pay back anything at all, a conclusion that few institutions will accept without data from an expertly designed and conducted cost analysis.

The use of cost study data in connection with grant applications is becoming increasingly necessary. One effect of the current shortage of outside funding for library projects is that granting agencies are scrutinizing cost projections much more critically. Budgets for funded projects frequently must be backed up by defensible estimates based on systematic cost analysis.

Technical services divisions and library systems as a whole are particularly susceptible to a type of inefficiency called in some management theory *suboptimization*. Suboptimization in this context occurs when a subunit of an organization optimizes its operations to meet unit goals to the detriment of the goals of the organization as a whole. A serials department, for example, may optimize its own procedures in a way that causes increased costs and service problems in departmental libraries and/or other units of the library. An active cost consciousness and a willingness to engage in focused costing methodologies are needed at the highest levels of library administration to settle the kinds of disputes that may arise in a large organization of energetic suboptimizers.

In that connection, cost studies themselves may sometimes result in modifications to organizations and procedures that have suboptimizing effects when the studies are confined to a single department or process. For this reason, proposed cost studies, their methodologies, and the interpretation of results should be reviewed by the highest administrative level in the library as a safeguard against this form of systemwide inefficiency.

The term *suboptimization* is sometimes used informally and less accurately to refer to a process of purposely accepting a less than optimum management practice, organization, or procedure because the cost of change to the optimum practice is greater than its value to the organization. This, too, is a useful concept for library management. Suboptimization in this sense implies that a decision to continue less than optimum practice may also reflect trade-offs based on quantified costs.

Payback studies, more precisely documented budgets for grants, and a more active attack on insidious forms of inefficiency such as suboptimization are just three additional areas where cost studies can be useful in libraries. These examples, like most of the case studies presented at the preconference, suggest specific objectives and methodologies.

A final, and more general, observation concerns the conditions at Vanderbilt, reflected in Malcolm Getz's paper. Here is a case in which a library must adapt to the general application of the willingness-to-pay principle for academic support services within an institution, thereby making cost accounting a basic and inevitable aspect of administering the library. This is a situation that most of us, I suspect, hope to avoid. Even as advocates of cost analysis, we prefer to choose and limit our applications, methodologies, and the manner in which we use and disseminate results. However, the Vanderbilt example may be cause for optimism, because it demonstrates that where cost study methodologies have been applied in a more general and fundamental manner than most of us would prefer, the library has not only survived but flourished. The Vanderbilt example illustrates that cost studies, even in their most extreme and what some might view as ominous manifestations, may be turned to the benefit of the library and its users. Such outcomes occur, however, only when librarians master the techniques of cost analysis and the art of using cost data effectively in a complex institutional setting.

# Reaction 4:
# Defining the Problem

## Jennifer A. Younger

The papers by Shillinglaw, Getz, and Williams accomplish several objectives. Collectively, the authors provide a description of costing methodologies and applications and reasons why costing methodologies are, or are not, important and useful to libraries. Both positive and negative positions are represented.

Shillinglaw's paper provides the necessary introduction. Although he does not presume to urge the use of cost accounting in libraries, he states there are two broad groups of decision applications for which costing activity is useful: resource allocation, including budget justification, and service pricing. Along these lines, a recent survey of research libraries found the most-cited reason for obtaining technical services operations cost data was to gain baseline information for anticipated changes as part of the planning process.[1]

In this context it is interesting that both Getz and Williams emphasize the use of cost data as a measure for evaluating the performance of libraries and library managers. The similarity ends there, as Getz believes "the performance of libraries will be improved if managers make greater use of analytic techniques," while Williams has major reservations about cost studies providing "the kind of information that contributes to the capacity of the organization to adapt to its surroundings."

Getz is optimistic for two reasons. First, he puts a high value on managerial efficiency, the measurement of which, he says, "involves the simplest application of cost concepts." According to Lancaster's typology, efficiency is a question of whether the job is being done as well as is possible.[2] The measuring of efficiency is ideally suited to cost analysis and one should expect to get usable results, provided the study relies on valid methods and data. Getz has, therefore, made a suitable match between his question and method of investigation, and laid a solid foundation for his optimism.

Second, Getz anticipates that more libraries will eventually undertake cost studies. This would, in his opinion, reduce the cost of analysis

Jennifer A. Younger is Assistant Library Director, Central Technical Services, at the University of Wisconsin, Madison.

for all libraries as well as create a databank for comparative study. In fact, the idea of a databank is one of the goals presented by Zweizig and Rodger in *Output Measures for Public Libraries*.[3] Although the perils to be found in comparing cost data across institutions are legendary, if sufficient care is paid to consistent definition, collection, and compilation of the data, it will be possible to make such comparisons.

Shillinglaw and Getz are convinced of the importance of understanding costs. In Getz's words, it "will help a library manager improve the quality of library services achieved with a given set of resources." Most important, in my opinion, they are aware of the pitfalls as well as the benefits of cost studies. Their papers do not contain glossy simplifications of methods or exaggerated claims for the importance of this modern management tool.

Williams is concerned that reliable cost data are not readily obtainable and that the role of cost data in decision making is commonly misunderstood. But in contrast to the first two papers, his suffers from his anticipation that his remarks will be unwelcome and unpopular. In his eagerness to impress upon his audience the limitations of cost studies (and there are critical restrictions), he does not separate the issue of poor cost studies from that of poor managers. His cynicism thus relates not to cost analysis, but rather to the perceived inability of library managers to conduct cost studies and use cost data properly.

The concerns he expresses over the difficulty of securing adequate cost data are legitimate. Yet the situation described at the hypothetical University of Northern South Dakota suggests more than anything else that incompetent managers make poor choices, not that cost data are necessarily inadequate. The selection of inertia, organizational survival, and rigidity as values preferred to efficiency is not mandated by a cost study.

Management determines what use, even if no use at all, will be made of a cost study. Williams is correct in his statement that costing is only useful as a beginning in an analysis of a library operation. But does anyone really believe otherwise? Getz and Shillinglaw, both proponents of cost analysis, certainly do not. Shillinglaw emphasizes that cost accounting requires estimates of what an activity costs; he does not propose using it to decide the value of an activity to the organization or its clients. Getz also considers the role of cost data in decision making. Why conduct cost studies when decisions revolve around shared trust and/or political criteria? This is the least satisfactory section of his paper in part because of the brevity of his answer but also because of his vision of costs as elements of an "objective database." The *American Heritage Dictionary* defines *objective* as not influenced by emotion or personal prejudice but by observable phenomena. Although costs can be observed, measured, and recorded, the question of which costs to measure is not without personal bias. Shillinglaw identifies that as the big question: "How to choose the costs we plug into these methods?" Getz fails in his conclusion to consider specifically that the original selection, collection, and analysis of data can and will affect the results of the cost study and the objectivity of the database. Data can be suspect, and databases are not always as objective as Getz suggests. Nevertheless, there is wisdom in focusing discussions of problems on information rather than on personal ideas or intuition.

While Getz offers a simple explanation—that objective data can serve a role as a base for political decision making—Williams explores the literature of management decision making. But what begin as interesting forays into the process of decision making end abruptly in unsubstantiated conclusions. Williams describes Baldridge's political model of decision making as the antithesis of Simon's rational decision making. He presents Baldridge's model as one in which coalition building replaces data gathering: "To function in Baldridge's model the manager must come to understand the values of those who work in the library and use that knowledge along with more objective data to plot the course of its operation." Is cost data one part of "more objective data"? Presumably, although he does not specifically say so. Securing reliable data may be difficult, but certainly not impossible. Yet Williams seems to endorse the statement that the "main reason for developing cost data in Baldridge's model is to sell a point after the decision has been made rather than to assist in the making of decisions."

Again, his eagerness to deflate the value of cost data has led him to overstate his case. Cost data may indeed be used to "sell a point." However, in the research process questions are asked and a hypothesis made about the results before the data are collected. To the uninitiated, it may appear that the data simply "prove the question" or justify the researcher's hypothesis about the question. (Williams's cynicism is again evident when he labels the library manager's thinking about his or her operation as prejudices rather than, for example, hypotheses.) Yet this is not the case. Speculation about the results is a necessary part of formulating the question.

## Notes

1. *Technical Services Cost Studies in ARL Libraries,* SPEC Kit 125 (Washington, D.C.: Association of Research Libraries, Systems and Procedures Exchange Center, 1986), 5.
2. F. Wilfred Lancaster, *The Measurement and Evaluation of Library Services* (Washington, D.C.: Information Resources Press, 1977), 1.
3. Douglas Zweizig and Eleanor Jo Rodger. *Output Measures for Public Libraries: A Manual of Standardized Procedures* (Chicago: American Library Association, 1982), 4.

# Reaction 5:
# Costs in
# Small-Town Libraries

## Pamela P. Brown

Before evaluating the papers by Shillinglaw, Getz, and Williams, we need an agreed-upon model of the average public library. Those of us who live in metropolitan areas with sophisticated library services have a different impression from the library revealed by statistics.

The 1982 NCES Survey of Public Libraries pictures the average public library:[1] It is in a small town (63 percent of public libraries in the United States serve a population of less than 10,000 people), its staff is two people who perform all the functions necessary to keep the institution running; it is open fewer than 40 hours a week, has a limited budget and a small book collection. Once a month a group of approximately seven citizens convene to establish policy, make decisions, and direct their chief executive officer, the librarian. To many Americans, this is the local public library. It is important to keep this model in mind, for only 10 percent of the public libraries in the United States serve a population of more than 50,000 people.

What does cost analysis mean to the typical library? It is unlikely that the staff has either an interest in statistics or the prerequisite level of sophistication—let alone the time—to be concerned with cost analysis. This is not to say there is no benefit from knowing what it costs to catalog a book, for example. But the reality is that circulation data and whatever "numbers" may be required for the insurance carrier and state library are frequently all the library's staff can handle.

In addition, few public libraries have a clearly worded, unambiguous statement or image of the role(s) they intend to play in their community. Public libraries often strive to be all things to all people. Their mission statements tend to be so broadly worded that nearly any imaginable program, service, or activity can meet the typical criteria of promoting informational, cultural, educational, and/or recreational objectives. In

Pamela P. Brown is Head of Technical Services at the Arlington Heights Public Library, Illinois.

fact, the expense of daily operations (what Shillinglaw calls "intermediate activities") is difficult to tack firmly onto any of the typical criteria. Yet it is possible to validate services as unusual as outreach to the local singles bar or the loaning of pet animals. Because of this prevalent lack of focus, and in recognition of the importance of long-range planning, the Public Library Association of the American Library Association is engaged in the Public Library Development Project, one element of which is to produce a role manual. This manual "will help librarians and trustees differentiate among the different roles a library might play in its community, identify the essential resources required to fulfill each role, and match performance measures to the roles selected."[2]

One of Getz's examples of decision making supported by cost data is the choice between a centralized facility and a diffused one. But is this primarily a matter of costs? Certainly cost is one element, but unless budget stability is threatened, a choice of this type actually concerns other issues, such as the goals of the institution, its long-range plan, community needs and concerns, and the philosophy or administrative style of the director and/or governing board. As Williams's paper suggests, these other matters help formulate the plan, which is then supported by favorable statistical data. Even if money were a prime motivator in a decision to open (or close) branches, the issue of money would have to be overwhelming in order to carry the change through to successful completion without the buttressing of community support.

Getz's example also brings to mind two areas of particular difficulty in the cost analysis of services for the public library: public relations and marketing. Calculating actual cost may be relatively simple. Determining benefit is another matter. This becomes quite evident when money needs to be reallocated, but it is impossible to project the effects of such actions as no longer providing pencils for patrons, removing a remote-site book drop, or closing a public meeting room.

None of the papers address the high cost of making changes. Even when budget cuts are of the immediate, cold-turkey variety, substantial resources at the administrative level are required to implement changes. Opening branches, centralizing services, and other such measures to increase efficiency require a public relations campaign, staffing adjustments, and so on after the decision to change is made. As any library system that has had to close a branch can attest, there is property to relocate, a collection to move, inventory records to update, personnel to terminate or relocate, and more. It is not simply a matter of locking the door and walking away. By the same token, libraries that face budget cuts (or increases) must make difficult decisions about where to effect the change and how. For this reason, although a change may appear cost-effective, the cost of making it (and the time required to realize the change) must be calculated as part of the decision process.

Getz discusses "willingness to pay." A few assertive patrons may be quick to demand service and special consideration on the grounds that they pay taxes, yet the general public has virtually no consciousness of what it takes to make materials shelf-ready. There is little awareness of how library dollars are spent, or even of what it takes to run a library. Any librarian who has experienced a bond levy to buy materials without a supporting increase in funds for additional staff or processing can readily attest to this fact, as can any librarian who has tried to explain why the latest best-seller is at the local bookstore but is not yet ready for circulation.

On the other hand, library administrators do not encourage public awareness of what particular services cost. Most prefer to discuss the library's budget as a whole, perhaps with personnel costs or the book budget isolated as a percentage. There seems to be a fear of publicizing, or an embarrassment concerning, what some particular service costs.

Library board members may be willing to pay for a very high level of service and to defend the total cost to their constituents, but usually they too prefer not to know individual service costs. They certainly do not wish to have their costs compared to those of neighboring institutions. Both Getz and Williams note the difficulties in comparing analyses from different institutions. Each library has its own salary range, quality standards, procedures, task definitions, and guidelines for task assignments. It is no wonder librarians and board members alike are protective of their cost data. It is threatening to give this information to the public, who lack the expertise to interpret it but do control the purse strings.

All of this is not to say that cost ignorance should be continued. Avoidance is precisely what perpetuates the free public library myth. Yet it takes hard cost data, a supportive environment, and effective public relations to correct this myth. We librarians must remember that the public pays our salaries and that our mission is to serve its needs. Serving the public's needs as effectively as possible also means being knowledgeable and realistic about costs and making cost information available for public scrutiny and understanding.

Notes

1. "The NCES Survey of Public Libraries, 1982: Final Report" as summarized in *The Bowker Annual of Library & Book Trade Information*, 31st ed. (New York: Bowker, 1986), 346–352.
2. Kathleen Mehaffey Balcom, "To Concentrate and Strengthen," *Library Journal"* 111, no. 11 *(June 15, 1986); 36–40.*

# 2
# Case Studies

# Introduction

## Gary M. Shirk

There is nothing more useful to anyone embarking on a new endeavor than assurance that a task can be accomplished. For those of us contemplating our own cost studies, the eight case studies that follow should provide all the assurance needed: two are case studies of acquisitions, one in a public library and the other in an academic library; two describe costing analysis in serials; two are cost analyses of various aspects of cataloging; and the remaining two are general studies of technical services costs.

In "Acquisitions Cost Study at Cornell University Library," Christian M. Boissonnas describes Cornell's experiences with technical services costing and describes in detail the acquisitions cost component of two studies conducted at different times. Although both studies yield valuable cost information, the information is inconsistent from one study to the next. Boissonnas points out some of the reasons for the differences in such studies, even when conducted in the same institution. Nevertheless, the cost information is valuable both for planning/budget presentations and cost recovery calculations.

Kenneth J. Bierman explores the cost of book acquisitions at the Tucson Public Library in "Acquiring Unit Time and Cost Study." His article illustrates the importance of looking beyond simple, gross costs per unit for acquisitions. Although his study is methodologically similar to the others, Bierman's approach differentiates the costs of acquiring several different functional types of materials—for example, multiple copies of popular material and single-copy titles from specialized vendors. Tracking costs of several different types of materials permits more sophisticated planning and decision making.

"Costs Associated with the Public Card Catalogs at the University of Oregon Library" is Karen Calhoun's account of maintaining both card catalogs and COM (computer output microfiche). Data were needed to determine if this situation should be continued until an online catalog could be installed. Conducting the study helped to identify and clarify

Gary M. Shirk is Vice President of Yankee Book Peddler, Inc., Contoocook, New Hampshire. He was formerly Acquisitions Librarian at the University of Minnesota.

many issues affecting management of the catalogs. The results of the analysis led not only to improved decision making but also to procedural simplification.

In "Three Public Catalog Formats Compared—A Cost Study," Elizabeth Hood and Ruby Miller provide insights into the costs of three catalog formats at the Maddux Library, Trinity University: the traditional card catalog, COM (computer output on microform), and online catalog. The study analyzes currently performed tasks, then extrapolates from these to determine the probable costs of each of the other alternatives. Their research led to the conclusion that an online public access catalog was the most cost-effective alternative in their situation.

With "No More Free Ride: Cost Analysis in the Serials Department," Sherry Anderson outlines a medical library's experience with serials cost analysis at Wake Forest University. The study uses direct measurement techniques to determine the costs of each task associated with serials check-in and provides sample forms. Although the paper primarily focuses on the methodology used, the results of the study were impressive. Imagine reducing serials staff by 43 percent and finding time to implement a new automated system that facilitates further reductions!

Linda Haack Lomker's "Serial Check-in Cost Study: A Methodology" reports the work of the Resources and Technical Services Division (RTSD)'s Serials Section Committee to Study Serials Records, 1984–1985. This report discusses the issues that affect the development of standardized serials costing methodology. Among these are the scope of the serials file, its size, its complexity, its content, variations in check-in procedures, the level of staff performing the tasks, wage scales, sampling methods, and assumptions about nonworked hours.

Gary M. Pitkin describes the utility of a single costing methodology in two different circumstances in "Technical Services Costs Case Study." It is first used by the library of Sangamon State University to analyze technical services costs in response to a cut in the personnel budget. This is a demonstration of functional cost analysis using a staff survey to determine the proportion of time for each task and tabulating the data by computer. The results of the analysis permit several organizational changes and a $25,000 reduction in costs without reducing technical services production. The same technique is used later at Appalachian State University to determine the savings that could be achieved by automating serials check-in.

In "Menu-Driven Processing: Cost Analysis Studies at Vanderbilt University," Douglas Phelps thoroughly describes the costing methodology used at Vanderbilt. This complex set of procedures is currently used to calculate the recovery costs required for an extensive array of technical services operations. Of special interest is the technique for finding a common denominator among different units of measure. The use of these data is unusual: Technical services bills each public services unit in proportion to the number of volumes processed through various costing modules. In addition, the results of the analysis impact on budgeting, organizing staffing patterns, setting production targets, and formulating management objectives.

## OBSERVATIONS

Despite the variation among the studies in terms of scope and methodology, several issues emerge in varying degrees in most of the articles. From these I have observed the following:

### Purpose Defines the Study

All case studies must address numerous methodological issues (for example, functional definition, scope of functions, level of specification, data collection techniques, nonproductive time assumptions, unit of measure, sampling techniques). The basis on which decisions are made for each of these issues is the intended purpose of the study. The eight cost studies in this section have one or more of the following general purposes: cost reduction, cost recovery, and evaluation of processing alternatives.

### Comparisons Are Risky

Comparing organizations is risky because of variations in the decisions I've described. No two studies are precisely the same, even if, as Cornell's experience shows, they are conducted in the same institution. Inevitably the scope of the study varies; the functions studied differ; or measurement methods are dissimilar enough to affect results. Choices are invariably made to maximize the study's value to the library as determined by what information is needed most at the time.

### A Pragmatic Approach

None of the case studies are "pure" research. All are conducted with a specific set of objectives in mind. It is entirely reasonable under these conditions to expect that methodological choices are influenced by the perceived risk associated with the decision at hand, the need to reduce disruption to continuing operations, and the limitations of cost analyses. Rules of thumb and methodological simplification are permitted, particularly if the alternative is to complicate the study in an area peripheral to the main issues.

## Simple Mathematics

There are no complex mathematical models in use here. For the most part, only rudimentary statistical techniques and simple formulas are used. Although not explicitly stated, the authors appear to recognize that the assumptions and simplifications made in the methodology do not justify sophisticated mathematics.

## Unexpected Benefits

Analysis of cost typically produces valuable, unanticipated results. For example, studies conducted for cost recovery purposes will probably reveal opportunities to simplify procedures and reduce costs. These may help in reorganization, budget preparation, planning, procedural analysis, and decision making. As a corollary, the studies also produce considerable data for which no useful purpose can be found—for example, the costs of intermediate steps in a function whose gross costs are used for cost recovery.

## Satisfactory, but Tentative, Data

All the librarians presenting their findings urge caution in using their data and, to a lesser extent, their methodology. They recognize the risk of comparing one institution's data with another's; they probably also lack complete confidence in the methodologies they have used. They recognize that the data represent an oversimplification and probably incorporate a significant range of error. Though satisfactory for the purpose of their cost study, the methodologies used are not sophisticated enough to indicate the range of error that may be due to inconsistent measurement or sampling.

## Shaky Theoretical Foundations

Costing theory for libraries is in its infancy. We are unclear about the appropriate scope for cost studies of technical services. For example, do we really know the value added to library material because of its processing? How can we be sure that we are measuring all activities that contribute to that value and should, therefore, be part of the measurement of its costs? As a result, critical assumptions are made without theoretical defense—Bierman's 100 percent overhead cost figure, for example.

Despite the lack of a firm theoretical foundation and sophisticated mathematics, these case studies are valuable examples of how much can be done by library professionals today. Nearly all the studies have served the purpose they were designed to fulfill and have yielded practical results. They are solid testimony to the value of careful scrutiny of library operations.

# Acquisitions Cost Study at Cornell University Library

## Christian M. Boissonnas

At Cornell, in the past ten years, we have conducted three internal studies of technical services costs and participated in one external. The external study was done by Tantalus, Inc. under a contract with the Council on Library Resources (CLR). We study ourselves for pretty much the same reasons as everybody else does.

First, we want to gather data to help us in the planning process. I am always overwhelmed with how persuasive our data are, how well they document our need for more of everything. I am therefore constantly surprised at the obtuseness of my university's administrators in not allowing themselves to be convinced and coming through with the cash. In other words, although I do share my colleagues' belief that these studies help in the planning process, I really cannot show what they contribute to our budgets that we would not have gotten without them.

The second reason we conduct technical services cost studies is to recover costs. At Cornell the Hotel School is not really owned by the university. Rather, it is operated by the university under a contract with the Statler Foundation. The Hotel School Library contracts out its technical services to the University Library Central Technical Services, of which my department is part. In order to know what to charge, we must have some idea of what the process costs.

Although I will limit my presentation to acquisitions costs, we have costed out all technical services operations from the time of receipt of packages in the shipping room to the time books leave technical services for their final shelving locations. I will present costs from the last study that we conducted, in 1984. I will then attempt to compare this study with the CLR study, which was conducted immediately after our own.

When we decide to do a cost study, we hire a person who has had formal training in statistical methodology and/or operations research. Our 1984 study was conducted under my direction, and I asked that it follow as closely as possible the format and methodology of our 1980

Christian M. Boissonnas is Acquisitions and Systems Librarian at Cornell University Library, Ithaca, New York. He is a well-known speaker on acquisitions and technical services costs.

study. I hoped that we could in this way obtain comparable automation costs. In 1980 we were in OCLC, and in 1984 in Research Libraries Group (RLG). Unfortunately, as far as acquisitions is concerned, we obtained no useful comparisons. In 1980 we had a batch/punch card acquisitions system, and in 1984 we used the Research Libraries Information Network (RLIN) Acquisitions System. The two were not comparable.

Our methodology follows the technique of functional cost analysis or activity costing described by Mr. Shillinglaw. In our study it involved five steps. The first was to define and identify tasks starting with the arrival of books in the shipping room. Exhibit 1 shows the tasks identified in the acquisitions department and how they are defined.

EXHIBIT 1.   Tasks Performed by the Acquisitions Department in Cornell University Library 1984 Cost Study.

| Task | Definition |
| --- | --- |
| Shipping room processing | Identify shipments, open packages, find the invoice and insert it in the first book in the shipment; then load the shipments on book trucks. |
| Preparation of orders for input | Sort orders received from selectors and users. Decide which need preorder searching beyond the automated system and which actually get ordered. Assign vendors, keep track of ordering statistics. |
| Preorder searching | Search using the RLIN Acquisitions System. |
| Ordering | Input, print, and mail the orders using the RLIN Acquisitions System. |
| Invoice approval | Check invoices against corresponding shipments, funding each invoice line. |
| Checking-in | Call up the acquisitions record in the RLIN database, update it to reflect that the book has been received, and print the record for inclusion in the book. |
| Precatalog searching | Verify the form of the main entry in the Cornell Union Catalog and verify any series in the Series Authority File and/or Union Catalog. Record the locations and call numbers of any other manifestations of the work in hand. |

The second step was to conduct a time study at each station. The data were gathered through two processes: self-timing and direct observation. Self-timing was used in tasks where long periods were spent at a single location, such as the card catalog, the receiving desk, or a computer terminal. It was also used in circumstances where the research assistant could not carry out observations covertly enough, which might result in disturbances of the subjects under observation and unrepresentative data. The research assistant also performed some independent checks by observing individuals while they were timing their own work. He found their observations to be accurate.

The third step was to identify as many overhead costs as possible. Exhibit 2 shows the components of these costs.

The fourth step was to compute a compensating factor to account for that time which was paid for but not worked (for example, vacations, sickness, breaks, rumor mongering). It required the computation of a "productive time ratio" or PTR (time worked *productively*/time paid for). The compensating factor was the amount that had to be added to the direct labor costs identified in the study to account for nonproductive time.

The fifth and final step was to compute costs at each work station using current costs and salaries.

The careful definition of the tasks that we carried out in the first step can result in substantial savings for future studies. If the tasks are defined precisely enough, the whole study does not have to be redone every time new cost data are needed. As long as the process involved is

EXHIBIT 2.  Components Used in Overhead Computations in Cornell University Library 1984 Cost Study.

| Component | Includes: |
| --- | --- |
| Administrative salaries | Technical services department heads, assistant heads, and secretaries; book accounting staff; assistant university librarian for automated and technical services, 40% of his secretary's salary, 50% of the system office staff's salaries. |
| Local computing charges system | Cost of running the book accounting system. |
| Telephone | Equipment and line charges, but not line charges related to the RLIN system. |
| Equipment rentals | Typewriters, copy machines, keypunch machines, but not RLIN terminals or associated printers. |

still the same, only that task for which new costs are required has to be studied.

The outcome of the study was a set of costs associated with the processing of one title, including library overhead and productive time ratio. It did not include university overhead (utilities, heating, cleaning services, or central administration salaries). These are real costs too, but we did not attempt to measure them because we did not need to factor them in our cost recovery formula.

In Exhibit 3, I have shown the results of our study. The size of the sample for invoice approval may appear a little small, but this is a very mechanical activity that goes fast and without much variation. It involves making certain that the book and invoice line match, and writing the fund number obtained from the order slip in the book on the appropriate invoice line. The real work of verification, in which such questions as "Is this the right book?" are asked, is done during checking-in.

Exhibit 4 shows the overhead calculation. Let me anticipate my critics and tell you why, for our purposes, this figure isn't much good, although it was valid for the study we did. Our study was to identify technical services costs, not acquisitions costs. The overhead identified includes components in the catalog and serials departments and all of the salary of the assistant university librarian for technical and automated services. So the real figure, for the acquisitions department, is something *less* than 18 percent, but we do not know how much less. It is inflated by the salaries of two department heads, two assistant department heads, two secretaries, and about two-thirds of the assistant

EXHIBIT 3.   Sample Sizes and Types in
Cornell University Library 1984 Cost Study.

| Activity | Sample Size | Sample Type* |
|---|---|---|
| Shipping room processing | n/a | n/a |
| Preparation of orders for input | 132 | s |
| Preorder searching | 114 | s |
| Ordering | 114 | s |
| Invoice approval | 77 | o |
| Checking-in | 701 | s |
| Precatalog searching: | | |
| Matching books and printouts | 100 | s |
| Verifying data on the printouts | 130 | s |
| Searching | 403 | s |

*s = self-timed, o = observed

EXHIBIT 4.  Overhead Calculation in
Cornell University Library 1984 Cost Study.

| | |
|---|---:|
| Overhead components: | |
| Administrative salaries | $333,105 |
| Local computing charges | 30,670 |
| Telecommunications | 12,826 |
| Equipment rentals | 4,300 |
| Total overhead | $380,901 |
| Total technical services budget | $2,111,085 |
| Overhead (Total overhead ÷ Total technical services budget) | $.180429 |

university librarian's salary. The overhead figure should be nearer 6
percent than 18 percent.

There is no such problem with the computation of the compensating
factor, which is shown in Exhibit 5. The key datum is computing the
PTR is the percentage of observations showing productive work, which
must be interpreted carefully. It is valid only if the people being
surveyed behave during the study as they normally do. So, it is very
important to allay their concerns long before the timing and observations start. We feel that this was accomplished in three ways.

First, before the study started the department heads explained the
study and its purpose to them, described in detail what data were being
gathered, and emphasized that no individual names would appear.

Second, the research assistant spent the better part of three weeks
dealing with the employees in each department on a one-to-one basis
having them describe their jobs, and explaining to them what he was

EXHIBIT 5.  Computation of Compensating Factor in
Cornell University Library 1984 Cost Study.

| | |
|---|---:|
| *Productive Time Ratio* | 990 |
| Total number of observations: | .824 |
| Percentage of observations showing productive work | 2,028 |
| Working hours in a year | 1,522 |
| Available hours less vacations, holidays, etc. | 1,254 |
| Total hours of productive work (1,522 × .824) | .6184 |
| Productive Time Ratio (PTR = 1,254/2,028) | |

95 percent sampling error = $\pm 1.96 \sqrt{(.618)(1 - .618)/990} = .03$

*Compensating Factor (CF)*
$CF = (1/PTR) - 1 = .617$

doing and why. He worked hard at establishing good working relations with them and ultimately succeeded.

Third, the research assistant was always on the production floor, watching as unobtrusively as he could. However, it was impossible to tell what he was watching. His target could have been five or ten desks away, or in the next department. The staff quickly got used to seeing him around and paid him no mind. It was only after three weeks had elapsed that the gathering of data began.

One indication of the fundamental soundness of the PTR is how the ratio compares with the one from the 1980 study, which was based on 1,008 observations, with all other variables the same. In 1984 the PTR was .618; in 1980 it was .610.

One cost that we were particularly interested in identifying was the cost per title of using the RLIN Acquisitions System. Exhibit 6 shows this computation.

One difficulty with this computation was that the terminals were not used only for ordering and checking in books. They were also used for preparing in-process records for books received on standing orders, blanket orders, and gifts. The above 58,706 records created include the latter as well as the former. Of these, 30,927 records were for orders.

Another problem concerned the depreciation period. Five years for such equipment is an accounting standard. However, it is certain that

EXHIBIT 6. RLIN Cost per Record Input in
Cornell University Library 1984 Cost Study.

|  | Unit cost per title |
|---|---|
| *Records created* (1983/1984): 58,706 | |
| *Hardware* Four terminals @ $1,595 each + one DEC printer @ $1,980, depreciated over five years. Cost per year: $1,672 | .028 |
| *Maintenance contracts* $36/mo. × 12 × 4 terminals = $1,728 | .029 |
| DEC printer = $384 | .007 |
| Telecommunications $290/month × 12 × 4 lines = $13,920 | .237 |
| *Total RLIN cost/record input* | .301* |

* This cost does not include RLIN charges per record for inputting or generating orders, claims, or cancellations. These charges are included in Table 7.

we will keep most, if not all, our terminals much longer than that, if our OCLC experience is any guide.

We are now ready to look at the per title cost of processing monographs in the acquisitions department, as shown in Exhibit 7.

At Cornell in the summer of 1984 it cost us $5.42 to order, receive, and send one monograph to the catalog department. Even if you accept my statement that this was a carefully conceived and executed study, you must view this result with great suspicion. You must ask yourself: "What does this result really tell me? What is it really an average of? What else do I need to know before I can compare it with some other number?"

Let me address some of these questions. Careful though we were, you already know that one number is artificial, at least as far as this presentation is concerned. The 18 percent overhead, as I have discussed previously, is not just an acquisitions department overhead. So you know that $5.42 is really inflated by something between six and twelve cents. However, this is only a 2 percent error. I can live with that. If that's the worst we did, we did very well.

EXHIBIT 7.   Per Title Cost of Acquisitions Process in Cornell University Library 1984 Cost Study.

| Function | Hours | Wage /hr. | Additional costs | Cost/ unit |
|---|---|---|---|---|
| Ordering | | | | |
| Preparation of orders for input | .028 | 9.430 | | .260 |
| Preorder searching | .021 | 5.830 | .030 | .122 |
| Ordering | .046 | 5.830 | 2.200 | .268 |
| Receiving | | | | |
| Shipping room processing | .004 | 7.260 | | .029 |
| Invoice approval | .021 | 5.380 | | .113 |
| Checking-in | .041 | 5.380 | .050 | .221 |
| Precatalog Searching | .065 | 5.830 | | .379 |
| Total labor cost | | | | 1.392 |
| Compensating factor (.617) | | | | .859 |
| Overhead (18%) | | | | .251 |
| Fringe benefits (24%) | | | | .334 |
| Total labor cost, overhead, & benefits | | | | 2.836 |
| RLIN cost per record | | | | .301 |
| Additional RLIN costs* | | | 2.280 | 2.280 |
| Per Title Cost of Acquisitions Process | | | | 5.417 |

*Includes first-time use, searching, and order-printing charges.

The real question is: What does this number really represent? It is not the average cost of processing one book in my department. It is not even the cost of processing one order among others from beginning to end. It is only the cost of processing one firm monographic order, from the time the order is placed, until the time the book is received and sent to the catalog department. It is not an average based on a sample of all orders, or even all firm orders. At Cornell, exchange requests, requests for gifts, and standing orders are also called orders. It is not representative of all firm orders because not all firm orders are received. Some have to be claimed, cancelled, reordered, or returned. None of these functions was factored in this study.

So, what good is it? Well, it may not be any good for you, but it is just what we ordered. Remember why we did this in the first place: to gain some information for planning purposes and for cost-recovery purposes. We gained some management information. Not much, but enough for now. Here, cost recovery was the driving force. And the fact is that the Hotel Library orders almost nothing beyond current trade publications, easily available, almost all of which eventually arrive. We rarely claim a hotel order, and I can't remember ever seeing a request to cancel one. Thus, the cost of studying these functions would have certainly exceeded any benefit that we might have derived from the data.

To illustrate the point that comparisons in this business can be very misleading, I'll now consider the study that was conducted by Tantalus, Inc., a few weeks after this one. At first sight, at least one of its purposes was the same: to gather data on what technical services cost. Exhibit 8 shows those data elements that can be compared at all. It is doubtful that the comparison is meaningful. There are several problems.

Tantalus included four levels of overhead: university, library, division, and department. In order to make the two studies comparable, data for university and library overhead have been omitted here. The Cornell study includes only technical services overhead.

Where the results are within a few cents of each other (as with comparable subsections of ordering and the receiving section), it is unfortunately impossible to draw the conclusion that both are accurate estimates of the real costs. It is necessary to apply certain statistical tests to determine whether the differences between the two sets of data are statistically significant. Although we have both sets of data and could do this, it is probably not worth the expense.

The data for comparable subsections within shipping room processing present us with serious problems; the differences are just too great to be ignored. Let us examine how the data were gathered. In the Cornell study, an actual count of the books in the shipping room was made. In the Tantalus study, a count of incoming *boxes* was one benchmark and outgoing *books* was the other. There is no way that the

Exhibit 8.   Tantalus and Cornell Cost Studies Comparison.

| Process | Tantalus | Cornell with PTR | Cornell Without PTR |
|---|---|---|---|
| Ordering and preorder searching | | | |
| Labor | .51* | .65 | |
| PTR (.617) | ** | .40 | |
| Fringes | — | .16 | |
| Overhead | .10 | .12 | |
| RLIN cost | 2.94 | 2.94 | |
| Other direct costs | .13 | — | |
| Total | $3.68 | $4.27 | $3.87 |
| Shipping room processing | | | |
| Labor | .09* | .03 | |
| PTR | ** | .02 | |
| Fringes/overhead | .02 | .01 | |
| Other direct costs | 0 | — | |
| Total | $ .11 | $ .06 | $ .04 |
| Receiving section (acquisitions dept.) | | | |
| Labor | .27* | .33 | |
| PTR | ** | .20 | |
| Fringes | — | .08 | |
| Overhead | .06 | .06 | |
| RLIN cost | 0 | .05 | |
| Other direct costs | .13 | — | |
| Total | $ .46 | $ .72 | $ .52 |

*Includes fringes
**Tantalus results do not include a productive time ratio
—Included elsewhere

two are comparable until the assumption that the conversion factor used by Tantalus (X number of books per box) has been established to be true for the study period.

So, where does this leave us? We have two studies, conducted at approximately the same time, that show contradictory data. Which is right? Ours? Tantalus's? Probably neither is completely right. One may be closer than the other, but there is no way ever to establish that for certain, and I doubt very much that it would be worth the effort. The studies may, in fact, show different facets of the same problem. All we are left with for certain is that the methodologies were different enough to account for the discrepancies.

Naturally, we will continue to use the results that we obtained on our own. In fact, the data presented here formed the basis on which a new contract between Cornell University and its Hotel School was negotiated. Some of them, such as the RLIN costs, can be, and have been, used for budget planning. As far as we are concerned, they were worth gathering. It does not mean, however, that they are, or should be, applicable to anyone else. The methodology, however, may be.

# What Does It Cost to Acquire a Book?: The Tucson Public Library Experience

## Kenneth J. Bierman

What does it cost to acquire a book at the Tucson Public Library? This report answers that deceptively simple question with an equally deceptively simple answer: $1.88. This is the "average" direct cost (excluding indirect costs of library and city support services), which is derived by taking the total direct annual cost of running the acquiring unit ($245,000) and dividing it by the total number of items acquired in an average year (130,000). As is so often the case with simple answers, this simple answer does not begin to tell the whole story. Read on to find a more complex, but also a more useful, answer to the question, "What does it cost to acquire a book at the Tucson Public Library?"

The Tucson Public Library, established in 1883, serves the City of Tucson and Pima County, one of the fastest-growing metropolitan areas in the country. The library serves 650,000 people in a geographic area covering 9,000 square miles from a main library and fourteen branch libraries and two mobile vehicles (Homebound Services to shut-ins and Bookmobile Services to rural areas of the county).

The collection consists of 800,000 cataloged items (750,000 print and 50,000 nonprint), as well as uncataloged mass market paperbacks. The library attempts to be a client-oriented institution providing a wide variety of popular library materials and services. The library does not attempt to be a research center or to have a research collection, although the main library attempts to fill the gap between what is available at the branch libraries and what is available at the University of Arizona Library, located in Tucson and open to the public. In general, however, the Tucson Public Library is more like the Baltimore County Library than the Enoch Pratt Library.

Kenneth J. Bierman is Assistant Director of the Tucson Public Library and has served on numerous RTSD and Public Library Association committees.

The collections of the library are heavily used. Over 300,000 residents have active library cards (that is, they have been used at least once in the past year) and over 4,000,000 items are circulated annually. The library takes great pride in getting current popular materials in the hands of the public as quickly as possible.

The acquiring unit of the Tucson Public Library is charged with obtaining materials for the library system. In this function it produces selection lists, places orders, and authorizes payment for books, periodicals, phonorecords, audiocassettes and videocassettes, and all other library materials. The current materials budget is $1,100,000.

The acquiring unit has a staff of 8.5 full-time employees: a librarian IV manager, a library technical assistant III, one and one-half library technical assistants II, four library technical assistants I, and one processing clerk.

The average annual salary of these employees, (excluding the librarian IV and the processing clerk), is $22,520. This includes 30 percent for fringe benefits paid by the city. For all tasks in this study except general administration and physical processing, this is the salary from which average unit costs were derived. General administration costs were based on the librarian IV's salary, and physical processing costs were based on the processing clerk's salary.

Except for high-demand popular titles, selection is done outside the acquiring unit and, therefore, the cost of regular selection is not included in this study. The selection costs for high-demand popular titles are included in the task called general administration, as this selection is done by the librarian IV.

The acquiring unit acquires approximately 130,000 items a year, representing 15,000 to 16,000 new titles. Of the total items acquired, approximately 92 percent (120,000) are print items, and 8 percent (10,000) are nonprint items (primarily records, audiocassettes, videocassettes, and mixed-media kits). Approximately 85,000 are ultimately cataloged, and the remaining 45,000 (mass market and juvenile paperbacks) are sorted and distributed uncataloged to the public service agencies.

## ACTIVITIES WITHIN THE ACQUIRING UNIT

Materials are acquired in a number of ways. The two most common are through Greenaway Plans or the submission of order slips for replacement titles and titles not expected to be received as Greenaways.

Greenaway plans are arrangements made to obtain single copies of books from selected publishers at the time of publication. Selection lists of these titles are reviewed by the acquiring unit and made available for purchase by age-level selection committees.

Other are judged on the basis of printed reviews or anticipated demand. Those selected are submitted by public service staffers, who copy the bibliographic information and citations on order slips. Order slips are sometimes used by the acquiring unit to compile subject-area or media selection lists. The chief use of these slips, however, is by the selectors who review them and determine the number of additional copies needed, marking their choices directly on the slips.

Some materials are obtained using standing orders (automatic shipment by publishers of updated editions of reference materials), book club memberships, and association memberships. All newspaper and periodical subscriptions for the library system are placed centrally by the acquiring unit.

Since 1972, the library has been using a computerized ordering system called BATAB. Bibliographic and order information are keyed onto diskettes, using special keying machines, and the diskettes are used by the city computer services department to produce selection lists, purchase orders, and open order and financial reports. As orders are placed, BATAB automatically assigns the order amount to the appropriate fund accounts. There is a BATAB computer run once a week.

Ordered materials are received, unpacked, checked in and stamped as property of the library by the acquiring unit, and the transactions necessary to clear invoices are keyed onto diskettes for computer input. The cleared invoices and matching computer output are forwarded to the city accounting department where another computer program automatically produces the city checks to pay the invoices.

As invoices are paid, the BATAB program deducts the expenditures from the budgets of the agencies that ordered the materials. Weekly fund status reports and summary reports are produced on two levels: the library system level as well as the individual agency level. The fund status reports show agency librarians the week's financial transactions and budgetary balance, while the open order reports show them which titles are still on order or in process for the library system.

Approximately two-thirds of our books come from Baker & Taylor and arrive processed (with a dust cover or plastic cover, detection strip, and date due slip) and are ready to be sent to cataloging. Those copies purchased from other sources are processed in the acquiring unit. This includes either covering with plastic jackets or reinforcing (for paperback books), inserting detection strips, and affixing date due slips. When invoices are cleared, the acquiring unit sorts titles according to adult/juvenile, fiction/nonfiction, new titles/added copies, circulating/reference and forwards them with the appropriate documentation to the cataloging unit.

In addition to acquiring and paying for materials, the unit performs a number of other services for the library system:

High-Demand Title Ordering
The acquiring unit manages the spending for very popular titles, mostly best-sellers. This function is budgeted separately within the overall materials budget, and the level of reserve/request fulfillment is based on the funding. Currently, we attempt to buy one copy for every two or three reserves, as determined from the automated circulation system (CLSI). The acquiring unit manager selects the titles and numbers of copies to be ordered using advance reviews, reports from public service librarians, purchase alerts from CLSI, and the total number of reserves as indicated by CLSI. A special system of telephone ordering and rush handling ensures speedy placement of these titles in all our locations.

Periodical and Mail Service
The acquiring unit receives, sorts, and dispatches all mail for the administrative office, technical services, and the main library. The periodicals and newspapers for these locations are part of the mail deliveries received. These are sorted and distributed daily.

Claims Service
The acquiring unit receives claims for missing issues of newspapers and periodicals from all agencies of the library system. These claims are organized and the problems are resolved in a number of ways, depending on their causes. An online claims service speeds delivery of replacement copies.

Gifts
Gifts of library materials are usually received at the agencies and forwarded to the acquiring unit. The unit also sends letters of acknowledgment for gifts received.


## METHODOLOGY FOR THIS COST STUDY

Because personnel costs account for almost 85 percent of the total direct cost of operating the acquiring unit, this study focuses on accurately reflecting these costs. For a two-week period in early December 1985 and another two-week period in late January 1986, each member of the acquiring unit recorded on daily log sheets time spent at various tasks and quantities of materials handled. Appendix A (pg 00), shows the daily log sheets that were used. Average weekly times and quantities for major tasks were developed from the four weeks of data. The average week is displayed in Table 1 and Table 2.

Personnel costs presented in this report are based on hourly rates. These rates were adjusted to allow for holidays, normal use of annual and sick leave, and breaks, by reducing the 40-hour workweek to 30 hours. Thus, the cost of these nonproductive times (holidays, vacation leave, sick leave, and so on) is amortized over the remaining time when productive work occurs.

Throughout this report, two cost levels are presented. The first cost level indicates direct personnel costs, which includes an additional 30 percent to cover fringe benefits paid by the city.

The second cost level adds 100 percent to the direct salary cost to cover the direct cost of general administration (librarian IV), other direct costs (computer charges, supplies, utilities, and so on), and indirect costs (library administration, library personnel support, library business office support, city personnel support, city purchasing support, city accounting support, city janitorial support, space, and so on). The assumption that the direct personnel cost of general administration, the nonpersonnel direct costs, and all indirect costs equal 100 percent of the direct personnel cost is based on intuition rather than research. The library plans to calculate indirect costs more precisely in a future study following methodology outlined in *Cost Finding for Public Libraries: A Manager's Handbook* by Philip Rosenberg (American Library Association, 1985).

This study concentrated on the cost of acquiring English and Spanish print material. Because nonprint is a relatively small part of what we acquire, no attempt was made to keep track of it separately—print and nonprint are averaged together. A more detailed study would probably reveal that nonprint material costs more to acquire on a unit or title basis than print.

Following is a summary of an average total weekly time and cost by task for four weeks:

| Major Activity | Total FTE Staff | Percentage of Total Staff | Annual Personnel Cost |
|---|---|---|---|
| Ordering | 3.2 | 38% | $ 72,067 |
| Receiving/Accounting | 3.0 | 35% | $ 67,563 |
| Processing | 1.3 | 15% | $ 19,874 |
| General Administration | 1.0 | 12% | $ 46,332 |
| Total | 8.5 | 100% | $205,836 |

TABLE 1.   Average total time and cost-per-week-by-task for two two-week sampling periods.*

| Task | Average Hrs. Per Week | Total Hours | FTE | Estimated Annual Cost Personnel | Total |
|---|---|---|---|---|---|
| *Ordering* | | | | | |
| Searching order slips in BATAB | 14.0 | | | | |
| Searching order slips in CLSI, ComCat, OCLC, BIP, etc. | 16.0 | | | | |
| Keying new-title bibliographic data | 31.0 | | | | |
| Establishing and keying new vendors | 2.0 | | | | |
| Keying orders | 10.0 | | | | |
| Typing order slips for gifts | 4.0 | | | | |
| Preparing computer run | 2.0 | | | | |
| Reviewing/mailing purchase orders | 3.0 | | | | |
| Reviewing selection lists | 4.0 | | | | |
| Misc. standing order work | 5.0 | | | | |
| Misc. correspondence with vendors | 5.5 | 96.5 | 3.2 | $ 72,067 | $144,134 |
| *Receiving/Accounting* | | | | | |
| Unpacking Baker & Taylor receipts | 19.5 | | | | |
| Unpacking and keying non– Baker & Taylor receipts | 12.0 | | | | |
| Property stamping | 7.0 | | | | |
| Bursting and filing order forms | 4.0 | | | | |
| Accounting report processing and distribution | 7.0 | | | | |
| Invoice handling | 13.0 | | | | |
| Distributing to cataloging | 4.0 | | | | |
| Unpacking, sorting, and distributing uncataloged material | 6.5 | | | | |
| General mail receipt and sorting | 12.0 | | | | |
| General periodical work (claiming, etc.) | 5.0 | 90.0 | 3.0 | $ 67,563 | $135,126 |
| *Processing* | | | | | |
| Processing clerk | 40.0 | 40.0 | 1.3 | $ 19,874 | $ 39,748 |
| *General Administration* | | | | | |
| Librarian IV | 30.0 | 30.0 | 1.0 | $ 46,332 | included above |
| *Total* | 256.5 | 256.5 | 8.5 | $205,836 | $319,008 |

*FTE based on 30-hour week to allow for holidays, vacations, sick leave, and breaks. Personnel cost based on average of all staff excluding processing clerk and librarian IV.

TABLE 2.   Average unit time and cost-by-task for two two-week
sampling periods.

| Task | Average Units Per Week | Average Time in Minutes | Estimated Unit Cost Personnel | Total |
|---|---|---|---|---|
| *Ordering* | | | | |
| Searching order slips in BATAB | 484 titles | 1.7 | $   .41 | $   .82 |
| Searching order slips in CLSI, ComCat, OCLC, BIP, etc. | 353 titles | 2.7 | .65 | 1.30 |
| Keying new-title bibliographic data | 415 titles | 4.5 | 1.08 | 2.16 |
| Establishing and keying new vendors | 9 vendors | 13.3 | 3.19 | 6.38 |
| Keying orders | 1,596 copies | 0.4 | .10 | .20 |
| Typing order slips for gifts | 135 titles | 1.8 | .43 | .86 |
| Preparing computer run | once-a-week | 120.0 | 28.80 | 57.60 |
| Reviewing/mailing purchase orders | once-a-week | 180.0 | 43.20 | 86.40 |
| Reviewing selection lists | once-a-week | 240.0 | 57.60 | 115.20 |
| Misc. standing order work | Daily | 60.0 | 14.40 | 28.80 |
| Misc. correspondence with vendors | 20 | 16.5 | $ 3.96 | $ 7.92 |
| | | | | |
| *Receiving/Accounting* | | | | |
| Unpacking Baker & Taylor receipts | 1,350 volumes | 1.2 | $   .29 | $   .58 |
| Unpacking and keying non– Baker & Taylor receipts | 210 volumes | 3.4 | .82 | 1.64 |
| Property stamping | 1,527 volumes | 0.3 | .07 | .14 |
| Bursting and filing order forms | 305 titles | 0.8 | .19 | .38 |
| Accounting report processing and distribution | once-a-week | 420.0 | 100.80 | 201.60 |
| Invoice handling | 15 invoices | 52.0 | 12.48 | 24.96 |
| Distributing to cataloging | 1,400 volumes | 0.2 | .05 | .10 |
| Unpacking, sorting, and distributing uncataloged material | 300 volumes | 1.3 | .31 | .62 |
| General mail receipt and sorting | daily | 144.0 | 34.56 | 69.12 |
| General periodical work (claiming, etc.) | daily | 60.0 | 14.40 | 28.80 |
| | | | | |
| *Processing* | 290 volumes | 8.3 | $ 1.33 | $ 2.66 |
| | | | | |
| *General Administration* | daily | 360.0 | $180.00 | included above |

Each of the major divisions can be broken down into individual tasks. Within ordering, for example, an average of 14 hours per week are spent searching in BATAB, 16 hours searching everywhere else, and 31 hours keying bibliographic data.

Table 2 shows the average *unit* time and cost by task, along with the average number of units for the four-week period. Average minutes per unit per task are derived by multiplying the average hours per week from Table 1 by 60 minutes and dividing this total by the average units per week from Table 2. Note that for some tasks (searching, keying bibliographic data, and so on), the appropriate unit of measure is title. For other tasks (keying orders, unpacking, property stamping, and so on) the appropriate unit of measure is volume or the number of copies. Finally, some tasks do not easily relate directly to either title or volume but are rather daily or weekly tasks (preparing the computer run, reviewing selection lists, distributing accounting reports, and so on).

Over the course of a year, the acquiring unit brings in 1,635 volumes per week of material that will be cataloged, representing about 300 new titles. In addition, approximately 865 volumes per week of mass market and juvenile paperbacks are acquired and distributed to the public service agencies uncataloged.

The remainder of this report provides further analysis based on these two tables.


OVERVIEW OF UNIT COSTS

The direct costs of operating the acquiring unit can be summarized as:

| | |
|---|---|
| Personnel (including 30 percent for fringe benefits) | $205,800 |
| BATAB Computer Costs | 17,200 |
| General Supplies | 5,000 |
| Processing Supplies | 5,000 |
| All Other Costs (such as equipment, training, utilities, and telephones) | 12,000 |
| Total | $245,000 |

Since personnel accounts for almost 85 percent of the total direct cost, this study concentrates on accurately allocating the staff time (and therefore, cost) to the various tasks performed.

Doing a unit time and cost study can become very complicated because so many variables can be considered. In this study we have tried to be fairly simplistic and keep the big picture in mind on the assumption that minor variations and details would not change the overall totals significantly.

Perhaps the simplest way to do a cost study is to take the total direct costs for an operation and divide that total cost by the number of units. In our case, this works out as: $245,000 divided by 130,000 items equals $1.88.

Thus, we can say that the average direct cost to acquire an item (one book, one record, or one cassette, for example) at the Tucson Public Library is $1.88. However, as the next section of this report shows, this average cost can be very deceiving in that the range of cost per item varies greatly from this average.

## UNIT COSTS FOR SPECIFIC SITUATIONS

Intuitively we know that the cost of acquiring one copy of a specialized title will be significantly greater than the per-copy cost of acquiring a popular title when twenty copies are acquired at the same time. This section of the report illustrates the magnitude of this difference by looking at four typical cases for the Tucson Public Library as follows:

- A single-copy new-title order to a specialized publisher that is not handled by Baker & Taylor
- A new title to a publisher handled by Baker & Taylor for which five copies are being ordered
- A new title to a publisher handled by Baker & Taylor for which 20 copies are being ordered
- An order for five copies of a title previously ordered for which bibliographic information is still in the BATAB file

For each of the following exhibits, major activities encompassing all the major acquiring unit tasks are presented as follows:

Searching

Searching includes all preorder searching to verify bibliographic information and price (if required) and to verify status at the Tucson Public Library (new title, currently on order, and so on). The amount of searching actually required per title can vary from none to a great deal. Potential places to search include the BATAB Book History Report (microfiche), BATAB Open Order Report (microfiche), ComCat (microfiche catalog), CLSI (online terminal), OCLC (online terminal), or any number of printed sources to resolve a problem such as *Books in Print* or *Publishers Trade List Annual.*

Establishing and Keying a Vendor

Orders for titles not available from Baker & Taylor from publishers that have not been previously established in our BATAB files will require establishing and keying an order vendor in the BATAB Vendor File. In addition, an entry in the City Accounting System Vendor File will also be required so that payment can be made. This activity most typically occurs for specialized material for a special collection in the main library.

### Keying Bibliographic Data

The most time-consuming of the keying transactions are those required to enter a new title. Once a title has been entered into the BATAB database, subsequent transactions regarding that title are simple and quick. Once entered, the title record remains in the BATAB database until 24 months with no activity (that is reordering) for the title.

### Keying the Order

Once the bibliographic title has been entered, a brief order entry is keyed for each copy of the title desired showing quantity, location, age level, and reference/circulation indicator.

### Miscellaneous Ordering Tasks

This includes preparing the weekly batch computer run, reviewing and mailing the printed purchase orders, reviewing and distributing the printed selection lists, miscellaneous standing order work, and miscellaneous telephoning of or correspondence with vendors.

### Unpacking and Keying

Receiving procedures begin with bursting and filing order set forms by vendor to await receipt of materials. When the materials are received, they are unpacked and checked against the order set forms and the invoice to verify that we received that which we ordered and for which we were billed. For Baker & Taylor shipments, invoice clearing transactions come keyed on computer tape and ready to be processed by the BATAB system. For all other orders, an invoice clearing transaction must be keyed by the acquiring unit staff.

### Accounting

Accounting procedures are almost entirely a matter of handling and analyzing BATAB output. Invoices are checked against the computer-produced invoice summary report before being forwarded to the city accounting department for payment. Fund status reports are checked before distribution to agencies. Input errors are corrected as they are discovered.

### Processing and Distribution

Materials from Baker & Taylor are received preprocessed and require only property stamping. Other receipts require processing and property stamping. Material is then sorted and delivered to cataloging,

EXHIBIT 1.   Cost estimates for specialized publisher orders.

| Task | Staff Cost per Copy* | Total Cost per Copy** |
|---|---|---|
| Searching | $1.06 | $2.12 |
| Establishing and keying vendor | 3.19 | 6.38 |
| Keying bibliographic data | 1.08 | 2.16 |
| Keying order | .10 | .20 |
| Misc. ordering tasks | .94 | 1.88 |
| Unpacking and keying | .82 | 1.64 |
| Accounting | .23 | .46 |
| Processing and distributing | 1.93 | 3.86 |
| Total | $9.35 | $18.70 |

*Including fringe benefits.
**Including staff cost with fringe benefits, general administration, and overhead.

if it is to be cataloged, or sent directly to the agencies, if it is not to be cataloged.

Unit costs are presented in two ways: direct staff cost (including 30 percent fringe benefits paid by the city) derived from Table 2; and total cost, including direct staff cost with fringe, a prorated portion of the general administration cost of the acquiring unit, all other direct costs (computer charges, supplies, etc.), and an estimate of the indirect costs. A single-copy new-title order to a specialized publisher that is not handled by Baker & Taylor is most typical of main, government reference, and special collection orders.

EXHIBIT 2.   A typical order for five copies of a new title to a publisher handled by Baker & Taylor.

| Task | Staff Cost per Copy* | Total Cost per Copy** |
|---|---|---|
| Searching | $ .21 | $ .42 |
| Keying bibliographic data | .22 | .44 |
| Keying order | .10 | .20 |
| Misc. ordering tasks | .19 | .38 |
| Unpacking | .29 | .58 |
| Accounting | .23 | .46 |
| Processing and distributing | .12 | .24 |
| Total | $1.36 | $2.72 |

*Including fringe benefits.
**Including staff cost with fringe benefits, general administration, and overhead.

A variation on this case would be a single-copy new-title order from a publisher that Baker & Taylor handles or from a publisher already established in our BATAB vendor file, in which case, the staff cost would be $5.63 and the total cost would be $11.26.

The cost per volume of a title being acquired is significantly reduced with multiple-copy ordering. This in itself is no surprise but the magnitude of the difference is. The cost of acquiring a single copy directly from a publisher is almost ten times the cost per copy of acquiring 20 copies of a title from Baker & Taylor.

## USING THE DATA

How can we use the information derived from this time and cost study? First, a formal written, documented cost study looks good to library and city management because it suggests that the acquisitions department "has its act together" and must know what it is doing. This may or may not be the case, but a written cost analysis looks good at budget time to the city's budget and research department in terms of recommending the requested budget.

Second, a cost study helps management focus on the most time-consuming activities and avoid spending a great deal of time concentrating on activities that take relatively little time. For example, management might feel that spending thirteen minutes just to establish and key one vendor is too long, but since only two hours a week are spent on this task, there is scant advantage in spending time to minimize it. Even if the unit time could be cut in half, only one hour a week would be saved.

EXHIBIT 3.   Ordering 20 copies of a popular adult or juvenile title by a publisher handled by Baker & Taylor.

| Task | Staff Cost per Copy* | Total Cost per Copy** |
| --- | --- | --- |
| Searching | $ .05 | $ .10 |
| Keying bibliographic data | .05 | .10 |
| Keying order | .10 | .20 |
| Misc. ordering tasks | .29 | .58 |
| Unpacking | .29 | .58 |
| Accounting | .23 | .46 |
| Processing and distributing | .12 | .24 |
| Total | $1.13 | $2.26 |

*Including fringe benefits.
**Including staff cost with fringe benefits, general administration, and overhead.

EXHIBIT 4. Ordering five copies of a title already in the database. One of the significant advantages of BATAB is the relative ease with which additional copies of a title can be ordered.

| Task | Staff Cost per Copy* | Total Cost per Copy** |
|------|---------------------|----------------------|
| Searching | $ .08 | $ .16 |
| Keying order | .10 | .20 |
| Misc. ordering tasks | .19 | .38 |
| Unpacking | .29 | .58 |
| Accounting | .23 | .46 |
| Processing and distributing | .12 | .24 |
| Total | $1.01 | $2.02 |

*Including fringe benefits.
**Including staff cost with fringe benefits, general administration, and overhead.

On the other hand, time might profitably be spent looking for ways to reduce the amount of searching and bibliographic keying required since the study reveals that significant amounts of staff time are devoted to these activities.

Third, a cost study helps management respond to changing conditions. For example, if a reorganization is being planned in which physical processing activities will be transferred from acquisitions to cataloging, the study tells exactly how much staff will have to be transferred (1.3 FTE) from acquisitions to cataloging along with the responsibility for these tasks. If management asks, "How much time would be saved if we stopped property stamping the books?" the acquiring unit manager can give a precise answer (one-third of a minute per book or about seven to eight hours a week at our present acquisition rate).

Fourth, a unit time study helps management respond accurately to "what if" questions about the future. For example, "What if the materials budget is increased next year by $100,000 beyond the inflationary increase to be used for single copy titles for the main library?" The study clearly documents that additional staff would be required to handle this increased load because of the significant unit times required to search, key, and unpack non–Baker & Taylor titles. On the other hand, the study reveals that if the money is going to be used to buy additional copies of popular titles, probably no increased staff will be required because the unit time required to order and receive additional copies of these titles is so very small. Without a unit time and cost study, "what if" questions are answered with guesses instead of facts. Time and cost

Exhibit 5.   Summarizing the data.

|  | Staff Cost per Copy | Total Cost per Copy |
|---|---|---|
| Single Copy/New Title/Specialized Publisher | $9.35 | $18.70 |
| Single Copy/New Title/Baker & Taylor | 5.63 | 11.26 |
| Five Copies/New Title/Baker & Taylor | 1.36 | 2.72 |
| Twenty Copies/New Title/Baker & Taylor | 1.13 | 2.26 |
| Five Added Copies/Baker & Taylor | 1.01 | 2.02 |

studies should help management make better decisions. If they don't, then they are not worth doing.

Although this study has answered some questions, it has left others unanswered. For example, "How does the cost of acquiring a book compare with the cost of acquiring a record, audiocassette, or videocassette?" or "What does it cost to acquire an English language book as compared to a Spanish language book?" These answers would require different data. First determine what you want to know and then collect the appropriate facts. We decided not to collect data to answer these questions because the volume of these materials is either small or the costs are believed not to be significantly different.

As this study demonstrates, there is no useful single answer to the question, "What does it cost to acquire a book at the Tucson Public Library?" It depends on the kind of book and the number of copies being acquired at the same time, as the summary in Exhibit 5 clearly illustrates.

# Appendix A

Appendix A contains copies of each of the four daily log sheets that were developed for the staff of the acquiring unit to use. The log sheets are roughly divided into ordering tasks, receiving tasks, BATAB handling and accounting tasks, and processing tasks. Staff members do a variety of activities, so, in reality, most staff members had to use at least two sheets per day.

| Acquisitions Unit Time-Study | | Date: |
|---|---|---|
| *Bibliographic Searching* | Time | Number |
| Order Slips | | |
|   BATAB | ———— | ———— (titles) |
|   Other (CLSI, ComCat, BIP, OCLC, etc.) | ———— | ———— (titles) |
| Standing Orders, Greenaways, Gifts, Here | | |
|   Billed, etc. | ———— | ———— (titles) |
|   BATAB | ———— | ———— (titles) |
|   Other | ———— | ———— (titles) |

*Keying and Verifying*

| | Time | Number |
|---|---|---|
| Order Slips and 30s | ———— | ———— (records) |
| Greenaways, Standing Orders, Documents, Gifts, Memo Orders, | | |
|   Here Billed | ———— | ———— (records) |
| Selection Lists | ———— | ———— (records) |
| Ordering Book in BATAB (multipurpose | | |
|   form) | ———— | ———— (records) |
| 51s | ———— | ———— (records) |
| Vendor, 32s, etc. | ———— | ———— (records) |

*Typing*

| | Time | Number |
|---|---|---|
| Gifts (51 form) | ———— | ———— (titles) |

*Other* (please specify, e.g., mailing POs)

| | | |
|---|---|---|
| ———————————————— | ———— | ———— |
| ———————————————— | ———— | ———— |
| ———————————————— | ———— | ———— |
| ———————————————— | ———— | ———— |

| Acquisitions Unit Time-Study | | Date: |
| --- | --- | --- |

| *Materials Receipt* | Time | Number |
| --- | --- | --- |
| Burst, file 51s | _____ | _____ |
| Unpacking | | |
| Baker & Taylor | _____ | _____ (volumes) |
| Directs | _____ | _____ (volumes) |
| Distribute to Cataloging | _____ | |
| Send Out Uncataloged | _____ | |

*Mail Receipt*

| | | |
| --- | --- | --- |
| Sorting | _____ | _____ (est.) |
| Periodical Check-in | _____ | _____ (est.) |
| Microfilm | _____ | _____ (reels) |
| Claims | _____ | _____ (no. of letters or forms) |

*Other* (please specify)

| | | |
| --- | --- | --- |
| _____ | ____ | ____ |
| _____ | ____ | ____ |
| _____ | ____ | ____ |

| Acquisitions Unit Time-Study | | Date: |
| --- | --- | --- |

| *Processing* | Time | Number |
| --- | --- | --- |
| Stamping | ____ | ____ |
| 3-M and Date Due Slips | ____ | ____ |
| Jacketing | ____ | ____ |
| Reinforcing | ____ | ____ |

*Other* (please specify)

| | | |
| --- | --- | --- |
| _____ | ____ | ____ |
| _____ | ____ | ____ |
| _____ | ____ | ____ |

Acquisitions Unit Time-Study                                   Date:

| *BATAB Handling* | Time | Number |
|---|---|---|
| Computer Run Preparation | _____ | |
| Selection List Review | _____ | |
| BATAB Reports Processing (exception, suspended invoice, invoice summary fund status) | _____ | |
| Purchase Order Processing | _____ | |
| Reproduction and Distribution of BATAB Reports | _____ | |

*Correspondence*

| | | |
|---|---|---|
| Vendors | _____ | _____ (no. of letters) |
| Gift Acknowledgment | _____ | _____ (no of forms) |
| Requests, Letters, Notes | _____ | _____ (no. of letters or forms) |

*Other* (please specify)

_____   _____   _____
_____   _____   _____
_____   _____   _____
_____   _____   _____

# Public Card Catalog Costs at the University of Oregon Library

## Karen C. Calhoun

In the spring of 1984, the University of Oregon undertook a research project to determine the costs of producing and maintaining its public card catalogs. The study was prompted by the catalog department's need for detailed documentation of what tasks were being performed, how, and by whom; how the available labor was organized to do the work; and how much staff time would become available for reassignment if the public card catalogs were closed.

Over the past ten years the University of Oregon Library, like many institutions, has made steady progress toward automating library services. It is in a particularly strong position with its database of machine-readable catalog records. Begun in 1975, it contains over 400,000 machine-readable records, a significant percentage of the library's cataloging. Records for most materials acquired before 1975 must be sought in the card catalogs, although a modestly staffed retrospective conversion project, begun in 1983, has added over 96,000 of these older cataloging records to the local database.

The local database is used to produce the library's COM (computer output microfiche) catalog, which is divided into author, title, and subject portions. In addition, the library continues to produce and maintain its author and title card catalogs. (The subject card catalog was closed in 1977.) Thus, the catalog department finds itself maintaining public access catalogs in both card and COM formats.

Faced with high expectations for service, limited staff, and a larger workload (as a result of increases in the book budget) the library administration had difficult decisions to make and needed quantitative cost data to inform its campuswide discussion of the issues involved in automating. The library administration supported closing the public

Karen S. Calhoun is User Documentation Specialist for OCLC (Online Computer Library Center). She was previously Catalog Librarian at the University of Oregon.

card catalogs and relying on the COM for access to current materials until an online catalog could be implemented. It was felt that the catalog department's limited staff resources would be more effectively used if they concentrated on building the local database, which was seen as the library's investment in the future.

Recognizing the need to gain the understanding and support of staff and users, the administration began to gather data, both to plan a course of action and to strengthen its arguments for change. The public card catalog cost study was requested as a part of this fact-finding process. At the same time, the administration did its best to stimulate campuswide discussion by circulating position papers, holding public meetings, and organizing educational demonstrations of several vendors' turnkey library systems.

## METHODOLOGY

At the outset, four catalog department supervisors were interviewed to gather information about the work flow and distribution of labor and to establish an appropriate list of tasks to be analyzed. Job logs were developed for data collection during the week of April 16–20, 1984 and, the information was used to create an up-to-date organization chart of the catalog department (see Exhibit 1). It was also used to chart the work routines associated with the flow of cards through the department (see Exhibit 2).

On the basis of information from the supervisors' interviews, two job logs were developed, one for clerical staff, and the second for professional staff. Both logs were used to record the time spent daily on tasks listed.

A meeting was held with clerical staff before the study week to explain the job logs and answer questions. In their regular weekly meeting, professional staff were informed and shown how to keep the logs. Study participants themselves kept the job logs and turned in their sheets daily. The data were then compiled from the log sheets to yield a snapshot of how the catalog department's time was spent on the public card catalogs. As it turned out, because vacation scheduling resulted in work substitutions, and because some tasks are performed monthly rather than weekly, some task times had to be reconstructed or estimated to achieve an average week. In all cases estimated were made in consultation with the staff member and appropriate supervisor. Finally, a list of study participants' salaries and a year's worth of filing statistics were collected from library administrators.

The data were analyzed using the CONDESCRIPTIVE and RE-PORT procedures of SPSSx (Statistical Package for the Social Sciences,

EXHIBIT 1.   Organization Chart, Spring 1984.

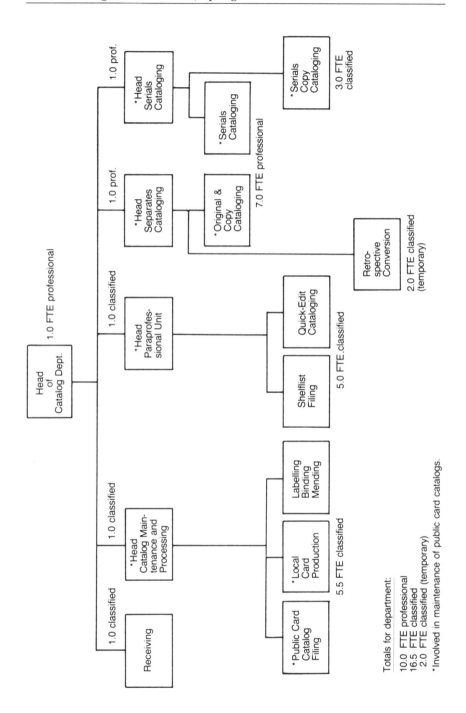

Head of Catalog Dept.

1.0 FTE professional

*Head Serials Cataloging — 1.0 prof.

*Serials Cataloging

*Serials Copy Cataloging — 3.0 FTE classified

7.0 FTE professional

*Head Separates Cataloging — 1.0 prof.

*Original & Copy Cataloging

Retrospective Conversion — 2.0 FTE classified (temporary)

*Head Paraprofessional Unit — 1.0 classified

Quick-Edit Cataloging

Shelflist Filing

5.0 FTE classified

*Head Catalog Maintenance and Processing — 1.0 classified

Labelling Binding Mending

*Local Card Production

Public Card Catalog Filing

5.5 FTE classified

Receiving — 1.0 classified

Totals for department:
10.0  FTE professional
16.5  FTE classified
 2.0  FTE classified (temporary)
*Involved in maintenance of public card catalogs.

version x), a package of programs that runs on the university's mainframe computer. A powerful and flexible set of analytical programs used primarily for social science research, SPSSx nevertheless has many practical applications in the library setting.

In the spring of 1984, the catalog department was maintaining more than ten public card catalogs:

| | |
|---|---|
| Main* (author, title) | Documents* (author, title) |
| Science* (author, title) | Oregon Collection* (author, title) |
| Map Room (author, title, subject dictionary catalog) | Juvenile Collection* (author, title) |
| Douglass Room (author, title, subject) | OIMB (author, title, subject) |
| IMC (author, title, subject) | Pine Mountain (author, title, subject) |

*Subject access provided by the COM catalog

It has long been recognized that providing access to a library collection is expensive and time-consuming. The means by which access is provided—card, COM, book, and online catalogs being some of the choices—are reflected in the organization of labor in a technical services department. Exhibit 1 shows the wide dispersal of tasks related to the public card catalogs. A major reassignment of personnel and duties would be required if the public card catalogs were closed.

One caution: the chart fails to show staff involvement in producing and maintaining the bibliographic database used to produce the COM catalog. In fact, the head of the paraprofessional unit took charge of coordinating needs and problems with the library's COM vendor, while the rest of the department added or adjusted routines to accommodate the needs of building and updating the COM database. These tasks were performed simultaneously with, and in addition to, the tasks related to the public card catalogs.

The flowchart in Exhibit 2 shows the progress of catalog cards through the department. Some routines have been simplified for ease of illustration. Like a library collection, bibliographic information is dynamic and changing. The impact of these changes on the catalogs is shown at the lower right of the chart.

The flowchart does not illustrate other tasks that help provide up-to-date bibliographic information, such as identifying problems or inconsistencies in new cataloging. A problem-solving role is part of the function of any catalog, regardless of format; therefore, the time and effort spent validating bibliographic information was not considered in this study's design and implementation.

Results of the analysis of the job logs are shown in Table 1. During

Exhibit 2.

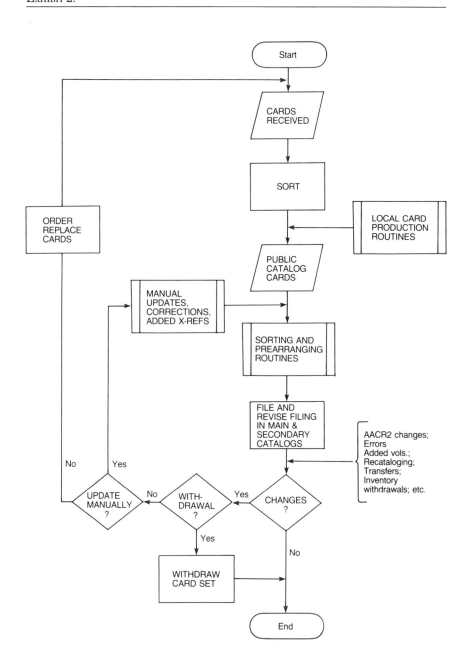

TABLE 1.    Estimate of Weekly Costs of Public Card Catalogs by
Employee Level.

|  | Clerical Hours | Professional Hours | Total Hours |
|---|---|---|---|
| 1. Taking statistics, sorting, distributing | 3.43 | 0.00 | 3.43 |
| 2. Preliminary arrangement of cards | 20.42 | 0.00 | 20.42 |
| 3. Filing in all catalogs | 31.70 | 0.00 | 31.70 |
| 4. Revising filing | 9.50 | 5.50 | 15.00 |
| Subtotal Filing Tasks* | 65.05 | 5.50 | 70.55 |
| 5. Local card production (cross-references and Orientalia) | 15.88 | 0.00 | 15.88 |
| 6. Changes and updates (added volumes, AACR2 changes, transfers, recats, corrections, etc.) | 21.37 | 1.00 | 22.37 |
| 7. Maintenance of card catalog cabinets | .23 | 0.00 | .23 |
| 8. Answering questions about filing; assisting staff using public catalogs | .68 | 0.00 | .68 |
| Subtotal Other Tasks* | 38.17 | 1.00 | 39.17 |
| Grand Total | 103.22 | 6.50 | 109.72 |
| Total in FTEs | 2.58 | .16 | 2.74 |

*Based on current salaries of study participants, weekly cost of filing routines is
$455.46; cost of other tasks is $241.08; total weekly cost $696.54.

the study week, 2.74 FTE staff were engaged in public card catalog
tasks. The routines involved were mostly clerical (2.58 FTE); professional librarians were involved as filing revisors and through their participation in the Anglo-American Cataloging Rules 2 (AACR2) change
procedures. Assuming that all the public card catalogs in the catalog list
(p. 99) were closed, this 2.74 FTE staff savings could be directed to new
projects, such as stepping up the retrospective conversion effort. However, since the 2.74 FTE is distributed among the jobs of 17 people (nine
clerical, eight professional), not one of whom engages solely in public
card catalog processes, reassignment of duties would not be a simple
task. (In fact, the minimum time spent on the card catalogs among the
clerical group was .08 FTE, the maximum was .77 FTE, and the mean
was .29 FTE.)

The weekly filing costs were calculated by applying the library
office's formula for determining a person's hourly wage, multiplying the
result by the number of hours that person spent on filing routines (tasks
1 through 4 in Table 1), then taking the sum of the products for all study
participants. Other weekly costs were calculated in the same way.

With this estimate of weekly filing costs, $455.46, one can go on to estimate a unit cost for filing a card by dividing the weekly cost by the average number of cards filed weekly. Department statistics showed that 150,717 cards (excluding shelflist) were filed the previous year, for an average of 2,989 cards per week. Thus the unit cost per card for labor may be estimated as $455.46 divided by 2,898, or 16 cents per card. Labor plus materials came to 22 cents per card in the spring of 1984 compared to the 65 cents the library was paying OCLC for each printed catalog card.

After the study was completed, the public card catalogs were kept open because funding problems impeded automation. However, staff members worked effectively to build awareness of the choices involved in closing them. This study's results were disseminated and discussed in the library and around the campus in both formal and informal settings.

The study identified problems that must be resolved before the public card catalogs can be closed or phased out. Charting the work flow provided immediate help in making the card production/maintenance routines more efficient. Although the catalog department must continue to divide its attention between the public card and COM catalogs, some new procedures streamlined maintenance of the public card catalogs, and some reassignment of duties has occurred. More resources are being devoted to maintenance and quality control of the local database that is used to produce the COM catalog. COM supplements are produced monthly, instead of bimonthly; more copies of the COM catalog are available in the main catalog area and elsewhere on campus; and new microfiche readers and better signage have improved accessibility. When the public card catalogs are finally closed, data from this study will help in organizing duties in the catalog department.

# Three Public Catalog Formats Compared: A Cost Study

Elizabeth Hood

Ruby Miller

During the spring of 1985, Trinity University's Maddux Library conducted a cost study of the cataloging department's operation. Costs of traditional card catalogs were examined, as well as online catalogs, for comparison with the existing COM (computer output on microform) catalog. U.S. documents had been added to the catalog in 1980, and during the study year represented about 82,000 records, about 20 percent of a catalog that contained 402,932 records.

The library did not begin the study with any preconceived choice of catalog form. We intended to assess our current costs in order to evaluate alternative catalogs. The study also served as a method of reviewing *organizational* patterns within cataloging. The costs of adding government documents to the catalog would be evaluated as well.

## METHODOLOGY

A survey of recent library literature revealed little theoretical discussion of cost study methods. SPEC Flyer 89 describes two basic types, the "top down" method and the "bottom up" method.[1] These are described by William J. Maher as "retrospective analysis" and "direct measurement,"[2] and each includes specific methodologies for individual case studies which vary markedly, depending on the scope and purpose of the study; the skills, sophistication, and time resources of the re-

Elizabeth Hood is Assistant Professor and Serials Catalog Librarian at Trinity University.

Ruby Miller is Associate Professor and Assistant Director for Technical Services at Trinity University.

searches; and the available statistics on expenditures and production. Because of these variations, the results must be used with the greatest caution and impartiality when making comparisons between libraries. Even when the express purpose of the study is comparison of measured costs, as in studies described by Mitchell, Tanis, and Jaffe in California State University system libraries[3] and by Getz and Phelps in three research libraries,[4] the analysts point out the difficulties of measuring exactly the same activities in different settings, since procedures and levels of processing vary greatly among libraries.

In very general terms, top down (retrospective analysis) methodology is appropriate for analyzing the costs of broad functions, such as circulation, cataloging, or reference, where expenditures devoted to the function can be defined easily. This method requires exact data on quantities of units produced; expenditures for personnel, materials, equipment, data, servicing, etc.; and estimates of institutional overhead costs, such as space and administration. Specific activities are not described qualitatively; therefore, it is difficult to make comparisons between libraries, or even within the same library, if tasks change radically over time because of new procedures, policies, or staff.

The bottom up methodology (direct measurement) is more appropriate for analyzing specific activities or procedures. It is most useful in comparing two means for accomplishing the same task of assigning staff to a specific activity. Techniques such as time and motion studies and work sampling fall within this method.

By far the most important factor affecting choice of methodology is the purpose for which cost data are being gathered. Maddux Library's purpose was to compare overall system costs of three catalog forms. The administration did not want to find out the specific amount of time required for an individual employee to perform a specific activity as part of a larger task that was itself a part of the even larger function of cataloging. Although the library did want to obtain a per-unit cost for volume equivalents, it was primarily interested in total system costs.

Since the information was expected to be of interest to budget planners both inside and outside the library, an annual cost was thought to be more accurate and more useful than costs for shorter time periods. Besides providing a more realistic overall cost for processing by avoiding seasonal fluctuations, a base period of one year simplified data collection. Annual production statistics have been kept for many years, and budget expenditures are also annual. Costs were calculated for the fiscal year June 1983 through May 1984.

Note that Trinity Library did not consider abandoning the use of automation as a means of acquiring and/or creating a catalog record. Trinity has relied for 15 years on automated cataloging sources for cataloging copy, and our processes reflect this dependence. We follow what we believe is efficient use of automated records: heavy use of well-trained and well-supervised support staff for searching; copy cataloging of titles with all types of copy including OCLC member copy; use of terminal operators rather than copy catalogers for input of changes to copy; and assignment of professional staff to such tasks as supervision of authority work, subject cataloging and classification in the absence of usable copy, original cataloging, catalog maintenance, and cataloging administration.

We did not include administrative costs, such as a portion of the library director's salary, space, desks, and electricity for any of the three options. Although we must obviously account for these costs in an accurate tally of the total cost of the cataloging operation, for purposes of the comparison they were assumed to be equal in each of the catalog alternatives. This assumption is not altogether valid, but the differences are extremely difficult to measure.

We depreciated equipment using a straight line, or constant annual depreciations, and we assumed a salvage value of zero. This method is simpler to calculate and served our purpose better than a "sum of years" method.[5] We did not need to know the exact value of equipment at any one time, but rather a simple average of the university's outlay over a period of years. On the other hand, we used our actual experience to estimate equipment maintenance costs not covered by maintenance contracts. These costs do change from year to year. In some cases the estimates were averaged to achieve a yearly "straight line" cost for maintenance.

DATA COLLECTION FOR THE COM CATALOG

The first step was to determine costs for the existing COM cataloging system. The types of data collected are similar to those delineated in the Research Libraries Group *Statement of Desired Data for Determining the Costs of Maintaining RLG Catalogs, 1976/77*.[6] The following categories were included in Maddux Library's cost study: salaries, including fringe benefits and student labor; OCLC costs; computer center charges for all use of the catalog database; charges for programming support; the cost of microform catalogs; the cost of microform readers and reader stations; card cabinet space for shelflist cards; equipment, including OCLC terminals, IBM 3278 terminals to access files and programs maintained at the computer center, and typewriters; supplies; and cataloging tools such as rule books and compilations of classification schedule changes. Exhibit 1 outlines these costs; next, we'll clarify how they were determined.

Determining salary costs was the most intricate challenge of the

Exhibit 1.   Cataloging Cost for One Year

| | |
|---|---|
| Salaries and fringe benefits | $330,992 |
| OCLC | 29,183 |
| Computer center charges | 253,525 |
| Programming support | 12,788 |
| MARCIVE products | 11,162 |
| Microform catalogs | 11,768 |
| Film and fiche readers, maintenance, and work stations | 3,930 |
| Card cabinet for card shelflist (1/3 cabinet) | 850 |
| Equipment | 4,934 |
| Supplies | 12,354 |
| Intellectual tools | 1,000 |
| Total | $672,486 |

60,624 titles cataloged in 1983–1984
Average cost per title: $11.09

study. An attempt was made to separate staff by function. Certain staff members have positions that are split among departments, so percentages of their time devoted to the cataloging function were separated and counted. Documents and music cataloging, manual processing of materials for the circulation system, and equipment maintenance all fall into this category. Also, we wished to obtain a figure roughly comparable to the Getz and Phelps study of labor costs for cataloging,[7] since that study was of interest to several Trinity librarians. Moreover, we wanted to determine the extent to which the total cataloging function relied on professional versus support staff.

Salary information is not generally available for individuals. Additionally, exact dollar amount (or even percentages) of salary paid for fringe benefits varies. Therefore, these costs were collected by discreet consultation with the library's administrative office and with the university office of personnel services.

Some interesting facts emerged. The cataloging department spends 31 percent of its staff costs for professional salaries, 65 percent for support staff, and 4 percent for student labor. These figures reflect the heavy use of support staff for copy cataloging and processing the bulk of materials added to the library.

The costs for OCLC data and related expenses were collected from AMIGOS library group invoices. Excluded from the total cost were noncataloging functions such as interlibrary loan. However, since the library utilizes OCLC primarily as a cataloging data source, the full costs for membership in the AMIGOS group—telecommunications charges, and modem leasing—were added, as well as the direct cataloging costs of data use, tape records, tapes, shipping, and tape frequency charges.

Computer center charges were the second most complex costs to collect. Computer costs were figured from monthly bills provided by the Trinity Computer Center for the value of the time actually used by the library. Since these bills are for a lump-sum cost that includes all library computer use, we could not distinguish exact costs for cataloging charges. Although the cataloging department keeps logs for its own use from JCL reports returned to us when jobs are submitted, the logs do not account for documents processing, production of printed periodicals holdings lists, computer runs to gather statistics for administrative use, runs for special projects for all purposes including acquisitions and public services, and such reports as new books lists. During the study year there were many such charges, notably a high Government Printing Office (GPO) tape-processing cost resulting from a retrospective government documents cataloging project and test runs for a subject authority system program. Some of these database uses are performed regularly at least once a year. Other special projects do not recur, but it seems that some new special project appears as soon as the last one is completed. The logs kept by the cataloging department account for less than half the total computer center charges. Furthermore, since the library is not actually billed for these charges, and since they do not appear as part of the library's budget, there is no attempt made to gain credit for runs that fail nor to receive university user or educational discounts of any sort. Thus the computer center bills include both successful and unsuccessful processing, as well as costs that might be attributed to programming development and to nontraditional use of the catalog database.

Because of the difficulty of extricating those costs that are directly related to the cataloging function, and because in a sense all these costs result from the existence of the catalog in its database form, it was decided to list the entire sum of billed charges as computer center charges. Had those charges been paid in real dollars, they probably would be lower. Nonetheless, they are a part of the university's cost for presenting a library catalog.

Programming support is another unbudgeted costs. This service is provided by MARCIVE, Inc. Developed by the Trinity Computer Center as a set of programs to derive catalog copy from MARC data sources, MARCIVE was divested in 1981 and became a for-profit catalog vending service. Because of the historical relationship between Trinity and MARCIVE, the library's contract includes free programming services of up to $50,000 annually. Therefore, programming support is not a real dollar cost. But since the contract provision is part of MARCIVE's financial obligation to the university for license to use software developed by the university, library use of the programming services may be considered a cost to the university. If MARCIVE did not provide this support, another source of such services would be needed.

The remaining costs were relatively simple to collect. MARCIVE products costs are real dollar costs paid for the production of shelflist cards and labels for processing. We gathered the costs of microform catalogs directly from records and invoices maintained in the library's administrative offices. This figure includes the cost of microfilm and microfiche masters and all fiche and film copies. We derived the cost for the twelve public service ROM microfilm readers from the actual cost of the equipment depreciated at seven years. Because the 24 catalog fiche readers are of various ages and costs, a replacement cost of $200 was used to estimate their average value. This cost was depreciated over a ten-year period. (Eight of these readers are for public access to the catalog; the remaining 16 are in public services office areas and in technical services.) We collected maintenance fees for the ROM microfilm readers from the actual bills for parts and maintenance. Because the ROM readers were about four years old, maintenance costs were beginning to increase, and were included in costs for the study year. Maintenance for the microfiche readers is such an incidental expense that a cost figure has not been kept, but we estimated an average of $10 per reader per year, which covers our actual expenses. For the 14 public catalogs that are placed on special work stations, an estimated cost of $400 per work station was depreciated over twenty years. Other catalogs are placed in locations that serve other functions, such as the reference desk and information stations in the stacks, so the cost of work stations for these catalogs was discounted.

Approximately one third of a 72-drawer card cabinet is used each year to accommodate Maddux Library's growing shelflist, so we counted this growth figure as an actual cost. The existing shelflist was not depreciated or added. The equipment category includes the actual cost of the two OCLC terminals that we own, depreciated at five years, the three IBM 3278 terminals (linked to the computer center) that we lease, nine typewriters estimated at a value of $400 each and depreciated over seven years, and three labelling machines and related equipment, estimated at $500 each and depreciated over a seven-year period. The "intellectual tools" category is an estimated cost for subscriptions to compilations of LC Classification Schedule changes, LC Rule Interpretation compilations, copies of AACR2, dictionaries, books on cataloging, and so on. Separate records for the cost of cataloging tools have not been kept.

At the time of the study, the documents department, not the cataloging department, cataloged government documents. To include government documents in the COM catalog, the cost of the salaries and fringe benefits related to the cataloging function in the documents department were simply added to cataloging salary costs. The library uses MARCIVE to search the GPO MARC tapes by item number and downloads the records into a government document database, which is merged with the nondocuments database at COM catalog production time. Thus, all the computer costs and MARCIVE costs for documents are already captured within the totals for the year.

## DIFFERENCES AMONG EXHIBITS 1, 2, AND 3

Exhibits 2 and 3 outline costs for producing a library catalog in card and online public access forms. These two charts differ somewhat from Exhibit 1, which describes costs for the system now in place. Exhibit 1 covers all costs, including COM viewing equipment. Since these microform and microfiche readers are already in place, and because the development expenses for our computer software were absorbed long ago by the computer center and are not available for study, no initial expenses to the university for installation of the COM catalog are described. Those costs that might be considered one-time costs are merely depreciated and added to ongoing costs. However, there would be substantial initial expenses to the university if the library changed to another catalog format. Therefore, Exhibits 2 and 3 include a second section on initial expenses. By separating the one-time costs, the two alternative catalog formats may be compared for the initial outlay that would be required should the university choose to install a different library catalog.

These initial expenses for installing various catalog formats may be depreciated over a reasonable system life expectancy to determine the way in which they would affect overall costs for ongoing cataloging. Thus Exhibits 2 and 3 include a third section combining the year's cataloging cost with depreciated one-time costs for card and online catalog formats.

## DATA COLLECTION FOR THE CARD CATALOG

Exhibit 2 shows the way in which costs would vary should a card catalog be reestablished at Trinity Library. It was assumed that if the library were to return to a card catalog, the automated cataloging procedures utilizing MARCIVE and OCLC would remain the same. We are convinced that these procedures are more cost effective for us than are other methods of card production. We also assumed that we would continue to maintain a machine-readable database, since products such as a periodical holdings book catalog are obtained from this database. Besides these products, maintenance, bibliography work, statistical counts, and catalog distribution to book vendors for acquisitions purposes depend on the continued use of a machine-readable database.

EXHIBIT 2.    Projected Cataloging Costs with Card Catalog Reestablished.

*Estimated Costs for 1983–1984 Processing*

| | |
|---|---:|
| Salaries and fringe benefits | $477,606 |
| OCLC | 29,183 |
| Computer center charges | 193,525 |
| Programming support | 12,788 |
| MARCIVE products | 14,982 |
| Card cabinets (7.58 cabinets at $2,550) | 19,329 |
| Equipment | 4,934 |
| Supplies | 12,354 |
| Intellectual tools | 1,000 |
| Total | $765,701 |

60,624 titles cataloged
Average cost per title: $12.63

*Initial Expenses to Reestablish the Card Catalog*

Cards
  320,932 nondocument titles × 8 cards per record  =  2,567,456
    cards
  82,000 document titles × 10 cards per record = 820,000 cards

| | |
|---|---:|
| Total 3,387,456 cards × $0.05 a card | $169,373 |
| Cabinets | |
| 55 cabinets × $2,550 a cabinet | 140,250 |
| Computer center charges | |
| 3,387,456 cards × $0.05 a card | 169,373 |
| Salaries | |
| 3,387,456 ÷ 60 cards filed per hour = 56,458 hours of filing, or 30 filers for one years × $11,426 each | 342,780 |
| Total | $821,776 |

*Estimated 1983–1984 Costs*
*Including Initial Expenses Depreciated over 15 Years*

| | |
|---|---:|
| Salaries and fringe benefits | $500,458 |
| OCLC | 29,183 |
| Computer center charges | 204,817 |
| Programming support | 12,788 |
| MARCIVE products (including cards) | 26,274 |
| Cabinets | 28,679 |
| Equipment | 4,934 |
| Supplies | 12,354 |
| Intellectual tools | 1,000 |
| Total | $820,487 |

Average cost per title: $13.53

Ongoing costs for a card format catalog would increase most in the area of staff. This cost figure reflects the labor-intensive nature of a card catalog. We estimated that four full-time filers, filing at the rate of thirty-two cards per hour, would be required for the current cataloging workload. The library would need one full-time equivalent filing reviser and an increase of at least one librarian to work with catalog maintenance.

The second largest cost increase in a card format catalog would be for card cabinets. At an estimated average of eight public catalog cards per title, the library would need almost seven-and-a-half card cabinets each year to accommodate public catalog growth, in addition to shelflist cabinet space. MARCIVE charges for catalog cards would increase also.

These cost increases would be somewhat offset by reducing or eliminating the cost of COM production, reading equipment, and computer center charges for COM tape production. Computer center charges would be reduced by $60,000 a year. This reduction is based on a cost of approximately $12,000 in computer center charges for each of five COM catalog cumulations done during the study year. Costs for computer runs to cumulate cataloging data for new catalogs were not kept separately. Since cost study data were collected, we have begun to keep this cost as a separate figure. Each cumulation costs about $12,000 in computer center charges. We used this estimate to reduce computer center charges by $60,000 in a card system. Note that a card system without a COM catalog will reduce seriously the catalog access of staff working at a distance from the catalog, whether the staff are located in public services or in technical services. Therefore, elimination of COM catalog production compromises the comparability of access envisioned for the cost study.

Certain costs would remain the same in a card system: OCLC costs, programming support, equipment, supplies, and cataloging tools. We delineated one-time set-up costs for reestablishing the card catalog. The cost of cards was estimated separately for the library materials budget (nondocument titles) and U.S. documents that we receive as a government depository library. We thought the typical document record would be longer and would contain more and longer access points than the average nondocument record. We used multiplier of eight cards for each nondocument title and ten cards for each document title to determine total card production. The total estimate for retrospective conversion to a card system was almost three-and-a-half million cards. We could then easily derive the number of card cabinets required from the number of cards.

We estimated computer costs for producing almost three-and-a-half million catalog cards at five cents per card. This figure is possibly an underestimate for current card production. Because computer costs for shelflist production have not been kept separately except for special instances (for example, rush cataloging, browsing collection titles, and replacement shelflist cards for maintenance), we do not know exactly how much these costs currently average. However, if we were to return to a card system, it is probable that economies of scale would bring down the computer costs of printing a card from the catalog database to a figure of five cents.

Initial computer costs for the production of a set of cards for each title in the catalog would not be a direct cost to the library, just as current ongoing computer costs are not billed to the library directly. However, they are a substantial expense to the university and are included in the initial costs of the card catalog. Moreover, the impact on the computer center staff and equipment to produce catalog cards for a database of over 400,000 titles would be enormous, and would have to be spread over a long period of time.

We based salaries for filing cards on the assumption that it would require one year to reinstall the library's card catalog. Although cards would be received in alphabetical order, it would be necessary to interfile various types of entries, batches of cards, and new filing that would continuously come in. There would most likely be a tremendous impact on catalog maintenance staff as well. With these considerations in mind, we estimated that on average we might be able to file 60 cards an hour. This would require 30 filers at $11,426 a year in salary and fringe benefits. This does not account for filing revision and maintenance carried on by higher-paid staff. If the university did in fact return to a card catalog, there might well be different mix of employees.

The third section of Exhibit 2 shows these initial expenses spread over the expected useful life of a card catalog. We believe that technological developments will almost surely dictate replacement of card catalogs within the next 15 years. Therefore, we depreciated the initial expenses over a 15-year period of time. The net effect on ongoing costs of returning to a card system is an increase in average yearly expenditures of nearly $150,000, or about $2.44 per title processed.

## DATA COLLECTION FOR THE ONLINE CATALOG

The library is in the process of developing its options for an online system and is working with an automation consultant to generate cost information from several vendors. Thus far, prices from turnkey vendors have ranged from a high of $650,000 to a low of $325,000. For the purposes of this study, however, we used the published costs for a software-based system, calculated for the number of terminals requested by the library for the cataloging operation alone. We also used estimates for the same system received as part of a formal request for information from the vendor and consultation with the university computing center.

We assumed that if the library were to pursue an online option, the automated cataloging processes would fall into patterns similar to what we have now, with copy catalogers working offline and terminal operators inputting data. We are concerned here with estimating the cost of replacing our present catalog with equivalent access. Therefore, estimates for terminals located in the technical services division and the circulation department were not made. We assumed that online catalogs would be available for library users and at the reference desk, but that staff would have access to a COM catalog, which would continue to be produced as a back-up system. Indeed, we might desire the enhanced cataloging and multipurpose system access that would be possible in an online setting, but we tried to estimate simple replacement costs to avoid a distorted comparison with the COM catalog. We assumed that we would maintain a card shelflist as well.

Although we are aware that organizational patterns would change in an online environment, we cannot determine the extent of the impact of those changes at this time. Some possible changes would be the ability to catalog and do maintenance work online and the ability to add bibliographic records at order time. However, we did not assume that these organizational changes would result in a reduced overall staffing cost for the cataloging function. Costs might simply be moved out of the existing cataloging department. We estimated that staffing costs for copy cataloging and processing of materials would remain the same. The costs for acquiring OCLC data would also remain the same; only the time frame in which the data are acquired might vary. Other costs that would remain at their current levels are MARCIVE costs for cards and processing labels, card cabinets, equipment, supplies, and cataloging tools.

The library would experience some new or increased ongoing expenses with an online catalog—annual maintenance fees for the library system program and the cost of leasing additional terminals for public access. Currently we have 12 microfilm catalogs and 24 microfiche catalogs, adding up to 36 catalog stations. We believe that equivalent access would be available with 17 online catalog terminals and 20 microfiche catalogs, for a total of 37 catalog stations. However, we estimated that we would need six more microfiche reader stations in public areas, so we adjusted the figures for microfiche catalogs and fiche readers accordingly. A total of eight extra work stations would be needed to house the resulting total number of public COM back-up catalogs. In order to compare these costs to microform reader costs in Exhibit 1, we have placed the figures in the first section of Exhibit 3, describing ongoing costs.

Exhibit 3.   Projected Cataloging Costs in an Online System

*Estimated Costs for 1983–1984 Processing*

| | |
|---|---|
| Salaries and fringe benefits | $330,992 |
| OCLC | 29,183 |
| Annual maintenance fees (software) | 10,000 |
| Computer center hardware maintenance fee | 11,000 |
| Computer center charges | 150,000 |
| MARCIVE products | 11,162 |
| Public access terminals (17 IBM 3178-C2) | 4,481 |
| Terminal maintenance | 1,241 |
| Microfiche catalogs | 1,075 |
| Fiche readers, maintenance, and work stations | 1,060 |
| Card cabinet for card shelflist | 850 |
| Equipment | 4,934 |
| Supplies | 12,354 |
| Intellectual tools | 1,000 |
| Total | $569,332 |

60,624 titles cataloged
Average cost per title: $9.39

*Initial Expenses to Establish an Online System*

| | |
|---|---|
| License fees | $ 95,000 |
| Additional computer hardware needed by the computer center | 110,000 |
| Installation, preparation, cabling, and so on | 10,000 |
| Modems (2 at $2,650) | 5,300 |
| Printers (8 and $400) | 3,200 |
| Printer switches (2 6-way at $100) | 200 |
| Total | $223,700 |

*Estimated 1983–1984 Costs*
*Including Initial Expenses Depreciated over 5 Years*

| | |
|---|---|
| Salaries and fringe benefits | $330,992 |
| OCLC-related membership and use fees | 29,183 |
| License fees | 19,000 |
| Annual maintenance fee (software) | 10,000 |
| Additional computer hardware needed by the computer center | 22,000 |
| Additional hardware maintenance fee | 11,000 |
| Computer center charges | 150,000 |
| MARCIVE products | 11,162 |
| Modems | 1,060 |
| Installation, preparation, cabling, and so on | 2,000 |
| Public access terminals (17 IBM 3178-C2) | 4,481 |
| Terminal maintenance | 1,241 |
| Printers | 640 |

EXHIBIT 3.   Cont'd.

| | |
|---|---:|
| Printer switches | 40 |
| Microfiche catalogs | 1,075 |
| Fiche readers, maintenance, and work stations | 1,060 |
| Card cabinet for card shelflist | 850 |
| Equipment | 4,934 |
| Supplies | 12,354 |
| Intellectual tools | 1,000 |
| Total | $614,072 |

Average cost per title: $10.13

Since the library would be able to use the university computing center's program compiler, no rental fee was added for this item. It would be absorbed in overall computing center charges assessed the Library.

Other expenses would be reduced in an online environment. Computer center charges would fall by an estimated $67,000. We made estimates for one additional computer operator, one applications programmer, one-fourth FTE systems liaison staff member at the computer center, machine maintenance contracts, disc storage fees, processing for a report generator, batch processing for file back-up, rebuilding indexes, offline products produced by batch process (such as the periodical holdings list), and COM data collection. We would make only two computer runs for COM tape generation, as opposed to five in the COM system. Since the COM catalogs would serve primarily as a back-up system, we assumed that we would want to reduce the number of catalog cumulations produced to two per year. The figure for microfiche catalogs was reduced similarly, and the cost for microfilm would be eliminated completely.

Just as eliminating COM access in the card catalog option would severely hamper staff access to the catalog, reducing the number of fiche catalogs produced annually would affect staff access, particularly in catalog maintenance and acquisitions. Some limited online access for these functions could be gained by increasing the time during which the two IBM computer terminals used for processing are available. In the event that access is enhanced by additional terminals in public and staff areas, the computer hardware configuration in the "initial expenses" chart would adequately support up to 75 terminals. Thus increased access gained by a greater number of terminals would increase the cost of the system by little more than the price of purchasing and maintaining or leasing the terminals themselves.

As with the card catalog, there are initial expenses to set up the new form of catalog. We isolated these costs as we did for the card catalog so that we could compare the two forms. The greatest expense is additional computer hardware for the computer center. The estimated computing capacity requirement is based on purchasing enough hardware to allow for the next five years of catalog growth. It discounts entirely the computer space that we currently use. Software license fees are a second large initial expense. The other initial costs of printers, printer switches, and modems are incidental to public catalog stations, and interfaces with MARCIVE and OCLC. Since the useful life of an automated system is relatively short, we depreciated these one-time costs over a period of five years and added them to the third section of Exhibit 3.

## RESULTS AND OBSERVATIONS

The primary result of the cost study is that we obtained a current cost for presenting the library's users with a catalog, including cataloging for government documents and all catalog database products. The results of the study were presented to the library administration in a useful form. Comparisons with other cataloging cost study results should be made very cautiously because of operational and organizational differences and differences in the method by which costs are collected.

Although a card catalog format proved to be considerably more expensive in Maddux Library's environment because of initial expenses and high labor costs, the present COM format and the online system studied are much closer together in total depreciated cost. Choice of catalog will also depend on non-cost considerations, for example, the ability of a system to provide other subsystems besides a catalog, or long-run efficiencies to be gained by lowering the size of the labor component relative to other costs.

We could not easily discern the cost of including government documents in the catalog, since salary costs were the only expense not buried in such items as computer center charges and microform catalogs. One result of the study is that we have begun collecting separate computer processing costs for documents. However, we did discover that including government documents in the catalog increased the total cost of the catalog, but significantly lowered the per-title cost. Because statistical counts for documents have not been based on volume equivalents, it was impossible for the study to use a volume count, the library's usual unit of measure, for comparisons of systems. But since catalogs describe titles and not volumes, perhaps a title count is a more useful measure.

Whereas the costs of including documents in a card catalog would have an even greater impact on the overall cost of the catalog, it is unlikely that documents inclusion would have as great an effect on online costs. It appears that in a card catalog (a manual data storage system) the per-title cost increases in proportion to the size of the catalog, whereas in either a COM or an online catalog (an automated storage system) the per-title cost decreases in proportion to size.

It is important to clarify the purpose of a cost study. The methodology chosen will be dictated by the use envisioned for the data. However, during the course of conducting the study, it might become apparent that the available data dictate a modification or expansion of the purpose, or that the end uses of the study might be broader or different in some way. It is important to maintain contact with those who will make use of the study, to be sure that the data being collected are suitable to the real needs of the library and to continue to clarify the goals of the study.

Another inescapable observation is that all the library catalog formats studied are expensive. Librarians who are not directly responsible for budget planning, sometimes lose sight of the fact that operating their libraries frequently involves very large expenditures. An average savings of a few cents per book in cataloging can add up to thousands of dollars when multiplied by the total number of titles processed. Even medium-sized cataloging operations are a big business.

This study did not account for public service costs of training personnel and users for any of the three catalog forms. These costs may prove to be substantially different for the three forms of catalog studied. Because instructions for use may be incorporated into terminal displays, the online option may well prove to be the least expensive.

Finally, note that these cost comparisons are for up-and-running costs. Should the library change cataloging format, it will need to continue providing a COM catalog during installation of a new system. Because a COM catalog would be produced as a backup catalog in an online option, this provision for a dual system would not increase costs. For the card catalog option, a dual system would need to be maintained for at least a year and would increase initial expenditures by about $60,000. This cost is not included in the comparison figures. Within the Trinity University and Maddux Libraries, an online public catalog including similar access to the same collections is least expensive. The COM catalog is next least expensive, and the most expensive is a card catalog. This is true both for ongoing annual costs and for annual costs including depreciated initial expenses. Even over a depreciation period of 15 years, the card catalog would continue to be the most expensive option.

We want to emphasize that these conclusions would not be the same for all online systems, only for the one that we used for our study. The system we chose to use for the comparison would not necessarily be the least expensive nor the most desirable in every library setting. Nor would every library find an online system to be the least expensive catalog format option. Finally, there are other important considerations for choosing a cataloging format besides cost. However, since cataloging costs are a major expense to all libraries, cost studies such as this one yield information that is important for administrative functions.

## Notes

1. *Technical Services Cost Studies in ARL Libraries,* SPEC Flyer 89 (Washington, D.C.: Association of Research Libraries, Systems and Procedures Exchange Center, 1982), unpaged.
2. William J. Maher, "Measurement and Analysis of Processing Costs in Academic Archives," *College & Research Libraries* 43 (January 1982):60–61.
3. Betty Jo Mitchell, Norman E. Tanis, and Jack Jaffe, *Cost Analysis of Library Functions: A Total System Approach* (Greenwich, Conn.: JAI Press, 1978), 3.
4. Malcolm Getz and Doug Phelps, "Labor Costs in the Technical Operations of Three Research Libraries," *Journal of Academic Librarianship* 10, no. 4 (September 1984):202–219.
5. For a discussion of straight line versus sum of years depreciation techniques, see Richard M. Dougherty and Fred Heinritz, *Scientific Management of Library Operations*(Metuchen, N.J.: Scarecrow Press, 1982), 191–198.
6. *Statement of Desired Data for Determining the Costs of Maintaining RLG Catalogs, 1976/77,* in *Technical Services Cost Studies in ARL Libraries,* SPEC Kit 89 (Washington, D.C.: Association of Research Libraries, Systems and Procedures Exchange Center, 1982), 26–43.
7. Getz and Phelps, "Labor Costs in the Technical Operations of Three Research Libraries."

# No More Free Ride: Cost Analysis in the Serials Department

## Sherry Anderson

Historically, library budgets have grown with little need to justify increases. Academia feels that it is different from business and that the same management guidelines do not apply. At the Coy C. Carpenter Library of the Bowman Gray School of Medicine, we were faced with evaluating our direction and identifying our priorities in terms of our budget. To plan effectively, we needed to determine what our services and operations actually cost.

Ultimately we wished to evaluate each department within the library. Several objectives were defined that summarized what each study should encompass. These were to:

- determine the amount of time required to perform an activity
- obtain the resulting cost
- develop performance measures for various activities to be used by supervisors in performance appraisals
- analyze the existing work flow for possible inefficiencies
- suggest any changes in work flow or materials used to process an item to be more cost-efficient

These objectives provided a good framework for our studies.

In the summer of 1984, the Carpenter Library hired an MBA student in the internship program from the Babcock School of Management of Wake Forest University to perform cost analysis studies of various library functions. He was given thorough orientation to each department. We then identified those specific activities in serials that we wished to study, including check-in, claiming, processing bindery, kardex maintenance, and ordering and renewing journal titles.

In conducting a cost analysis study, all relevant factors need to be

Sherry Anderson is Associate Director of the Bowman Gray School of Medicine Library at Wake Forest University and is active in the Medical Library Association.

reviewed and costs per unit determined. Such a study includes the recording and analysis of all expenses related to production: all materials, labor, and overhead. This was not difficult to obtain for bindery services, nor for materials and supplies purchased for use by the serials section only. Assessing costs for personnel-associated activities was harder to isolate.

First, we carefully evaluated the existing serials work flow and procedures to see if there were any aspects that had changed or possibly needed to be changed for more efficiency. In a work flow analysis it may be best to chart each step on paper. List each activity in its logical progression through the department, indicating which employee is involved at each point.

After determining work flows, time studies were performed to learn how long each person takes to do a certain activity. A recommended method is to have each employee log all activities done during the work day. Just a few days of observations should yield enough data to determine an activity's average time. Employees should be encouraged to be as accurate and fair as possible, working neither too fast nor too slow. Short interruptions (two to three minutes) are normal and should be included in the recorded time for an activity.

An example of a good time study log is shown in Exhibit 1. It includes the date for each activity, the number of items being processed, beginning and ending times, and any comments pertaining to problems encountered. The log is kept by the employee and periodically verified by the project coordinator. If too many problems seem to have occurred that would skew the data, the observation may need to be reevaluated.

EXHIBIT 1.   Sample time study log.

*Time Study Log:*
*Susan Smith*

| Date | What | No. | Start Time | Stop Time | Total Time (in minutes) | Comments |
|------|------|-----|-----------|-----------|------------------------|----------|
| 5/10/85 | Search OCLC and printout | 26 titles | 8:00 | 8:32 | 32 | |
| 5/10/85 | Edit printout | 26 titles | 8:35 | 11:40 | 185 | 2 phone call interruptions |
| 5/10/85 | Proof book cards | 32 titles | 11:45 | 12:40 | 55 | |

The project coordinator totals the time spent on each activity. Each block of time is considered one observation period. Five to ten such observation periods are recommended; certainly there should be no fewer than three. Each observation period is divided by the number of items processed during that period to arrive at an average time per item:

$$\text{Time per item} = \frac{\text{Total Time Per Activity}}{\text{Total Number of Items Processed}}$$

Once an average time per item is found, all items are averaged together to determine an overall average for that activity. Once we have that, the averages for all activities in the work flow are added to determine the total length of time it takes to process an item through serials.

To determine an item's actual labor cost, each employee's labor cost per minute must first be derived. To compute this, you need each employee's salary plus fringe benefits. Then determine the total number of minutes of work per employee per year by applying the formula:

$$\frac{\text{Labor Cost}}{\text{Per Minute}} = \frac{\text{Salary and Fringe Benefits}}{\text{Total Minutes Worked Per Year}}$$

To determine the number of minutes an employee works in a year, first multiply a five-day work week by 52. Then subtract the number of vacation days, holidays, and sick days. Multiply the remainder by 7.5 hours (allowing for two 15-minute breaks) to get the total number of hours worked per year. Finally convert this to minutes by multiplying by 60:

$$\frac{60 \text{ Minutes}}{\text{Per Hour}} \left[ \frac{\text{Work Hours}}{\text{Per Day}} \left( \frac{52 \text{ Weeks/}}{\text{Year}} \times \frac{5 \text{ Days/}}{\text{Week}} \right) - \left( \frac{\text{Vacation Days,}}{\text{Sick Days, Holidays}} \right) \right]$$

52 Weeks/Year × 5 Days/Week = 260 Days
20 Vacation Days + 8 Holidays + 5 Sick Days = 33 Days
260 Days − 33 Days = 227 Work Days
227 Days × 7.5 Work Hours/Day = 1,702.5
1,702.5 Hours × 60 Minutes/Hour = 102,150 Minutes

With a labor-cost-per-minute figure for all activities, the total labor cost per unit can be determined:

Labor Cost Per Unit = Activities [Average Time/Activity × Labor Cost/Minute]

If multiple employees perform the same serial activity, a weighted average of their labor cost per minute should be used.

A second cost element is supplies, which includes departmental and general supplies. The most accurate method of assigning supplies cost to each journal title processed is to first add up the unit cost of each security strip, book pocket, card, and so on. Then the cost of all other departmental supplies ordered should be totaled and divided over the total number of titles processed during the year. General supplies ordered for the entire library's use should also be taken into account. The most equitable means of allocating general supplies expense is to divide the FTE number of serials staff by the total FTE for the entire library, and multiply this percentage by the general supplies expense for the year. The serials department's share of the general supplies expense is then divided by the total number of titles processed during the year. The total of all these supply figures provides a supplies cost per journal title processed.

Our library is billed for long-distance as well as basic telephone service. The serials department's portion can be determined by evaluating the total cost for each extension in their department. Total telephone charges for the year should be divided by all items processed and added to the other costs.

Some libraries may need to include an occupancy or overhead cost in their analysis. This is based on the square feet occupied and may include rent, electricity, telephones (if not billed directly), maintenance, and housekeeping. Within the library, this cost should be allocated appropriately to each section. The portion allocated to serials should be divided by the total number of titles processed per year to determine the occupancy cost per title.

Once we have identified all appropriate components for an activity, the information is incorporated into a formula that can generate our cost information. Since such numbers as salaries change, it is easy to substitute the new information and arrive at current cost information. As long as the procedure remains the same, and the time to perform the procedure has not changed, the formula can be used over and over. Periodically, the time studies are generated to confirm that the time per activity has not changed. If the time variables have changed, then the appropriate corrections are made in the formula and new time and cost information are generated. The formulas we have established are set up using Lotus 1-2-3.

Several management decisions were based on the results of our studies. For example, at first glance it seemed to be more expensive to have our bindery insert security strips into journal volumes, actually, it was more cost-effective. Therefore, a change in procedures was implemented.

Another change was made in the physical processing of bound volumes. Self-adhesive book pockets are considerably more expensive than plain pockets, which must be glued in. Our research proved that savings in labor costs offset the more expensive pockets.

We have been able to reduce the serials staff (through attrition) from 3.5 FTE to 2.0 FTE. Along with this reduction, we were able to implement an automated serials management system. Once the automated system replaces all the various manual files, even this level of staffing will be a little more than required.

Careful cost-benefit analysis has been very helpful in planning our budgets and future staffing needs. We think this model can be used by other libraries when it is tailored to meet their specific needs.

# Serials Check-in Cost Study: A Methodology

## Linda Haack Lomker

With the costs of serials skyrocketing, determining the expense—in both time and money—associated with their processing becomes even more critical. To study check-in time and costs effectively, first consider variations among libraries. Each library has its own list of activities that are part of the check-in process. Obviously, a greater number of activities or a greater complexity of procedures will increase check-in time and costs. Procedural complexity may be as much the result of the size of the institution as of anything else.

A larger, more complex file increases the time required to locate the appropriate record. For example, searching a large file containing all types of serials—including journals, monographic series, and annuals—takes longer than searching a smaller file containing only newspapers.

Other factors are the professional level of staff performing check-in tasks; salary, which may vary depending on geographic location, type of library (public, special, or academic); and the job categories (clerical, technical, professional, or managerial) used within the library.

## CHECK-IN ACTIVITIES

Describing the file or the level and salary of staff members is easier than comparing check-in procedures. In our library we divided check-in into three stages: the pre check-in stage (often referred to as mail sorting), the check-in-proper stage (which usually includes both records work and materials preparation), and the post check-in stage (which generally deals with distribution of checked-in materials). We made lists of possible activities within each stage in order to give an idea of what might be involved. In each case some or all of the activities listed could be included.

Linda Haack Lomker is Head of the Serials Acquisitions Section at the University of Minnesota Libraries and recently chaired the RTSD Serials Sections Committee to Study Serials Records.

## Pre Check-in:

- Rough sorting of mail (separating out material not for the serials department).
- Removing wrappers and boxes.
- Rough sorting of mail into alphabetical order.
- Sorting by language.

Some or all pre check-in may be done by the receiving room staff. The amount of sorting, if any, required for check-in varies among institutions.

## Check-in Proper:

- Searching files.
- Comparing record found to item in hand (verification of hit).
- Finding the citation (for example, volume and issue numbers, date) in piece.
- Recording the issue.
- Recording other information.
- Preparing the claim.
- Preparing the binding slip(s).
- Preparing the processing slip for cataloging.
- Marking the piece in some way.
- Recording invoice payment.
- Recording statistics.

The size, type, and number of files searched affect the cost of this stage greatly. It was agreed that snags, or serials that cannot be checked in immediately, would not be included in this stage. However, the cost of dealing with snags is of great concern.

## Post Check-in:

- Stamping and sorting.
- Recording more statistics.
- Inserting protection devices such as tattletape.
- Pulling binding slips (if batched and done after check-in proper).
- Placing materials on shelves, in bins, or in bags.
- Delivering materials

What is included as check-in proper at one institution may be part of the post check-in stage at another. It depends on work flow and staff assignments.

Activities performed at some libraries may have been missed, but the lists indicate the level of specificity suggested. Other activities may be added if necessary.

For simplicity, all the processing of problems such as title changes, shipment errors, and snags have been considered outside the confines of this study. However, materials that cannot be checked in immediately require more time than those that can be. This area needs further study.

Sampling Method

The sample required for a check-in cost study would vary depending on the purpose of the study and the time available to run it. In many institutions, seasonal fluctuations in the check-in work load have been identified. Therefore, if projections were needed for a year, a one-week sample in the spring, one in the summer, and one in the fall would be better than a two- or three-week sample during one month, if there was time to conduct the study over a period of a year. If comparative figures are required, testing times should be matched so that the seasonal fluctuation does not affect the results. A two- or three-week sample would yield more accurate results than a one-week sample. Taking a sample of more than two weeks at one time could overburden staff members, probably creating backlogs in other department activities, or perhaps even in the check-in activities being measured.

The basic time figures that follow were determined by simple calculations. For example, the amount of time it takes to do check-in divided by the number of pieces checked in equals the time-per-piece. Costs can be calculated just as simply, of course.

The problem is that performing a time study, particularly one that eliminates many of the interruptions and complications of daily operations, sets up abnormal working conditions. On top of that, test conditions affect the speed at which people work—figures shown here are definitely low. This may be in part because they do not reflect interruptions in using the files, requests for assistance that would be honored if a test were not being conducted, and personal time for such things as trips to the fountain and the rest room. Therefore, a factor of 10 percent was added to the simple calculations to more closely approximate the actual time required for direct check-in. However, adding the 10 percent still may not account for the fact that people speed up whenever a study is being done.

RESULTS OF THE TESTING

Using the methodology just described, check-in cost studies were done at three academic libraries during the early part of 1985. The exhibits and commentary that follow give an idea of what the application of the methodology can provide. However, the studies were performed to test the methodology, not as definitive measures of check-in time at the libraries. Therefore, they have not been identified.

FACTORS AFFECTING TIME AND COSTS

The type of files and the level of staff members differ among the test libraries. Library A has a kardex of over 14,000 titles; it is organized in one alphabet. However, newspapers and government documents are separate. The kardex at Library B contains over 18,500 titles, including documents, in one alphabet. Newspapers are separate. Library C has a revo file of 32,905 items, including periodicals, continuations, monographic series, and sets. It does not include government publications, most newspapers, or microforms. Libraries A and C used technical or paraprofessional staff members to perform the test. Library B used clerical and technical or paraprofessional staff members. All three had well-trained staff members who had been performing the check-in activities on the job for six months or more.

Exhibit 1 shows the activities included in the pre check-in stage. Although basically the same procedures are performed in Libraries A and B, the steps involved in the performance of them may be different. On the other hand, the receiving room at Library C handles all the activities done by serial staff members at the other two institutions, except for the rough sorting of mail into alphabetical order.

Exhibit 2 covers the check-in proper stage. The activities at the three institutions differ after the fourth step. Only Library B records ISSNs, if they are listed in the piece but not on the records. At Library A, claims are prepared during check-in; a dummy is prepared and the records are pulled for claiming at Library C. No claiming is done at Library B during the check-in activities. Both Library A and Library C prepare binding slips; Library B does not. Library C processes new orders, types new check-in cards when necessary, processes title changes, and prepares dummies for added volumes during the check-in proper stage. Similar activities are done at other times in the other two institutions. Libraries A and B take statistics on continuations and monographic series, authorize payment on any invoices that arrived in the volumes, and distribute them to the appropriate shelves during check-in proper. Thus this stage is quite different in the three institutions.

Exhibit 3 shows the activities of the post check-in stage. Six different activities are performed at Library A, four at Library B, and two at Library C. Some of what is done during post check-in at Library A was done during check-in proper at the other two institutions. At the time of the study, only Library A tattle taped items during post check-in and entered continuations on the RLIN Acquisitions System. Libraries A and B stamp and sort journal during this stage; Library C has done so already. This stage is also quite different among the three institutions.

EXHIBIT 1.   Pre Check-in Stage.

| Procedure | Institution | | |
|---|---|---|---|
| | Library A | Library B | Library C* |
| 1. Rough sorting of mail. (that is, separating out material not for serials dept.) | X | X | |
| 2. Removing wrappers. | X | X | |
| 3. Rough sorting of mail into alphabetical order. | X | X | X |
| 4. Sorting by language. | (Chinese sorted out) | (Chinese and Arabic sorted out) | |

*The other functions are performed by the receiving room.

Exhibit 2.    Check-in procedures in three academic libraries.

| Procedure | Institution | | |
| --- | --- | --- | --- |
| | Library A | Library B | Library C |
| 1. Searching file(s) | $X^1$ | $X^2$ | $X^3$ |
| 2. Comparing record found to item in hand. (Verification of hit) | X | X | X |
| 3. Locating citation in issue. | X | X | X |
| 4. Recording citation and check-in date on check-in card. | X | X | X |
| 5. Recording ISSN if necessary. | | X | |
| 6. Preparing claim notification if necessary. | X | | |
| 7. Preparing dummy and pull card for claim. | | | X |

1. Library A has a kardex of 14,000 + titles, which is organized in one alphabet. Newspapers and government documents are separate.
2. Library B has a kardex of 18,500 + titles, which is organized in one alphabet. Newspapers are separate.
3. Library C has a manual check-in file of 32,905 items.

EXHIBIT 2.   Con't.

| Procedure | Library A | Library B | Library C |
|---|---|---|---|
| | | *Institution* | |
| 8. Preparing materials to be forwarded. | | | |
| a. Marking the issue or volume in some way. | X | X | X |
| b. Preparing processing slips or flags. | X | X | X |
| c. Stamping property and location information. | | | X |
| 9. Preparing binding slip. | X | | X |
| 10. Processing new order. | | | X |
| 11. Typing new check-in card. | | | X |
| 12. Processing recognizable title change and forwarding to cataloging. | | | X |
| 13. Preparing dummy for added volumes. | | | X |
| 14. Counting continuations forwarded to serials. Cataloging (serials cataloged as separates) and recording the count on statistics sheets. | X | X | |
| 15. Placing the volumes on the proper shelf. | X | X | |
| 16. Paying invoices received with shipments. | X | X | |

Exhibit 3.   Post Check-in stage.

| Procedure | Institution | | |
|---|---|---|---|
| | Library A | Library B | Library C |
| 1. Taking statistics. | X | X[1] | X[2] |
| 2. Stamping journals with the property stamp. | X | X | |
| 3. Tattle taping selected items. | X | | |
| 4. Sorting journals by location. | X | X | |
| 5. Distributing to appropriate shelves, bins, bags, etc. | X | X[3] | X |
| 6. Entering continuations into the RLIN Acquisitions System. | X | | |

1. Includes statistics for journals and volumes to be delivered to the marking room. The volumes destined for cataloging are counted during check-in proper.
2. This is done during check-in proper.
3. Those volumes to be cataloged are placed on appropriate shelves during check-in proper.

EXHIBIT 4.   Library A, Time Figures.

|  | Actual Test Results | Projected Time |
|---|---|---|
| Institution | Library A | Library A |
| *Stage* | *Pre Check-in* | *Pre Check-in* |
| Number of pieces | 1,196 | 1,196 |
| Time | 480 min./8 hrs. | 528 min./8.8 hrs. |
| Time per piece | .40 min. | .44 min. |
| *Stage* | *Newspaper Check-in* | *Newspaper Check-in* |
| Number of pieces | 357 | 357 |
| Time | 42 min. | 46 min. |
| Time per piece | .12 min | .13 min |
| *Stage* | *Journal Check-in* | *Journal Check-in* |
| Number of pieces | 1,051 | 1,051 |
| Time | 1910 min./31.83 hrs. | 2101 min./35 hrs. |
| Time per piece | 1.81 min. | 2 min. |
|  | *Continuation* | *Continuation* |
| *Stage* | *Cat Sep Check-in* | *Cat Sep Check-in* |
| Number of pieces | 91 | 91 |
| Time | 460 min./7.67 hrs. | 506 min./8.4 hrs. |
| Time per piece | 5 min. | 5.56 min. |
| *Stage* | *Post Check-in* | *Post Check-in* |
| Number of pieces | 948 | 948 |
| Time | 460 min./7.67 hrs. | 506 min./8.4 hrs. |
| Time per piece | .49 min | .53 min |

## RESULTS OF THE TRIAL RUN

The actual time figures are summarized in three charts, one for each institution. (See Exhibits 4, 5, and 6.) For Libraries A and B, activities were recorded and figured in these stages: pre check-in, newspaper check-in, journal check-in, continuation/cat sep check-in, and post check-in. Because of differences in procedures, Library C's activities were recorded and figured in theses stages: pre check-in (unbounds), pre check-in (bounds), check-in (unbounds), check-in (bounds), post check-in (unbounds) and post check-in (bounds). Even if the pre check-in and post check-in figures for Library C were figured together, the activities within the stages are very different from those at Libraries A and B.

EXHIBIT 5.   Library B, Time Figures.

| Institution | Actual Test Results | Projected Time |
|---|---|---|
| | Library B | Library B |
| *Stage* | *Pre Check-in* | *Pre Check-in* |
| Number of pieces | 2,685 | 2,685 |
| Time | 1,100 min./18.3 hrs. | 1,210 min./20.2 hrs. |
| Time per piece | .41 min. | .45 min. |
| *Stage* | *Newspaper Check-in* | *Newspaper Check-in* |
| Number of pieces | 563 | 563 |
| Time | 327 min./5.45 hrs. | 360 min./6 hrs. |
| Time per piece | .58 min | .64 min |
| *Stage* | *Journal Check-in* | *Journal Check-in* |
| Number of pieces | 1,367 | 1,367 |
| Time | 1,211 min./20.19 hrs. | 1,332 min./22.2 hrs. |
| Time per piece | .89 min. | .97 min. |
| | *Continuation* | *Continuation* |
| *Stage* | *Cat Sep Check-in* | *Cat Sep Check-in* |
| Number of pieces | 139 | 139 |
| Time | 512 min./8.53 hrs. | 563 min./9.4 hrs. |
| Time per piece | 3.68 min. | 4.05 min. |
| *Stage* | *Post Check-in* | *Post Check-in* |
| Number of pieces | 1,697 | 1,697 |
| Time | 360 min./6 hrs. | 396 min./6.6 hrs. |
| Time per piece | .21 min | .23 min |

The actual test results column in each chart gives the results of the trial run made at each institution. The projected time column adds 10 percent to the time figures, to better approximate the actual time spent on these activities—staff members may have worked at a faster pace than can be maintained on a regular basis because of the study, but more important, problems were set aside. Check-in of straightforward materials takes a lot less time than checking-in problem items.

Where the time figures differ greatly among the institutions, it is because the activities performed are different. The test directors found the individual results useful for institutional information on operations and for charting changes in costs when routines change as a result of automation or other circumstances.

Exhibit 6.   Library C, Time Figures.

| | Actual Test Results | Projected Time |
|---|---|---|
| Institution | Library C | Library C |
| *Stage* | *Pre Check-in (unbounds)* | *Pre Check-in (unbounds)* |
| Number of pieces | 3,304 | 3,304 |
| Time | 247 min./4.1 hrs. | 272 min./4.5 hrs. |
| Time per piece | .07 min. | .08 min. |
| *Stage* | *Pre Check-in (bounds)* | *Pre Check-in (bounds)* |
| Number of pieces | 965 | 965 |
| Time | 50 min. | 55 min. |
| Time per piece | .05 min. | .06 min. |
| *Stage* | *Check-in (unbounds)* | *Check-in (unbounds)* |
| Number of pieces | 5,875 | 5,875 |
| Time | 7,570 min./126.2 hrs. | 8,327 min./138.8 hrs. |
| Time per piece | 1.29 min. | 1.42 min. |
| *Stage* | *Check-in (bounds)* | *Check-in (bounds)* |
| Number of pieces | 387 | 387 |
| Time | 856 min./14.3 hrs. | 942 min./15.7 hrs. |
| Time per piece | 2.21 min. | 2.43 min. |
| *Stage* | *Post Check-in (unbounds)* | *Post Check-in (unbounds)* |
| Number of pieces | * | * |
| Time | * | * |
| Time per piece | .12 min. | .13 min. |
| *Stage* | *Post Check-in (bounds)* | *Post Check-in (bounds)* |
| Number of pieces | * | * |
| Time | * | * |
| Time per piece | .38 | .42 |

*Numbers not available.

# Technical Services Costs Case Study

## Gary M. Pitkin

Early in the 1980 fiscal year, the library of Sangamon State University, Springfield, Illinois, was notified by the administration that $25,000 had to be cut from the personnel budget. Library administrators were faced with determining how and where these cuts would be made. The library's organizational structure at that time is shown in Exhibit 1. Faculty positions—university librarian, library systems coordinator, and instructional services—would not be affected by this budget cut. Over 75 percent of the library's paraprofessional or staff positions were in technical services, so most of the cuts would have to be made there.

To best determine where in technical services these cuts could be imposed with minimal impact on production and work flow, the library administration decided to study that work flow, and, at the same time, determine how much the library was spending in personnel costs to purchase, fully catalog, and prepare a document for use.

The methodology used to conduct the study was originally designed by Dr. H. William Axford in 1969 while he was university librarian at Florida Atlantic University. He analyzed internal costs as an approach to performance budgeting. The same methodology was later used at Arizona State University and at the University of Oregon. In each case, all job functions of entire technical services divisions were analyzed. Each study showed several functions to be unnecessary or repetitive, and appropriate reorganization followed.

For application of this methodology at Sangamon State University, we obtained a copy of the control deck, written in FORTRAN IV for IBM equipment, from the University of Oregon. It was modified to operate on Sangamon State's Hewlett-Packard 3000. Some changes were also made to the program and to the forms used for gathering information.

The first step in the process was to identify job functions in each department. Each staff member compiled a detailed list of his or her

Gary M. Pitkin is Director of University Libraries at the University of Northern Colorado. He has served as chair of the RTSD Technical Services Costs Committee and is editor of the Haworth Press journal *Technical Services Quarterly*.

EXHIBIT 1.   Organization before budget cuts.

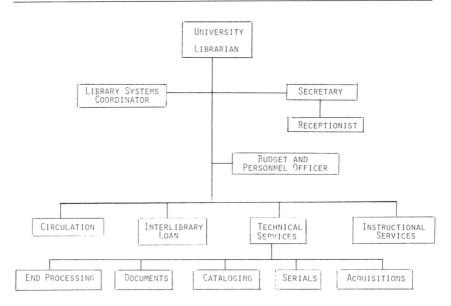

responsibilities. Individual lists were then compared and combined into departmental lists (see Appendix A). Each function was assigned a function number, as shown in the left-hand column.

In the second step each staff member assigned a percentage of time to each function that applied to his or her responsibilities. The log shown in Exhibit 2 was used for this purpose. Position number is not filled out by the employee. The function numbers are taken from the function lists and only those pertinent to the individual's responsibilities are listed. The total amount of time must equal 100 percent. The time period analyzed is a fiscal year. This information was then entered onto the preprinted form shown in Exhibit 3. The first field, listed as "ID#," is the position number. The second field is the annual salary. Hours represented by that salary are listed in the next field. The "C" column identifies staff position: a 1 in this column indicates professional, 2 indicates staff, and 3 indicates a student assistant. The rest of the line is taken directly from the function number/percentage sheet shown in Exhibit 2. A separate coding sheet was generated for each department.

Also coded, and attached to the sheet just completed, is the job function identification sheet shown in Exhibit 4. Both fields, job number and job title, were taken from procedures lists. The computer then analyzed each job function, in terms of cost per volume and minutes per volume, against the number of volumes processed in fiscal year 1980,

EXHIBIT 2.   Log form for job analysis.

Department or Section _____

Name _____

Position Classification _____

Position Number (*Do Not Fill In*) _____

Function Number                     Percentage of Time

| | |
|---|---|
| _____ | _____ |
| _____ | _____ |
| _____ | _____ |
| _____ | _____ |
| _____ | _____ |
| _____ | _____ |
| _____ | _____ |

which was 23,500. On the basis of information provided by the computer, analyses were made of costs and work flow. Costs are summarized in Exhibit 5.

Work flow was analyzed by comparing the procedural lists for redundancy and then examining the printouts to obtain total time figures for the redundant areas. For example, filing in the card catalog was listed as a job function for each technical services department. The time spent on this function in each department, except for cataloging, was minimal.

Evaluating redundant or repetitive work flow resulted in consolidating procedures into single departments. At the technical services administrative level, it was discovered that a substantial amount of time was spent on administrative matters including hiring, training, supervising, and evaluating personnel. This was done by the head of technical services and by the five department heads. Library administration felt that this function could also be consolidated.

The result was the reorganization shown in Exhibit 6. The budget and personnel officer had resigned. That salary was cut from the library's personnel budget, and the head of technical services was

EXHIBIT 3.   Data Input Coding Sheet.

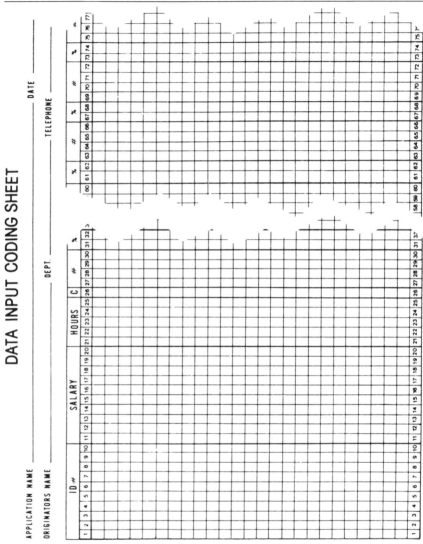

moved into that position. The receptionist in the administrative office was transferred to the cataloging department and the head of acquisitions was transferred to the administrative office as bookkeeper. The serials and documents departments were consolidated into the acquisitions department. A staff member in documents was appointed head of acquisitions, and a vacant position in the serials department was eliminated. The end processing department was consolidated into the cataloging department. The net effect was to cut $25,000 from the library's personnel budget, as directed by university administration,

EXHIBIT 4. Data Input Coding Sheet.

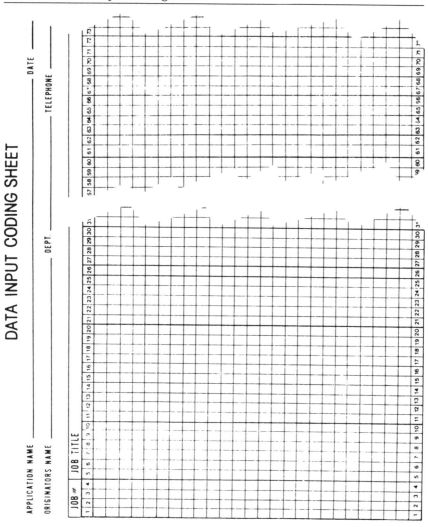

and to streamline work flow so that the cuts would not have a negative effect on production.

Until 1981, the methodology just described had been used solely to analyze production costs and not to compare different methods of production. One of the test sites for Faxon's LINX system was Appalachian State University, Boone, NC, and we wanted to determine the cost-effectiveness, if any, of the automated system. We consequently duplicated the control deck used at Sangamon and applied it at Appalachian. As in the Sangamon study, the first step was creating job function lists for both the manual and automated

EXHIBIT 5.   SSU Library Technical Services: Summary of Personnel
Processing Costs.
(23,500 volumes processed) Fiscal Year 1980

|  | $ | $ per Volume | Hours | Minutes per Volume |
|---|---|---|---|---|
| Acquisitions | $ 25,287 | $1.08 | 5,289 | 13.50 |
| Serials | 30,870 | 1.31 | 6,780 | 17.31 |
| Catalog | 61,617 | 2.62 | 11,434 | 29.19 |
| End Processing | 40,297 | 1.71 | 10,209 | 26.06 |
| Head Technical Services | 14,900 | .634 | 1,695 | 4.32 |
| Subtotal | $172,971 | $7.35 | 35,407 | 90.38 |
| OCLC | 22,346 | 1.12 | | |
| Grand Total | $195,317 | $8.47 | | |

systems. The various functions were listed under general headings
to facilitate the gathering and reporting of data and are provided in
Appendix B.

The function heading titles for both lists are: 1) check-in
procedures, not including newspapers or microfilm, 2) check-in
procedures for newspapers, 3) check-in procedures for microfilm, 4)
new subscription and title change procedures, 5) claiming procedures, and 6) training procedures. Again, each function is assigned a
function number.

Since each person in the serials department worked with both
the manual and LINX systems, each person needed to complete
function number/percentage sheets for each system. In this way
time percentages and, consequently, costs for similar functions could
be compared across systems per staff position. Again, the total had
to equal 100 percent. In this case, however, the time period analyzed
was not a fiscal year but a theoretical week in which all job
functions were performed.

To this data were added the number of hours and respective salary
per staff position per week for the manual and Faxon systems. The
information was coded onto the same forms discussed earlier. The
computer then analyzed each job function, in terms of cost per issue and
minutes per issue, against the average number of issues checked in per
system per week. For the manual system, this total was 615 issues. For
the Faxon system, 818 issues.

The computer gave us two printouts. One analyzed the manual
system job functions; the other analyzed the Faxon system job functions. The results which use the six function headings described earlier,
are in Exhibit 7.

According to these results, the Faxon system is $0.08 cheaper per

EXHIBIT 6. Reorganized library staff after costs and work flow analysis.

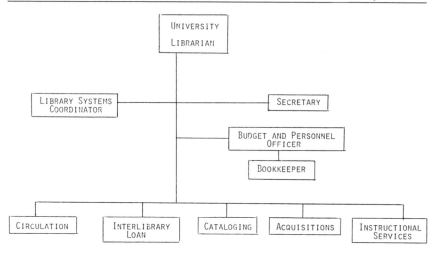

issue. Based on 4,878 current subscriptions and an average of eight issues per year per title, the total savings in staff time is $3,121.92 annually.

This was used to justify keeping the LINX system after the one-year test period had been completed. After the third year we conducted the study again and found a cost savings of over $10,000 per year. The savings in staff time has been used to increase the efficiency of the serials department's public service.

This methodology has been used at other institutions, including

EXHIBIT 7.

| | Manual | | Faxon | |
|---|---|---|---|---|
| Function Headings | $/ Issue | Minutes/ Issue | $/ Issue | Minutes/ Issue |
| Check-in Procedures (does not include newspapers or microfilm) | $.18 | 1.70 | $.16 | 1.55 |
| Check-in Procedures—Newspapers | .02 | .16 | .02 | .25 |
| Check-in Procedures—Microfilm | .00* | .10 | .00* | .06 |
| New Subscription and Title Change Procedures | .06 | .83 | .03 | .38 |
| Claiming Procedures | .05 | .50 | .02 | .27 |
| Training Procedures | .00* | .04 | .00* | .02 |
| Total | $.31 | 3.33 | $.23 | 2.53 |

*Functions measuring less than one-quarter hour per week factor to less than $.01 in cost.

Boston University and Boston College, to justify the replacement of manual systems with automated systems.

Analyzing internal costs as an approach to performance budgeting is effective. But it is successful only if you have enough confidence in the technique and in the results to use them efficiently for the betterment of the organization.

## APPENDIX A.

### Coding: Cataloging Unit Cost Study

300–Hire, train, supervise, evaluate personnel.
301–Verify order requests.
302–Receive and distribute books.
303–File (including temporary slips in title catalog).
304–Catalog major revisions.
305–Catalog matching copy & minor revisions.
306–Catalog original.
307–Add copies and volumes.
308–Check in OCLC cards.
309–Recat, reclass (snags).
310–Revise shelflist.
311–Campus obligations.
312–Opening & closing unit.
314–Statistics.
315–Blackwell project (preparation of books, filling out sheets, searching microfilm, filing).
316–Filling out OCLC duplicate and error reports.
317–Developing & maintaining in-house manuals.
318–Consultation on interpreting & applying cataloging rules (includes time with liaison).
319–Unit meetings.
320–Reading professional literature.
321–Breaks.
322–Miscellaneous.
323–Coordinating work flow with other unit heads.
324–Planning and organizing.

### Coding: Acquisitions Unit Cost Study

101–Hire, train, supervise, evaluate personnel.
102–Prepare invoice vouchers for all expenses charged to library accounts.
103–Xerox invoices needing additional copies for files.
104–Maintain ledger for library accounts.
105–Prepare monthly & yearly accounting reports.
106–Clear statements.
107–Prepare requisitions for all equipment, commodities, travel & contractual services requested from library accounts.
108–Maintain files on library accounts.

109–Open and sort unit's mail.
110–Coordinate work flow with Cataloging.
111–Clear purchase orders & complete receiving report as equipment and commodities are received.
112–Answer department telephone.
113–Type order request cards.
114–Date and alphabetize request cards.
115–Check order requests against card catalog, shelflist, and standing order file.
116–Verify order requests in BIP or Forthcoming Books in Print.
117–Type six-part multiple order form.
118–Type cover letter & FEIN request card, send envelope to vendor.
119–Distribute order form parts.
120–File orders in card catalog; obligation packets in obligation files.
121–Type order form for gifts.
122–Tear apart and distribute approval selection forms to appropriate ISLs.
123–File invoices and invoice vouchers for supervisor.
124–Clear old purchase orders from card catalog.
125–Send out-of-print search requests to vendors.
126–Unbox and arrange approval books on truck.
127–Tear apart approval forms and insert into books.
128–Remove prior week's shipment from shelves & alphabetize on truck.
129–Shelve current approval books in categories per ISL.
130–Type date received on form, separate, and distribute. Clear invoice for payment.
131–Pull selection slips from obligation file for items in current shipment.
132–Type credit memo & insurance form for approval returns.
133–File archival slips & return slips.
134–Unwrap or unbox regular flow of ordered materials.
135–Pull order and invoice, indicating date of receipt, invoice #, and cost on order. Send items to appropriate location. Clear invoice for payment.
136–Correspond with vendors concerning problems, errors, etc.
137–Process status reports, clear cancelled orders.
138–Maintain archival files.
139–Miscellaneous.
140–File order requests for future ordering.
141–Statistics.
142–Breaks.

## Coding: Serials Unit Cost Study

200–Hire, train, supervise & evaluate employees.
201–Sort & deliver library-wide mail.
202–Wrap & mail library-wide packages.
203–Open & distribute unit mail.
204–Check-in routines.
205–Record bound volumes.

206–Record microfilm.
207–Claiming routines.
208–Request replacement & backfile quotes from vendors.
209–Prepare binding notifications.
210–Prepare binding slips.
211–Assemble volumes for binding.
212–Unbox bound volumes from bindery.
213–Search missing issues & volumes.
214–Complete order request for missing issues and backfiles.
215–Put newspapers on sticks; discard newspaper backruns.
216–Maintain file for index and reference volumes.
217–Pull records on dead/canceled titles.
218–Answer user/staff inquiries.
219–Set up new serial records.
220–Correspondence.
221–Filing.
222–Record invoice information for renewals.
223–Prepare order requests for new titles.
224–Maintain duplicate & exchange file for missing issues.
225–Process duplicate & exchange lists.
226–Statistics.
227–Kill titles, NST changes.
228–Sort & check gifts.
229–Order & route sample issues.
230–Update printout.
231–Breaks.
232–Weed collection.
233–Transfer titles to different vendor.
234–Organize & prepare duplicate & exchange lists, wrap & ship requests.
235–Campus obligations.
236–Miscellaneous.
237–Inventory project.
238–Shelflisting project.
239–Match bindery slips with invoice.
240–Check bound volumes for accuracy.

## Coding: Documents Unit Cost Study

400–Hire, train, supervise, evaluate personnel.
401–Train & supervise students.
402–Open & sort mail & packages.
403–Search and verify requests.
404–Type multiple order forms.
405–Pull outstanding orders.
406–Check in ordered materials.
407–Claiming routines.
408–Correspondence.
409–Filing.

410–Answer user/staff inquiries.
411–Check weeding lists.
412–Copy cataloging.
413–Original cataloging.
414–Added copies and volumes.
415–Recat, reclass.
416–OCLC searching.
417–Set up new serial records.
418–Search for su-docs.
419–Pull cards for correction.
420–Type corrections on old cards.
421–Weed collection.
422–Inventory withdrawals.
423–Prepare binding slips.
424–Assemble volumes for binding.
425–Check-in binding.
426–Revise filing.
427–Revise card typing.
428–Revise processing typing.
429–Record renewals.
430–Conversion project.
431–LCS training and inputting.
432–Reference desk.
433–Breaks.
434–Miscellaneous.

## Coding: End Processing Unit Cost Study

500–Hire, train, supervise, evaluate personnel.
501–Type labels.
502–Apply labels, pocket, security strip & property stamp.
503–File.
504–Revise filing.
505–Revise typing.
506–Card maintenance.
507–Book repair.
508–Book maintenance (ref. to stacks, changes & corrections).
509–In-house bindery & preparation for out-of-house binding.
510–Statistics.
511–Snags—cards & books.
512–Missing books—pull cards.
513–Withdrawn books—pull cards & prepare book for property control.
514–Consultation on work flow.
515–Deliver books.
516–Special projects—author/title series, record reclass, dup. drawers,
       oversize inventory, portfolio/oversize dummies.
517–Breaks.
518–Miscellaneous.

519–Workshops, training sessions, meetings.

## Coding: Administrator for Technical Services

600–Hire, train, supervise, review & evaluate personnel.
601–Consult with unit heads.
602–Coordinate procedures among units.
603–Evaluate present procedures, investigate possible alternatives, implement new procedures if determined to be necessary.
604–Establish workload priorities.
605–Serve as a member of library cabinet, administrative council & task forces.
606–Consult with department liaisons.
607–Prepare monthly statistical & narrative reports.
608–Read professional literature & attend conferences, workshops & seminars.
609–Monitor all library accounts. Approve invoice vouchers & requisitions.
610–Attend unit & departmental meetings.
611–Salespeople.
612–Consult with director.
613–Maintain attendance records & monitor department student-help allocation.
614–Conversion discussions.
615–Examine order requests after bibliographic search is complete. Assign vendor on items to be ordered.
616–Miscellaneous.

## APPENDIX B

### Serials Check-in Study: Manual System

Check-in Procedures (does not include newspapers or microfilm)
101–Alphabetize serials to be checked in.
102–Locate title record in Kardex file.
103–Enter volume and number information.
104–Determine correct location for each serial and sort accordingly; place in campus mail issues to be sent to other library departments.
105–Sort titles that do not have Kardex cards.
106–Check order file to determine status of titles that do not have Kardex cards.
107–Record receipt of serials for reference/cataloging.
108–Record call number or shelf location on the serial for reference/cataloging; search the card catalog if necessary.
Check-in Procedures—Newspapers.
109–Alphabetize newspapers to be checked in.
110–Locate title in check-in file.
111–Enter receipt information.
112–Determine correct location for each newspaper and sort accordingly; place in campus mail issues to be sent to other departments.

113–Sort titles that do not have check-in cards.

114–Check order file to determine status of titles that do not have check-in cards.

Check-in Procedures—Microfilm

115–Alphabetize microfilm to be checked in.

116–Locate title in check-in file.

117–Enter receipt information.

118–Determine correct location for each microfilm and sort accordingly; place in campus mail reels to be sent to other departments.

119–Sort titles that do not have check-in cards.

120–Check order file to determine status of titles that do not have check-in cards.

New Subscription and Title Change Procedures

121–Set up the Kardex card for all new subscriptions and title changes; for the latter, this includes removing and filing the old card.

122–Set up new title card for new subscriptions and set up new title card and record information on old title card for title changes in the subscription file.

123–Prepare updates for the holdings printout.

124–Determine Faxon title number and record on Kardex card.

125–Determine how often title will be bound and record on Kardex card.

126–Set up oblique folders for new titles.

Claiming Procedures

127–Determine nonreceipts while checking in daily mail.

128–Scan Kardex file to determine nonreceipts.

129–Compile claim forms and mail to Faxon or publisher.

130–Record claim date and issues claimed on Kardex card.

131–Record received claim information on Kardex card.

132–Maintain claim correspondence file.

133–Erase notations on Kardex card when claimed issue arrives.

Training Procedures

134–Train students to check in materials.

135–Train students to claim materials.

## Serials Check-in Study: Faxon System

Check-in Procedures (does not include newspapers or microfilm)

201–Locate correct title matrix, including combinations and memberships.

202–Enter receipt information.

203–Determine correct location for each serial and sort accordingly; place in campus mail issues to be sent to other departments.

204–Sort titles that do not have matrices.

205–Check order file to determine status of titles that do not have matrices.

206–Record receipt of serials for reference/cataloging.

207–Record call number or shelf location on the serial for reference/cataloging; search the card catalog if necessary.

Check-in Procedure—Newspapers

208–Locate correct title matrix overriding daily matrices; include combinations and memberships.

209–Enter receipt information.

210–Determine correct location for each newspaper and sort accordingly; place in campus mail issues to be sent to other departments.

211–Sort titles that do not have matrices.

212–Check order file to determine status of titles that do not have matrices.

Check-in Procedures—Microfilm

213–Locate correct title matrix overriding daily matrices; include combinations and memberships.

214–Enter receipt information.

215–Determine correct location for each microfilm and sort accordingly; place in campus mail reels to be sent to other departments.

216–Sort titles that do not have matrices.

217–Check order file to determine status of titles that do not have matrices.

New Subscription and Title Change Procedures

218–Search ATTL and BRTH functions for a title number.

219–For a located number, fill in appropriate data, record receipt information, and send "title addition" message.

220–For a nonlocated number, send "title addition" message; after number is assigned, record receipt information.

221–Determine how often title will be bound and record in appropriate field.

222–Set up oblique folders for new titles.

Claiming Procedures

223–Determine nonreceipts while checking in daily mail and record "CG."

224–Scan holdings screens to determine nonreceipts and claim through electronic mailbox.

225–Compile claim forms for titles not received through Faxon.

226–Maintain claim correspondence file, including Faxon reports.

227–Erase notations on screen two when claimed issue arrives and check in issue.

Training Procedures

228–Train students to check in materials.

229–Train students to claim materials.

# Menu-Driven Processing: Cost-Analysis Studies at Vanderbilt University

## Douglas Phelps

The general technical services division of the library at Vanderbilt markets technical processing in a cost-recovery environment to the 11 libraries within the system. Not all libraries purchase processing at the same level. Some purchase full processing; others purchase only the accounting function as it pertains to book funds. Still others purchase full processing but also maintain a small amount of direct purchasing and localized cataloging.

Given the environment of the marketplace, library administrators at Vanderbilt recognize the need for accurate, current data on the cost of the services they market. Deans and directors of the various division libraries make budget decisions based on these data. These decisions affect processing the work flow and staffing within technical services. With so much at stake, technical services administrators are constantly trying to improve the accuracy and applicability of the data. A description of the methodology now used follows. Except for a few enhancements, it is the approach used for the past three years.

DIRECT COSTS

Labor, hours and wages
    Within the general technical services division, processing activity has been segmented into 20 processing modules shown in Table 1. Technical services administrators assign every nonadministrative position in the division to one of these modules. Nonexempt classified staff and student employees are required to submit biweekly time sheets,

Douglas Phelps is Director of General Technical Services at Vanderbilt University, Nashville, Tennessee. He is a member of the RTSD Technical Services Costs Committee and is active as a consultant on technical services costs.

TABLE 1.   Processing Modules.

| | |
|---|---|
| 1. Verification | 11. Monograph Binding |
| 2. Data Entry | 12. Serial Binding |
| 3. Ordering | 13. Periodical Binding |
| 4. Receiving (nonserial) | 14. Marking |
| 5. Serial Receiving | 15. Monograph Maintenance |
| 6. Periodical Receiving | 16. Card Sorting |
| 7. Invoice Payment | 17. Public Catalog Card Filing |
| 8. Copy Cataloging (monograph) | 18. Public Catalog Card Revising |
| 9. Original Cataloging (monograph) | 19. Shelflist Filing |
| 10. Serial Cataloging | 20. Shelflist Revising |

which are used to determine paid hours. For the exempt staff, a 40-hour work week is the norm. Therefore, an eight-hour day is multiplied by the number of working days in each month. At the end of the month, each person reports any time spent in modules other than the assigned primary module. This time is recorded and subtracted from the total work hours calculated for that month.

A list of time spent by staff members in each production module is produced each month. Table 2 shows the preliminary calculations to obtain a figure for labor costs.

Wages plus benefits are added to obtain a "budgeted total" for each person listed in a module. Next to the "budgeted total" are the number of hours for each position. For each staff category within the module, the total budgeted cost is divided by the total budgeted hours. The result is a mean hourly cost for each staff category in that module.

TABLE 2.   Module Labor Cost by Staff Category.

| | Budgeted Wages | Budgeted Benefits | Budgeted Total | Budgeted Hours | Hourly Cost |
|---|---|---|---|---|---|
| Exempt #1 | 23,000 | 4,800 | 27,800 | 2,080 | |
| Exempt #2 | 18,000 | 3,200 | 21,200 | 2,080 | |
| Exempt #3 | 17,000 | 4,000 | 21,000 | 2,080 | |
| Total | | | 70,000 | 6,240 | 11.22 |
| | | | | | |
| Classified #1 | 12,000 | 2,700 | 14,700 | 1,950 | |
| Classified #2 | 9,500 | 2,450 | 11,950 | 2,080 | |
| Classified #3 | 10,300 | 2,500 | 12,800 | 1,664 | |
| Total | | | 39,450 | 5,694 | 6.93 |
| | | | | | |
| Student #1 | 1,742 | 0 | 1,742 | 520 | |
| Student #2 | 2,730 | 0 | 2,730 | 780 | |
| Total | | | 4,472 | 1,300 | 3.44 |

Management is responsible for deploying staff most cost-effectively. Using lower-paid staff to the maximum, thereby freeing higher-paid staff to perform more specialized tasks, is one mark of a cost-effective organization. The different levels of staffing within a production module, the "staff mix," must be considered to get an accurate analysis of labor costs (Table 3).

The mean hourly cost for each staff classification is taken from Table 2. Hours worked in each module are reported on bimonthly time sheets. The percent of the total hours represented by each of the staff categories is identified and then multiplied by the mean hourly cost for that category. Assume 20 percent of the hours reported by the staff represented in Table 2 were exempt staff hours, 70 percent were classified staff hours, and 10 percent were student hours. The weighted labor cost per hour for this particular module is $7.43.

## Cost per Unit Produced

The weighted cost per hour times the number of hours paid in each module yields the total labor cost for that module. Note that the measure used is *hours paid* rather than hours worked. As described earlier, hours worked in secondary modules are subtracted from the total hours recorded for each staff member. Primary module hours, however, include not only hours worked but also sick leave, holiday, vacation, meetings, bereavement leave, etc. Since administrators are interested in cost rather than simply production rates, *total hours paid* is the primary unit of measure. To determine the labor cost to produce one unit, the total labor cost (hours paid times weighted labor cost per hour) is divided by the number of units produced.

## Supplies and Equipment

Nonlabor costs are determined by reviewing the year-end budget statements. When a budget encompasses more than one processing module, the expenditures are rationed on the basis of the number of staff hours, the amount of production, and/or the type of activity. (For example, original cataloging would incur few, if any, OCLC first-time use charges; copy cataloging would be the primary source for these

TABLE 3.   Weighted Labor Cost Per Hour.

|  | Mean Hourly Cost per Classification | Percent of Total Hours | Weighted Cost per Hour |
|---|---|---|---|
| Exempt | 11.22 | 20% | 2.24 |
| Classified | 6.93 | 70% | 4.85 |
| Student | 3.44 | 10% | 0.34 |
| Total |  |  | 7.43 |

costs.) On the other hand, costs between ordering and receiving are rationed on the basis of staff hours reported in each module. OCLC costs are the exception to the use of year-end budget statements. Instead, the charges billed by OCLC and SOLINET are used since these indicate the real expenditures. The year-end university budget figures simply record the deposits made into the library's SOLINET account.

The same equation for determining cost per unit is used with supplies and equipment as is used for labor costs—cost divided by the number of units equals cost per unit.

## INDIRECT COSTS

Systemwide Administration

Every library division in the system receives a library administration overhead cost assessment based on the number of budgeted nonstudent hours. The administration divides the bottom line of administrative costs by the number of budgeted nonstudent hours outside the administration, then assesses each division its share, on the basis of the total nonstudent hours budgeted for that division. Table 4 shows the method of allocating this assessment within technical services.

When the systemwide administration assessment for general technical services is received, the number of nonstudent hours in each budget is combined. This total is divided into the assessment to obtain the cost per hour. Technical services administration hours and the hours budgeted for department heads are listed along with the nonstudent hours for each processing module, and the assessment is allocated.

Space Maintenance

The same approach is used to determine other indirect or overhead costs. The library administration, working from the total library assessment levied by plant operations, assigns a square footage maintenance cost to each division in the library system. In general technical services, appropriate footage is assigned to each processing module, to the technical services administration, and to department heads. The number of square feet is multiplied by the cost per square foot to determine each module's portion of this indirect cost assessment. Again, once the cost has been determined, it is divided by units produced to get cost per unit.

Automation Assessment

The library administration assesses the ongoing costs of the library's integrated online system based on the number of terminals assigned to each library division. Technical services administrators identify the

TABLE 4.    Allocated Costs: Library Administration

Assessment to General Technical Services: $125,840
Total Nonstudent Hours in GTS: 81,562
Cost per Budgeted Nonstudent Hour: $1.543

| Processing Module | Budgeted Nonstudent Hours | Allocation |
|---|---|---|
| Gen'l. Technical Svcs. Administration | 4,030 | $   6,218 |
| Dept. Heads | | |
|    Monograph Services | 2,080 | 3,209 |
|    Serial Services | 2,080 | 3,209 |
|    Support Services | 2,080 | 3,209 |
| | | |
| Verification | 9,074 | 14,000 |
| Data Entry | 3,536 | 5,456 |
| Ordering | 3,900 | 6,017 |
| Receiving | 3,900 | 6,017 |
| Invoice Payment | 624 | 963 |
| Monograph Binding | 2,100 | 3,240 |
| | | |
| Serial Receiving | 7,904 | 12,195 |
| Periodical Receiving | 1,950 | 3,009 |
| Serial Cataloging | 6,240 | 9,628 |
| Serial Maintenance | 2,990 | 4,613 |
| Serial Binding | 708 | 1,092 |
| Periodical Binding | 1,344 | 2,074 |
| | | |
| Copy Cataloging (monograph)* | 8,476 | 13,077 |
| Original Cataloging (monograph)* | 12,480 | 19,255 |
| Monograph Maintenance* | 5,018 | 7,742 |
| Marking | 1,048 | 1,617 |
|    Total | 81,562 | $125,840 |

*For convenience, the relatively few nonstudent hours for card activities (sorting, filing, revising, etc.) are absorbed into copy cataloging, original cataloging, and monograph maintenance. Correction for rounding error is assigned to the GTS administration allowance.

processing modules within the division that uses the terminals and determine what share each should be charged. For example, verification has two shares (two terminals dedicated to verification), serial receiving has one terminal, also used by periodical receiving; therefore each of these modules has half a share. The terminal fee is multiplied by the assigned share.

Technical Services Overhead

Technical services overhead has two components: division administration and department heads. Division administration includes the direct costs for the director of general technical services and office support staff, supplies and equipment, and travel. It also includes the indirect assessment costs which are reallocated to the processing modules and to department heads in the division on the basis of total hours budgeted, including student hours.

Department head costs include the personnel and supplies/equipment costs budgeted specifically for them, plus their portion of indirect systemwide assessments and technical services administration costs. The cost of each department head are distributed among the processing modules he or she supervises, based on total number of hours budgeted, including student hours.

## AGGREGATE COST

Dividing the cost of each of these line items by the number of units produced leads to itemized data for cost per unit on each unit produced in the various production modules. These are shown in Table 5. However, this figure is of little value in determining total processing costs since each production module has a different unit of measure: The unit for verification is the number of first-time *searches* made; the unit for copy cataloging is the number of *titles* cataloged; and the unit for periodical binding is the number of *volumes* bound. There is need for a common denominator—a common unit of measure. Technical services administrators have chosen to use the total number of volumes received and have termed this the *volume base*. In this cost analysis, the volume base for each library is obtained from two sources: the number of gift volumes processed and the number of volumes purchased. The sum of these individual volume bases should approximate the number of volumes entering the technical services work flow.

After the *cost per volume* for each module is determined, figures can be put together. The equation used to determine cost per volume was generated by Malcolm Getz in 1983 for a study of processing costs in three academic libraries:[1]

$$\frac{\text{Units Produced}}{\text{Volume Base}} \times \frac{\text{Cost}}{\text{Units Produced}} = \frac{\text{Cost}}{\text{Volume Base}} = \text{Cost per Volume}$$

Note one major exception to this generic format. In setting up the production modules, monograph cataloging was separated into copy cataloging and original cataloging so the different work mix of these two

EXHIBIT 5.   Itemized Cost Per Production Unit.

Table 5. ITEMIZED COST PER PRODUCTION UNIT

AGGREGATE

| Unit | Ratio of Units/Vol Base | Weight Factor | Library Admin. | Space Maint. | Library Automation | GTS Admin | GTS Dept Mgmt | Sub-Total per Unit | Weighted Sub-Total per Unit | Indirect Cost per Vol. | Labor | OCLC Supplies | OCLC Activity Charges | OCLC Fixed Cost | Equipment Maintenance (excl. OCLC) | Sub-Total per Unit | Weighted Subtotal per Unit | Direct Cost per Vol. | Total Cost per Volume |
|---|---|---|---|---|---|---|---|---|---|---|---|---|---|---|---|---|---|---|---|
| **Input** | | | | | | | | | | | | | | | | | | | |
| Verification | 1.009 | 120.2 | .35 | .05 | .21 | .26 | .27 | 1.14 | 1.37 | 1.38 | 2.47 | .03 | .02 | .11 | .02 | 2.65 | 3.19 | 3.22 | 4.60 |
| Data Entry | .875 | | .16 | .04 | | .10 | | .30 | .30 | 0.26 | 1.03 | .19 | | | .02 | 1.24 | 1.24 | 1.09 | 1.35 |
| Ordering | .433 | | .35 | .08 | | .23 | .49 | 1.15 | 1.15 | 0.50 | 2.20 | .24 | | | .01 | 2.45 | 2.45 | 1.06 | 1.56 |
| Receiving | .605 | | .25 | .08 | | .17 | .37 | .87 | .87 | 0.53 | 1.53 | .02 | | | .01 | 1.56 | 1.56 | 0.94 | 1.47 |
| Invoices Paid | .235 | | .11 | .02 | | .07 | | .20 | .20 | 0.05 | .68 | .13 | | | .01 | .82 | .82 | 0.19 | 0.24 |
| Monograph Bind | .176 | | .47 | .11 | .30 | .29 | .62 | 1.79 | 1.79 | 0.32 | 2.35 | .04 | | | .01 | 2.40 | 2.40 | 0.42 | 0.74 |
| | | | | | | | | | | 3.04 | | | | | | | | 6.92 | 9.96 |
| **Serials** | | | | | | | | | | | | | | | | | | | |
| Serial Rec'ving | 1.593 | | .20 | .05 | .04 | .12 | .20 | .61 | .61 | 0.97 | .92 | .03 | | | .01 | .96 | .96 | 1.53 | 2.50 |
| Periodical Recv | .932 | | .09 | .01 | .06 | .09 | .15 | .40 | .40 | 0.37 | .50 | .03 | .12 | | .02 | .71 | .71 | 0.66 | 1.03 |
| Serial Catalog. | .060 | | 4.06 | .48 | 7.00 | 2.49 | 4.23 | 18.26 | 18.26 | 1.10 | 42.99 | .44 | 1.89 | .04 | .37 | 46.83 | 46.83 | 2.81 | 3.91 |
| Serial Binding | .041 | | .66 | .04 | | .41 | .89 | 2.00 | 2.00 | 0.05 | 2.83 | .02 | | 1.14 | .03 | 2.88 | 2.88 | 0.12 | 0.20 |
| Periodical Bind. | .055 | | .95 | .03 | | .59 | 1.28 | 2.85 | 2.85 | 0.16 | 4.07 | .02 | | | .02 | 4.11 | 4.11 | 0.23 | 0.39 |
| | | | | | | | | | | 2.68 | | | | | | | | 5.35 | 8.03 |
| **Output** | | | | | | | | | | | | | | | | | | | |
| Copy Cataloging | .691 | 58.8 | .81 | .32 | 1.03 | .50 | .52 | 3.18 | 1.87 | 1.29 | 5.57 | .04 | 1.99 | .14 | .03 | 7.67 | 4.51 | 3.12 | 4.41 |
| Orig Cataloging | .448 | 41.2 | 2.62 | .71 | 2.26 | 1.64 | 1.71 | 8.94 | 3.68 | 1.65 | 21.84 | .13 | 1.35 | .31 | .06 | 23.69 | 9.76 | 4.37 | 6.02 |
| Monograph Maint. | .128 | | 1.52 | .14 | .82 | 1.44 | 1.50 | 5.42 | 5.42 | 0.69 | 7.73 | .15 | 17.51 | .27 | .12 | 25.78 | 25.78 | 3.30 | 3.99 |
| Marking | 1.301 | | .04 | .02 | .04 | .09 | .18 | .37 | .37 | 0.48 | .42 | .04 | | | .01 | .47 | .47 | 0.61 | 1.09 |
| Card Sorting | 5.080 | | | | | | | | | | .04 | | | | | .02 | .02 | 0.10 | 0.10 |
| Shelf List File | 2.606 | | | | | | | | | | .04 | | | | | .04 | .04 | 0.10 | 0.10 |
| S. List Revise | 1.290 | | | | | | | | | | .06 | | | | | .06 | .06 | 0.08 | 0.08 |
| | | | | | | | | | | 4.11 | | | | | | | | 11.68 | 15.79 |

Total Processing Cost per Volume

| Input | $9.96 |
|---|---|
| Serials | 8.03 |
| Output | 15.79 |

Projects  $33.78

A. Maintaining Public Catalog

| | Ratio | ... | | Labor | ... | Sub-Total | Weighted | Indirect | Direct | Total |
|---|---|---|---|---|---|---|---|---|---|---|
| PC Card Filing | 4.673 | | | .05 | | .05 | .05 | 0.26 | 0.23 | 0.23 |
| PC Card Revise | 8.699 | | | .08 | | .08 | .08 | 0.05 | 0.70 | 0.70 |
| | | | | | | | | 0.31 | 0.93 | 0.93 |

B. Processing invoices for material not ordered via Gen'l Technical Services

| Data Entry | .875 | | .16 | .04 | | .10 | | .30 | .30 | | 1.03 | .19 | | | .02 | 1.24 | 1.24 | 1.09 | 1.35 |
|---|---|---|---|---|---|---|---|---|---|---|---|---|---|---|---|---|---|---|---|
| Invoices Paid | .235 | | .11 | .02 | | .07 | | .20 | .20 | | .68 | .13 | | | .01 | .82 | .82 | .19 | 0.24 |
| | | | | | | | | | | | | | | | | | | | 1.59 |

cataloging tracks, which we find in the various libraries, could be examined. Since the two modules together reflect total activity of titles cataloged, technical services administrators determined it was inappropriate to measure each production unit against the entire volume base. Therefore, the number of searches producing Library of Congress cataloging copy was obtained from preorder verification. In 1984–1985, LC copy was found for 58.8 percent of the total number of nonduplicate searches recorded. Using this standard, technical services administrators project that 58.8 percent of the volumes received are subject to copy cataloging. (We recognize that LC copy will be found for more titles prior to cataloging, but we also recognize that some LC copy titles will require the attention of a catalog librarian. For purposes of the model, a trade-off is assumed.) For copy cataloging cost analysis, the total volume base figure is replaced with 58.8 percent of the volume base to determine the cost of that portion subject to LC copy cataloging. Similarly, when original cataloging costs are figured, the remaining 41.2 percent of the volume base is used as the common unit of measure. This provides a means of tracking monograph cataloging costs either as an entity or as two separate cost factors. (This second option becomes important when determining cataloging costs of the various libraries.)

Processing activity and processing costs have been segmented. In order to put these figures together in a fashion that makes sense, the processing modules are restructured into three tracks:

• Input (acquisitions)
• Serials
• Output (monograph cataloging)

Three modifications are made after putting these processing module costs together. First, the work impact on verification is noted. Production data used in determining verification cost are the number of nonduplicating searches. In determining cost, however, the number of searches that do not go beyond verification because they are unintentional duplicates of titles already in the system must also be considered. For example, if a library submits 10,000 requests and 20 percent are unintentional duplicates, the verification data used in calculating cost would be 8,000 searches (10,000 minus 20 percent). Obviously, the work impact on verification is 10,000. Therefore, to reach a more accurate total cost for that particular library, this activity must be added back into the total. The number of searches can be increased when searches are multiplied by cost, or the cost per unit can be increased by this duplication factor and then the weighted cost is multiplied by the number of nonduplicating searches. Technical services administrators found it more convenient to do the latter. To give the appropriate weight to a duplication factor of 20 percent, the Processing subtotal (that is, the direct cost subtotal) is multiplied by 120 percent. (Table 5.)

The other two lines modified are copy cataloging and original cataloging. As indicated earlier, for each library the ratio of LC copy to non-LC copy is identified in the initial search of nonduplicating orders and books by verification. Also, the equation for monograph cataloging is broken down into copy cataloging cost and original cataloging cost. The unit production cost of the segment subject to LC copy cataloging is calculated (58.8 percent of the total volume base) as is the segment not subject to LC copy cataloging (41.2 percent of the total volume base). It is necessary to view these costs in terms of the total volume base in determining the cost per volume. The equation for this is:

$$\frac{\text{Production Units}}{\text{Volume Base} \times \text{LC\%}} \times \frac{\text{Cost}}{\text{Production Units}} \times \text{LC\%} = \frac{\text{Cost}}{\text{Volume Base}} = \text{Cost per Volume}$$

This is done in Table 5 by multiplying the per unit cost times the LC copy weighting factor and then multiplying this amount times the ratio of production units per weighted volume base.

Table 5 presents the aggregate data of all libraries served by general technical services. Specific costs for each individual library will vary somewhat depending on the rate of unintentional duplication in verification and on the work mix between copy cataloging and original cataloging. The data shown on this table represent projections for 1985–1986 costs.

From Table 5, the weighted indirect and weighted direct subtotals per unit for the serial cataloging function can be added to determine that it costs $65.09 to catalog one unit (that is, serial title); however, the volume cost of serial cataloging is $3.91 per volume received. Similarly, for 1985–1986 a copy cataloging cost of $10.85 per title is anticipated (here, the subtotals per unit rather than the weighted subtotals are added); $4.41 per volume received is the volume cost expected. And original cataloging cost should be $32.63 per title, but $6.02 per volume received. (To emphasize, these are the aggregate costs. Actual costs per library will vary.)

## USING THE DATA

Now it's time to ask, "So what?" Are these all just mental gymnastics to keep technical services administrators busy and out of trouble? Depending on how the data stack up, it *may* have just the opposite effect for some managers. However, here are some additional uses for the information:

### Budgets

The acquisitions accounting system provides the mean purchase price for volumes bought by Vanderbilt. This information is available for each library in the system. When a library plans its materials budget for the coming year, the number of volumes this money is going to purchase can be projected. That figure added to the number of gift volumes that the library proposes to submit for processing in the coming year results in a projected volume base. Using the method described and substituting proposed cost data, administrators can predict the processing cost per volume. The environment dictates that if one is to recover costs for service, one must place a price tag on that service. Therefore, each library can predict what its technical services processing cost will be for the coming year, given the number of volumes it expects to enter into the processing track. As a result, there has been improvement in support for technical processing from the school deans. In part, this is because Vanderbilt technical services administrators are able to show them where their money is going. Perhaps, to some extent, it is also because administrators are showing deans how poorly they have supported technical processing costs in the past. Certainly, it has not hurt to be able to chart how the libraries have been getting a lot more production out of technical services than their deans had been purchasing. Through these cost studies, library administrators have become more aware of how much they have depended on "soft money" to underwrite technical services costs in past years. That is a trend the library is now taking steps to correct.

Staffing

One of the essential calculations in this model is determining the processing cost of each unit. To do this, cost is divided by the number of units produced. To determine labor costs, the weighted staff cost per hour could be multiplied by the number of paid staff hours recorded (or projected). Another way to do this is to set up the number of paid hours divided by the number of units produced and multiply this amount by the weighted staff cost per hour. Technical services administrators use the latter method and, as a spin-off, derive the number of units produced per paid hour. Use the data shown in Table 5 and assume a volume base of 50,000. The production ratio for the ordering module is 0.433 orders placed per volume received. With a volume base of 50,000, it is anticipated that 21,650 orders will be placed (50,000 x 0.433). The production ratio for this module is 4.290 units per paid hour. (This does not mean that employees produce 4.290 orders per hour. It means that, given vacations, sick leave, holidays, breaks, meetings, and other activities required in acquisitions, such as opening mail, claiming, responding to reports, and handling problems, the ratio of orders produced is 4.290 orders per paid hour.) For 21,650 orders, 5,046.6 staff hours are required. Since currently only 4,030 paid staff hours are budgeted for order operations, it should not be too surprising to see some back-up of work.

Through the model it has been possible to identify those areas that appear to be overstaffed or understaffed. Resolving the financial and space problems to correct such problems is another matter, but at least there is a tool to help us reach correct conclusions. At Vanderbilt, the technical services department has been somewhat successful in moving staff to more critical areas as well as adding some staff. In certain areas staff had to be cut. When the budget required cutbacks, the model helped analyze which positions to eliminate.

## Projects

Projects take many forms. Some are even anticipated. At Vanderbilt, whether it's a grant, a large gift collection, or a request to recatalog and reclassify 300 serial titles, we put a price tag on it. Grant proposals carry stronger weight because technical services can validate production cost data. Libraries in the system are well aware that processing costs money. They can get that large collection processed if they pay the processing costs or if they substitute these volumes for other items for which processing has already been paid. The university is committed to providing processing funds as part of the total cost of adding titles to the library's collection.

## Production Targets

From the model, technical services managers know the previous rate of units produced per paid hour. By knowing how many hours there are—or how many there are going to be—in a given module, managers can have expected production targets for that module. These targets are based on previous experience rather than on some ideal. They can always be modified. By measuring monthly production against the target, managers at Vanderbilt feel they are in a better position to evaluate where the department is and where it's going. Providing both the production statistics and the target data to the libraries is also a move toward better communication and, the department hopes, less distrust and anxiety about the services technical services provides.

## Management Objectives

The data also allow a more accurate determination of where technical services has improved or failed to improve over the years. In the study by Getz and Phelps cited earlier, it was shown that by making one element in the equation model—salaries, for example-consistent across libraries, one could determine more objectively the relation between processing costs at one library and another. This approach can also be taken for the same library across time. The model can be used to review progress or lack of it in the work production of the different modules.

Cost analysis and its various spin-offs do not provide all the answers. But it does go a long way toward moving us away from "seat-of-the-pants" management or "crisis" management or any of the other styles endured in the past. It is another tool that, when used wisely, helps us to be better managers, more accountable to those we serve as well as to our own highest standards.

## Notes

1. Malcolm Getz and Douglas Phelps, "Labor Costs in the Technical Operations of Three Research Libraries," *Journal of Academic Librarianship,* 10, no. 4 (September 1984): 209–219.

# 3
# Standardization

# Introduction

## Douglas Phelps

The limited number of cost studies that focus on library operations have come primarily from narrowly defined analyses of one particular aspect of technical services. Rarely have these studies attempted to encompass multiple functions within technical services, much less within the library at large. Even more rare are attempts to expand the scope to determine costs across libraries. The following articles describe two such attempts. While the intent and the methodology of each is quite different, they share a common identity as pioneer studies in a new approach to understanding library functions in order to bring them under more effective managerial control.

Why measure the cost variations among libraries? Each chapter offers a valid response: because management skills and organization of work differ among libraries, and this difference does indeed contribute significantly to the variation in production and production costs (less effective libraries can then identify and learn from the more effective ones); and because if we as librarians do not take it upon ourselves to measure and manage our own operations, someone else, possibly with less awareness and less sensitivity to the problems, may attempt to do it for us.

Measuring costs among libraries requires consistency in defining terms and procedures. It also requires consistency in collecting production and cost detail. Until librarians and/or their parent boards or institutions acknowledge the value of such comparisons, there will be no motivation for working toward consistency. Even if the motivation were evident, American libraries and librarians are independent about developing and perpetuating their local variations of organization and procedure. If consistency within the same library system is scarce, how much less is to be found across institutional boundaries?

In both studies, the authors point to the critical role of differing quality standards among libraries as a major factor in the variation of production (quantity) and, therefore, of production costs. Yet, we are barely at the threshold of developing methods for quantifying quality variation; we have not yet approached the sophistication that permits factoring-in qualitative elements.

Methodologies for analysis and comparison are still in the early stages of development. Application of these methodologies beyond the single unit or department stands a distant "next in line." In the face of the work yet to be done, the following chapters offer a faint ray of hope for library managers of the future. Recently Paul Kantor described as "glacial" the progress of work being done to determine costs of library operations. Although he referred specifically to the relatively few studies published in this area, his comment provides additional insight. As glaciers moved over the earth, altering its surface, so incorporating cost factors into future management portfolios will restructure the landscape of library administration.

# Standardization: The British Approach

## Theresa Bomford
## Sue Howley

As early as 1977, the British Library, through its research and development department, funded a number of research projects on costing particular library operations, generally using a single institution as their base. However, various critics advocated that cost (and other) data should be collected and published in a standard way so that comparisons and collations would be possible. The Centre for Interfirm Comparison (CIFC) was chosen for the job.

It was established in 1959 by the British Institute of Management and the British Productivity Council as a nonprofit organization to help improve management standards by designing and conducting comparisons among the operations of firms in manufacturing industries. Later, the Centre broadened its activities, accepting commissions from many professions and public bodies. CIFC comparisons show management how the operations of its organization compare with those of similar organizations, and indicates the most fruitful actions to improve performance. The Centre is an independent, neutral, and expert body, internationally recognized as a leader in its field. Its method obliges participating organizations to pool their key data confidentially in the Centre. CIFC then processes the information and provides each participant with a set of ratios showing comparative results of all the organizations involved. Anonymity is preserved.

To initiate CIFC into interlibrary comparisons, the British Library Research and Development Department (BLR&DD) commissioned a short feasibility study. In July 1977,[1] the Centre reported that there was demand for interlibrary comparisons and that such comparisons were feasible. It stressed that comparisons should be seen primarily as a

Theresa Bomford is a member of the research and development department at The British Library in London, England.

Sue Howley is a member of the research and development department at The British Library in London, England.

management tool The report outlined a basic approach appropriate for interlibrary comparisons using cost/output measures for various functions and the factors affecting those measures. Costs would be compiled on a comparable basis and output measures expressed in units of work done from the library viewpoint rather than in units representing the value of activity to users.

The overall performance measure recommended was the sum of a number of individual measures for each library function that could reasonably be measured. These functional measures would be calculated by taking the library's functional cost/output ratio as a percentage of the average cost/output ratio for all other participants. Examples illustrating an individual library's figures and the layout of results tables appeared as an appendix to the report. Another appendix listed possible functional activities to be covered.

Other recommendations in the report concerned the size of libraries to be included in future comparisons and the mix of library types. It proposed excluding small libraries—those with fewer than six to ten staff members. Academic, public, and special libraries should take part, although special libraries where information-officer work was paramount should be excluded. Interlibrary comparisons should be carried out annually.

In establishing interlibrary comparisons, the report stated that potential participants must be consulted. The involvement of top management was important. A study should start with a relatively simple comparison that could be added to over the years. It would be necessary to distribute promotional literature and to arrange meetings and seminars.

Data should be collected using questionnaires accompanied by comprehensive notes and definitions. The results of the survey would be presented anonymously with tables of code numbers accompanied by a general report and user's guide. It was recommended that a discussion with and among participants follow the distribution of the report.

The Centre concluded with a proposed program of interlibrary comparison work. As a result of these recommendations, BLR&DD funded a design study and field trial for public libraries,[2] followed by a pilot study of 31 public libraries in 1979.[3]

A similar project for academic libraries was launched in the spring of 1981, when CIFC staff visited 12 academic libraries that had agreed to cooperate. CIFC later produced a discussion document about possible ratios for academic library comparisons. A consultative committee comprising representatives of the Standing Conference of National and University Libraries (SCONUL), the Council of Polytechnic Librarians (COPOL), the Library Association, and the Office of Arts and Libraries (the government agency responsible for libraries) met on a number of occasions in 1981. In the latter half of the year, the comparison exercise was launched. Basic guidelines laid down in the report of the feasibility study were followed throughout. For example, participants were consulted, especially about definitions to be used.

Twelve university and eight polytechnic libraries took part in the comparison. Most of the completed forms were received by the Centre in November 1981; the last in January 1982. Reports were issued to participants in March 1982. Participants received a full set of results for both university and polytechnic libraries. Each library was identified by a code letter to preserve anonymity. A composite report was later published by BLR&DD.

The report stressed that two types of ratios were involved—those relating to cost structures and those relating to costs and output. The cost structure ratios were intended to indicate the pattern of resource allocation. They showed, for example, the general management and administration staff costs as a percentage of all staff costs. The cost/output ratios, on the other hand, attempted to relate the resources to the work accomplished in certain functional or service activities. In the same example, the cost-output ratio would be the general management and administration staff costs per *number* of total library staff. In order to help interpret the results, each heading included further background information such as the general management and administrative function as a percentage of all staff employed and the average annual cost per staff member.

## CRITICAL PROFESSIONAL RESPONSE

Given such rudimentary output measures, it was inevitable that the resulting comparisons would be criticized for not producing meaningful effectiveness data. But they never set out to do this. The CIFC looks at costs data in terms of an input/output process in libraries on a function-by-function basis; they go little further than that and no way at all into the complete problems of service evaluation and performance or the relationship between usage and users. Nevertheless, their techniques do lead to the creation of external yardsticks, based on the actual experience of other libraries, which a librarian can use as a management tool to help evaluate the activities of a particular library. The yardsticks help library managers to see how they compare in the operation of various important activities; where and why there are differences; and the most fruitful actions for improving services and controlling costs.

Since 1982, professionals have debated the value of the technique. Many have criticized its practicality, pointing out that it fails to solve many of the technical and operational problems of costing—especially with respect to estimates of staff time input. Some have concluded that the results do not justify the considerable amount of staff time required to collect the data. The suspicion was voiced that there were differences and difficulties in interpreting or applying the method, despite the fact that the Centre staff took great pains to ensure that the method was applied in the same way by all participants. This suspicion was strengthened by the fact that the range of costs recorded for a particular activity was often very wide. Not infrequently, the highest functional cost recorded was five or six times the lowest. This could, of course, be due to basic dissimilarities in the libraries being compared, or perhaps even to genuine differences in efficiency, but many suspected it was due to lack of consistency in the way in which the comparative method was applied. Some even more fundamental worries about yardsticks were expressed. Critics stressed that there is little point in following the most commonly found practice if that practice is unsound. Comparative tables might show what the average is—but not whether it is sensible. Concerns were also expressed that although the comparison technique was developed for library managers, the resulting tables would inevitably fall into the hands of those outside the library profession, whose responsibility is to obtain value for money and who may well place the least favorable interpretation on the data. What would such people make of the fact that in 1981 one library spent 72 percent of its funds on staff or that, in another, it cost less to buy the average British academic book than to catalog it when bought?

For the proponents of comparison, such arguments held little weight. They pointed out that, as the search for economic management techniques intensified, more and more outside eyes would be scrutinizing library accounts and it was imperative for library managers to be prepared for this. It was significant in many ways that the academic library comparison exercise took place in 1981, a year that marked the start of a decline in library grants of quite unprecedented severity. A number of participants believed that this made the collection of data for the study a truly educational experience, reinforcing the often-expressed view that the real value of exercises such as these is forcing librarians to think systematically about the problems that confront them. Of course, it is true that many of the trends that are currently affecting academic libraries are not under the control of the librarian— falling student numbers, decline in the purchasing power of acquisition funds, wage and salary awards, static staff establishments, and so on— but not all problems are as "external" as these, and, in any case, the librarian needs the support of meaningful cost and other data in order to devise a strategy for coping with these external forces.

In response to this debate, related to both public and academic library programs, BLR&DD funded further work in public libraries to develop a simplified version of the comparison technique, which would be less difficult and costly to apply. The outcome was significant. Libraries involved in both studies reported that the results of the earlier version[4] were more valid and useful than those of the simplified comparison,[5] but that the earlier one took up too much time. The results of the simplified comparison, however, were probably adversely affected because the definitions were broadened and the analysis of staff time simplified, although variation in exactness of data was also a likely cause. In short, the simplified version tried, in CIFC's terms, to reconcile the conflict between accuracy and simplicity, or to put it another way, between validity and manageability.

## SCONUL AND COPUL CONSIDER THE REPORT

By 1983, the programs were complete, except for the production of overview reports[6] and other dissemination activities. During the year the mood among both public and academic librarians was much less favorable than the initial enthusiasm of 1977. Discussions on academic library and comparisons took place at separate general meetings of both SCONUL and COPOL during 1983. On both occasions, a representative of the Centre recommended that comparison should be run on an annual basis at a cost of about £500, which is, very roughly, $700 per participant. It was felt this fee could be reduced if the Centre were retained solely in a consultant capacity. Responses of librarians at the SCONUL and COPOL meetings were similar. The comparison work carried out was considered interesting and useful, but they thought the methodology would need modification before it could be utilized regularly and comprehensively. In particular, the narrowness of detail had made certain discrepancies apparent. Although the test exercise had been worthwhile, the technique as applied in the test required effort that was disproportionate to the value of the results. Moreover, there was a problem related to the definitions. This somewhat less than enthusiastic response disappointed the proponents of comparison, who feared that much that was undoubtedly of value in the exercise would be lost.

This did not prove to be the case. Developments in the last few years have given impetus and purpose to the rather fainthearted intentions expressed in 1983 to continue the quest for quality cost data and standardized measures and to build on the exercise rather than discard it. These developments constitute much more than a mere continuance of the recession and of economic constraint. In particular, there have been, and are, strong pressures from central government on all public sectors to improve efficiency.

Central government strategy was to set up an Audit Commission to investigate local government services, including public libraries. Although the commission's actions are frequently perceived as just another government program of reductionism and cost cutting, this is far from reality, for the commission can be seen to be as critical of central government as it has been of local government.

The challenge for libraries is how well placed they are to answer the questions that will inevitably be posed by the commission. How well, for example, do the services provided by libraries match such qualities as vision, strategies and plans, staff management, systems for performance review structures, communications, and style? The commission seems to recognize that different solutions are required for different problems but is it looking for evidence of good practice in terms of effectiveness, efficiency, and economy. Can research give us the answers to match the questions likely to be posed by the commission? If it does not, the answers will be provided by other means.

Auditors and policy-makers understandably wish to use readily available information when making judgments about library effectiveness, even though what's available may be flawed or incomplete. There is evidence of this in a recent Audit Commission study, which states: "Libraries serve a number of objectives other than simply lending books. . . . Nevertheless, the most direct single measure of the service provided by libraries is the number of books issued to the public."[7] Meanwhile the work already started by the commission suggests that research should be focusing on the determination and clarity of our mission with its related objectives. Catch-alls will not suffice, and the frequently quoted "objective of providing" a comprehensive and efficient service under the terms of the 1964 Libraries Act is meaningless as an objective.

## DEFINING TERMS WITHOUT BLOODSHED

At present the clarity of the terminology and the librarians' understanding of it is also problematical. For example, it is important to distinguish between efficiency (an input/output relationship) and effectiveness (an output/outcomes relationship) in determining performance indicators. Questions to be answered include: What are the key indicators? How can these be properly defined? What kind of management information do libraries need?

In 1986, the BLR&DD awarded a grant to Essex County Library not only to develop and test a set of performance indicators but also to devise systematic ways of incorporating such indicators of performance into the management processes of library service. Later this could serve as a model for other public libraries wishing to work along similar lines.

There is also a possibility that recommendations outlined in the American manual of standardized procedures *Output Measures for Public Libraries* by Zweizig and Rodger, published by the American Library Association in 1982,[8] might be tested in the British environment in order to produce an applicable set of guidelines for the use of libraries in the United Kingdom.

A number of recent publications, such as the Jarrett Report[9] and the Green Paper on Higher Education,[10] stress the necessity for greater efficiency and measurement of efficiency throughout higher education, including libraries in high education. In such a climate, the pressure is intense to produce cost data—whether they relate to unit costs or service costs of new developments, such as new courses and their implications for the library. The emphasis on service costs is particularly noticeable. The costs of library activities need to be expressed in terms of services to users and not in terms of operations, which may have only internal housekeeping validity. Hence, the pressure is on knowing, for example, the extra costs that a public library incurs because it has a high ethnic minority representation among its potential clientele rather than on knowing (directly) about catalog costs. There is, therefore, considerable interest in a large-scale project, funded by the Office of Arts and Libraries and administered by the BLR&DD, to develop, test, and disseminate better methods of costing public library services and also of measuring their performance. The objective of this project is that decisions on priorities, which public libraries are increasingly being compelled to make, can be informed by data about the costs and benefits attached to the various options being considered. An important aspect of this is the intention to produce a standard method of costing, which, although it will cater to local circumstances, can be used across the board and can therefore permit comparisons once compilations have been made.

SCONUL, working in collaboration with COPOL, plans to move toward standard costing methods by expanding its collection and analysis of statistical information. These plans involve progression from the present expenditure statistics through a systematic collection of output measures (currently being developed and tested at Southampton University) to an eventual costing exercise that will draw heavily on the CIFC technique and permit a comparative approach.

In Britain, costing activities and comparisons are very much back in fashion. The public sector is being urged to increase its efficiency, and a comparative approach is widely regarded as a substitute for the competition to which private sector efficiency is often attributed. Because meaningful comparisons cannot be made without standardized collection methods, the pressure to achieve those is also being felt. Although such methods cannot be imposed, central bodies controlling (however indirectly) certain purse strings, have considerable powers of persuasion. There are also, of course, fewer libraries in Britain than in the United States to persuade. Whether standard costing methods will soon prevail depends perhaps not so much on those powers of persuasion as on the ability of current research to overcome some of the technical and separate problems which have bedeviled the interlibrary comparison program. Certainly, if some progress is made, the experience gained during the years that the program ran and the discussion it stimulated will help pave the way toward acceptance and implementation of standard costing methods.

## Notes

1. *Inter-library Comparisons: Report to the British Library on a Feasibility Study, July 1977*, British Library Research and Development Department report no. 5608 (London: Centre for Interfirm Comparison, 1981).
2. *Inter-library Comparisons: Design Study and Field Trial Relating to Public Libraries*, British Library Research and Development Department report no. 5489 (London: Centre for Interfirm Comparison, 1979).
3. *Inter-library Comparisons: Pilot Comparison with Public Libraries*, British Library Research and Development Department report no. 5638 (London: Centre for Interfirm Comparison, 1981).
4. *Inter-library Comparisons in Academic Libraries*, British Library Research and Development Department report no. 5763 (London: Centre for Interfirm Comparison, 1984).
5. "Inter-library Comparisons: Test of Simplified Version of Public Library Comparison (County Libraries)" (Unpublished report prepared by the Centre for Interfirm Comparison, 1983).
6. R.F. Atkins, *Overview of the Inter-library Comparison Programme with Special Reference to Public Libraries*, British Library Research and Development Department report no. 5847 (London: Centre for Interfirm Comparison, 1984).
7. Cleveland County Council, "Review of the Library Service." (Unpublished report prepared by the Audit Commission for Local Authorities in England and Wales, 1985).
8. Douglas Zweizig and Eleanor Jo Rodger, *Output Measures for Public Libraries: A Manual of Standardised Procedures*, (Chicago: American Library Association, 1982).
9. Alex Jarrett, *Committee of Vice Chancellors and Principals Report on Efficiency Studies in the Universities* (London: Committee of Vice Chancellors and Principals, 1985).
10. "The Development of Higher Education into the 1990's," Command Paper 9524 (London: HMSO, May 21, 1985).

# The Association of Research Libraries Experience: Precursor to Standards?

## Paul B. Kantor

The Association of Research Libraries (ARL) has sponsored or helped with many studies undertaken by Management Consultants, and costs have come under consideration in several ways. In a study sponsored by the National Science Foundation, we looked at 65 scientific and technical libraries to study the relationship between the cost of operating specific branch units and the volume of service provided to their supporting institutions. In this study, no effort was made to define the quality of the service rendered. The results were reported in *Library Research*.[1]

In a second study sponsored by the National Science Foundation, we gathered more extensive data on over 100 operating units at academic libraries to study further the relationship between operating costs and services rendered, and to identify, to the extent possible, the impact of computerization and networking on those costs. The results of this study are available in a series of technical reports and have been presented in some detail in a recent article in *Advances in Library Administration and Organization*.[2]

A study for the Council on Library Resources attempted a microscopic examination of the costs of acquisition of new materials, specifically single-order monographs in English and western European languages, with the goal of identifying significant variations and possible management factors in those variations. Along the same lines was an investigation of the cost and quality factors in microfilm preservation, carried out at four research libraries during the winter and spring of 1986.

Paul B. Kantor is President of Management Consultants, Cleveland, Ohio. He was a 1987–1988 Visiting Distinguished Scholar in the OCLC Office of Research.

## CONSIDERATIONS OF QUALITY

*Quality* must be considered whenever the cost of library operations is examined. It seems quite obvious that costs can almost always be reduced if quality is thrown overboard. On the other hand, a complex system for the storage and retrieval of human knowledge (which is, after all, the engineer's description of a library) is worth practically nothing if it does not function with remarkably high levels of quality. The book that has been mis-shelved more than a yard from its proper location is effectively lost. The book whose main entry card in the catalog carries the wrong call number is virtually lost. I could add many more examples.

Even more disturbing are the problems having to do with intellectual quality. A library that has systematically failed to acquire important and up-to-date materials in any particular field dooms the students and scholars it serves to mediocrity. Providing quality in library services obviously costs money, but we are not very well equipped to say how much it costs. In fact, we are still learning how to say how much it costs to provide the quantity of service, almost without regard to quality.

Quality of Process

Although we are still learning the costs of quantity, we can begin to consider quality and break it down into two broad areas. The first is *quality of process*. A process induces, by its very nature, certain delays. If the product is the same, the process with fewer delays is of better quality. In the same way, access to materials represents a quality of library operation. If users have a 70 percent chance of finding the materials, the library is doing better than if they have a 60 percent chance, whether or not it is actually stocking the very best materials that it could.

Every process imposes some barriers to access that must be overcome by the users of the library. If a user can find his or her way from the card catalog to the shelf in four minutes, he or she is served better than if it takes 12 minutes, other things being equal. (Obviously, one of the ways in which other things might not be equal is that it will take longer to walk to a book in a very large library than in a very small library. These obvious considerations are taken into account in any study of the quality of library processes.)

The prospect for consistent and rational determination of the costs associated with quantity of service, and of the costs associated with quality of process, is quite good. Previous chapters in this book have reported that this kind of study can now be conducted in-house, by a library, without recourse to expensive, and sometimes incomprehensible, outside consultants. It was shown that a manual can be used to support this process at public libraries. (I admit to the iconoclastic view that most of what is true for accounting costs at public libraries is true at other types of libraries as well.)

## Quality of Product

The second broad area of quality is *quality of product,* an area that will continue to be studied more and more. Judging the quality of product requires expensive and time-consuming review of the work done by librarians. Whether the product is a catalog entry, a selection decision, or a complete reference interview, it cannot be evaluated without considering the background that gave rise to the question or decision and the context in which it is to be answered.

A selection decision at a major research library, in an area of concentration, is obviously quite different from a decision about the same item made in the library of a small independent college. The kind of reference service required by users of the medical library at a large university will probably be quite different from the kind of answers required by freshmen taking a survey course in health and hygiene.

### Sequential Analysis: A Very Efficient Technique

Given that expensive professional time must be applied to evaluate the quality of a product, we must then ask for the most efficient means to evaluate that quality. Libraries can benefit from a technological fallout from World War II studies of quality control for military products, as will be discussed later. A very powerful technique called *sequential sampling or sequential analysis* can cut the costs of monitoring quality by as much as a factor of three. The cost does not go away, but neither does the obligation to measure quality, and it is imperative to have the most efficient method.

## TALKING ABOUT COSTS

The discussion of costs turns out to be an enormously complicated problem, which is, in its own way, as challenging and complex as any other problem of librarianship. Most of us assume that a product, an object, or a process has a cost and a value. Essentially we will buy it at a stated price if that price (the cost to us) does not exceed the value as we perceive it. It is immediately clear, then, that no commerce or monetary exchanges will take place unless people and institutions differ in their judgments of cost and value. For a library, the value of a particular book is greater than the cost of acquiring it, while, for a publisher or jobber, the cost (as income received) exceeds the value of holding the book. If this did not occur, it would be difficult (even more difficult than it is now) to buy books.

## Accounting

Our experience with problems of cost generally comes from some encounter with accounting processes. Accounting is the art and science of keeping track of expenditure. Accounting is aided by certain mathematical formulas that must hold. Every penny that comes into an organization can, in principle, be accounted for as either spent or held. Most of us are familiar with the idea that money may either be spent immediately (the check is in the mail) or encumbered ( a firm contractual commitment is made to pay at a future date).

## Expenditure and Expense

Expenditure refers, quite simply, to money going out of the organization to somewhere else. The concept of expense, which is the basis for determining cost, is more subtle. A particular expenditure, such as the purchase of the building, or the salary for a good reference librarian, may serve many operating goals. Thus, the expenditure contributes to the expense of each of those goals. The key problem of cost accounting is to reasonably assign the expenditure to the various goals, processes, products, or whatever.

The difficulty of the cost accounting process is reflected in the variety of names that are used to describe it. In some circles it is called *cost finding,* with the seductive implication that the right answers are there, and all we need to do is keep looking until we find them. In others, it is more frankly called *cost allocation.* This, to me, implies that the decisions assigning expenditures to particular goals, products, or processes may be somewhat arbitrary.

Perhaps the most attractive term is *cost determination,* which implies a certain ambiguity. Take, for example, the judicial process. We say that a trial by jury *determines* the guilt or innocence of the accused. In some cases this may really mean uncovering facts that reveal the truth. In other cases, it results in a somewhat arbitrary, legalistic determination of guilt or of innocence.

## Motivations for Cost Determination

What we talk about, then, is generally cost determination rather than simple accounting. In a library this determination is particularly complicated because, except for sharply defined technical processes, most of the expenditures serve more than one goal or purpose, so that some allocation must be made. Accounting theorists agree that a key factor in the soundness of the cost determination is its consonance with the purpose of the determination. The most important purposes for cost determination are *justification, management,* and *motivation.*

*Justification.* We may do a cost study in order to justify the costs of our operation to those who must pay the bills. Although the costs originate in the technical details of our work, it is very important that we eventually express them in a language that is clear to those who pay. Ideally, management would have defined for us some standard unit of "library goodness" and all we need to do is tell them how much it costs to provide it. Unfortunately, whatever their prejudices may be, those who pay the bills know a great deal less about library goodness than do librarians.

*Management.* A more satisfying reason for cost determination is to improve the management of those activities for which we are responsible. A skilled manager often comes to suspect that some parts of his or her domain are not functioning quite as well as they could. A carefully planned cost study makes it possible to identify some of the reasons for this, and to put them objectively when dealing with staff.

*Motivation.* Although it may seem strange, one of the important current trends in accounting theory suggests that the arbitrariness in cost determination be used to motivate parts of an organization. Essentially, a top manager who feels that one part of his or her organization is not producing well enough may adopt a cost analysis scheme that throws a somewhat larger share of the overhead onto that part of the organization, so that it is compelled to find ways to trim the fat.

Although we are not advocating that cost analysis be used in this way, it is good to be reminded that any choice of a cost analysis scheme has motivational impacts, and those must be considered before the scheme is put into place.

## ACQUISITION COSTS AT EIGHT LIBRARIES

A study of acquisition costs at eight research libraries was based on systematic application of three central ideas: delay analysis, application of labor effort to daily production, and allocation of support costs against the annual product or activity.

*Delay Analysis.* As described in detail in *Objective Performance Measures for Academic and Research Libraries,*[3] the delay engendered by any library process can be very efficiently studied by sampling techniques and a technique called *flow analysis.* We used flow analysis throughout the study to determine average processing delays, even when those delays were longer than the ten-week span of the study itself. (We will not go into technical details of the process here. It is explained in the ARL publication and is supported by software available from Tantalus, Inc.)

*Application of Labor Effort to Daily Production.* Library staff recorded statistics on many kinds of activities, including both total activity for the day and the total time spent by all the people who contributed to that activity. Labor was broadly classified into professional, technical, and student. In making cost comparisons, we used average wage scales for these three groups to compensate for differences in local wage scales.

Among the more interesting technical points of the study was the determination of the unit of product for activities such as selection. The product of selection activity is "decisions," whether those decisions are positive or negative. Even so, some selectors felt that they could not quantify the number of decisions associated with browsing through the catalog and deciding to order two of the items. Thus, data on selection costs do not include all of the eight libraries in the study.

*Allocation of Support Costs Against the Annual Product or Activity.* For costs such as space, computer services, supplies, and materials, it is not practical to do accounting during a short study span. Instead, we divided the total annual cost (or budgeted expenditure) for those cost categories by the most recent year's product in the corresponding category. In addition, we determined overhead at the departmental, divisional, library, and institutional levels. In the final analysis, it proved impossible to obtain reliable figures for the cost of space, so we did not include them.

Findings of the Study

The principal result of this study was the determination of two statistics: the representative cost for processing a copy catalog item ($15.34) and the number of working days involved (38.3). For an item requiring original cataloging, the representative cost is $33.01 and the processing time is 85.3 working days (17 weeks). Of course, this processing time does not include the time spent waiting for the vendor to deliver the book. It also does not include the estimated mean of 206 working days in a holding area for those books that are not immediately cataloged, but are held waiting until they appear on the database. The detailed data supporting this study are reported in *Advances in Library Administration and Organization* (see note 2).

## Problems of Comparative Cost Study

The library study described above suffered from a number of procedural problems. The intention was not to paint a clear and detailed picture of each individual library, but to find those general categories that would permit comparison between them. The narrowness of focus was intended to answer the question, "Are there significant differences in costs for accomplishing the same activity at different libraries?"

The answer is clearly "yes." Unfortunately, the greatest benefit that might have been derived was not available to us. We assured each library of confidentiality and then unwisely presented all the costs for a given library in a single row. Thus, if we identified by name the library with the lowest cost for book ordering, we would also have revealed all of that library's secrets. Unfortunately, we did not recognize this error in design until after we had released preliminary data to a number of libraries.

On the other hand, the range of variations makes it clear that there are differences in the management of these processes and that these differences have significant cost impact. I would urge anyone responsible for the management of acquisitions to consider his or her own processes, and to contact some or all of the eight libraries involved in this study to see if they are willing to share their data on a confidential basis.

Comparability was also somewhat damaged by the fact that, although each library had been asked to begin data collection during the summer of 1984, two of the libraries greatly delayed the start of data collection, so that their data are not clearly comparable to others.

## THE MEASUREMENT AND CONTROL OF QUALITY

The currently available techniques for measuring quality of process are well summarized in the ARL publication cited. For measuring the quality of product, there is no way to avoid the expenditure of skilled professional time in monitoring the work of others. This is obviously true during the training period and, for good management, it is desirable from time to time even for the work of the most skilled and experienced staff.

This principle applies throughout the college or university. It would be most desirable if department chairpeople could routinely review the quality of the work of the teachers in their departments by interviewing students, observing classes, and soliciting critical comment on scholarly papers. However, such activities are regarded as unacceptable intrusions on the academic freedom of faculty members.

Librarians share some of the burdens, and some of the perquisites, of college and university faculty. The professional librarian is accorded, and expects, a good deal of autonomy in carrying out his or her day-to-day tasks. Thus, many librarians reject the ideas that I am about to discuss.

## Sampling to Evaluate the Quality of Library Product

Sampling techniques can be applied to pick up random examples of a person's work and review them for quality. We are usually hindered from doing this by the expense of collecting a large sample. To obtain high precision in our estimates of whether work is or is not up to standard, we need samples of 300 to 400 items. The review of 300 or 400 reference queries is very time-consuming, as would be the review of a similar number of selection decisions or catalog entries.

A very powerful and efficient technique for this kind of quality control is sequential analysis. It makes it possible to monitor quality without expending too much time or effort. The basic principle is set forth in semitechnical terms by Dixon and Massey,[4] and is laid out in great technical detail in Wald's original monograph.[5] Its application to the library field is described by Kantor and Kantor.[6]

## LOOKING TOWARD THE FUTURE

We are still struggling with the problem of determining the cost of producing a given quantity of library product. The techniques for measuring the quality of library processes are at hand, and the techniques for measuring the quality of library products (if we can obtain cooperation for this type of task) are just around the corner.

However, an enormous difficulty still faces us. Only when we have measured the cost and quality of an operation at scores or even hundreds of different institutions may we begin to develop explanations for how quality necessarily increases costs. The tool for this is what economists call *regression analysis*.

Regression analysis, first used to study the biological phenomenon of regression to the norm, looks for a general underlying trend in a large set of data. Having conducted a number of such regression analyses, I must report that there is a large gap between an analysis that is successful from a statistician's point of view and an analysis that is useful from a manager's point of view.

In our studies of the relationship between cost and quantity of service, the most successful regression analyses still left fully one-third of the libraries more than 65 percent off the prediction. That is, one-sixth of them had budgets that were at least 65 percent higher than the best formula could predict, and another sixth of them had budgets that were at least 65 percent lower. This is not a suitable basis for planning and management.

At the time, many critics suggested that these variations were only to be expected, since there are enormous variations in the quality of both process and product at the various libraries studied. At the time, we could not answer that criticism. We can now hope that, within the next five to seven years, there will be enough data generated, and shared, so that the validity of this explanation will be tested. Then, and only then, will libraries be able to provide documentation to their supporting institutions that the cost of running a library is what it is because of the quantity and quality of services that the library provides.

## Notes

1. Paul B. Kantor, "Levels of Output Related to the Cost of Operation of Scientific and Technical Libraries," *Library Research* vol. 3 no. 2, 1981, 1–28; 141–154.
2. Paul B. Kantor, "Three Studies of the Economics of Academic Libraries," vol. 5 of *Advances in Library Administration and Organization* (Greenwich, Conn.: JAI Press, 1986), 221–286.
3. Paul B. Kantor, *Objective Performance Measures for Academic and Research Libraries* (Washington: Association of Research Libraries, 1984).
4. Wilfrid J. Dixon and Frank J. Massey, Jr., *Introduction to Statistical Analysis*, 2nd ed. (New York: McGraw-Hill, 1957).
5. Abraham Wald, *Sequential Analysis* (London: John Wiley, Chapman & Hall, Ltd., 1947).
6. Anne G. Kantor and Paul B. Kantor, "Managing for Quality in Library Services." (Unpublished article available from Tantalus Inc., Suite 218, 2140 Lee Road, Cleveland, Ohio).

# Annotated Bibliography, 1970–1988

Jeanette Mosey

Lee Weston

## INTRODUCTION

This annotated bibliography covers the literature of library and information science from 1970 through 1988 and selected business and economics literature on costing methodologies. It is a supplement to *Management and Costs of Technical Processes: A Bibliographical Review, 1876–1969* by Richard M. Dougherty and Lawrence E. Leonard (Scarecrow Press, 1970). A few pre-1970 items which were not cited in the previous bibliography are included. Items excluded are those in languages other than English.

Arrangement of items is by type of information found in the reference cited: bibliographies, background information on technical services costs in general, methods of conducting cost studies, and applications are further divided by functional area with studies covering more than one function in the multiple category. Other categories are cataloging, which includes catalogs and conversion of data; acquisitions; serials and binding; and general technical services. The latter is a potpourri of topics which do not fit into the other functional areas.

Items are numbered consecutively throughout the bibliography. Within each section, items are arranged alphabetically by author, or by title if there is no author. There is a name index for all personal and corporate authors or editors.

Jeanette Mosey is Head of Technical Services for the Arapahoe Library District in Littleton, Colorado. She was formerly on the faculty of the School of Information and Library Studies at the University of Michigan.

Lee Weston is Assistant Professor and Reference Librarian at the University of Northern Colorado.

1. Clark, Lenore. "Acquisitions, Budgets, and Materials Costs: A Selected Bibliography." In *Acquisitions Budgets and Material Costs,* edited by Sul H. Lee, pp. 145–162. New York: Haworth Press, 1988.

   Bibliography focusing on escalating costs and increasing demands amid austere budgets and a weakened dollar (for example, dwindling purchasing power). Readings are grouped under the headings of "Approval Plans", "Rising Materials Costs: Impact and Management", "Discriminatory Pricing", and "Acquisition of New Information Formats".

2. Cooper, Michael D. "The Economics of Information." *Annual Review of Information Science and Technology* 8 (1973): 5–40.

   A review of the literature on the economics of information from production through dissemination to use. Of special interest are the sections on cost-benefit analysis, demand analysis, cost-effectiveness analysis, cost analysis, operations research models. One hundred forty-four documents published from 1969–1972 are cited.

3. Dougherty, Richard M. and Leonard, Lawrence E. *Management and Costs of Technical Processes: A Bibliographic Review, 1876–1969.* Metuchen, N.J.: Scarecrow Press, 1970.

   An historical survey of more than 850 cost studies and related materials. Covers areas such as research methodology, work simplification, systems analysis and evaluation of technical processes or library activities. Items excluded are materials on systems analysis and design and automation. Sources used in compiling the bibliography of mainly published materials are: *Library Literature, Library Science Abstracts* and *Cannons Bibliography of Library Economy* along with bibliographies from numerous sources.

   Organized alphabetically by subjects which are divided into historical (1876–1945) and current (1946–1969) sections. Within each section entries are alphabetical by author or issuing agency. There is an author index which references the first citation of an article, although articles may be listed several times. There are no annotations.

4. Hayes, Sherman. "On Account: Costs, Costs, Costs . . . Give Me a Break: A Brief Bibliography." *Bottom Line* 2 (no. 3 1988): 30–31.

   Listing of materials selected from the past ten years where cost is the significant or entire emphasis of the material. Categories include "General Articles", "Automation", "Circulation", "Collection Management", and "Online Database Searching".

5. Hindle, Anthony and Raper, Diane. "The Economics of Information." *Annual Review of Information Science and Technology* 11 (1976): 27–54.

   Measures of costs and benefits plus modeling for collection control are among the topics addressed in this review. Approximately one hundred fifty items appearing in the literature from 1965–1975 are cited.

6. Landau, Herbert B. "The Cost Analysis of Document Surrogation: A Literary Review." *American Documentation* 20 (October 1969): 302–310.

   The literature on costs of descriptive cataloging, subject classification, subject heading indexing, coordinate indexing and abstracting is reviewed. Landau discusses the general lack of literature on information system costs, the general cost elements involved in document surrogation and the relation of surrogation to overall document handling costs. Literature on

"Specific Cost Factors for Surrogation Systems" is divided into five areas: classification and descriptive cataloging, manual indexing, automatic indexing, abstracting, and automatic abstracting.

Forty-one items, with publications dates ranging from 1955 to 1968, are cited in the reference.

7. Leimkuhler, Ferdinand F. *Evaluation of Costs and Benefits of Libraries: Paper Presented at the Annual Conference of the Special Libraries Association (Kansas City, Missouri, June 1978).* 1978. (Eric ED 163 947)

Briefly reviews the literature of quantitative analysis including economic models, systems analysis, program planning and budgeting, cost-effectiveness, and cost-benefit analysis.

8. Leimkuhler, Ferdinand F. and Billinsley, Alice. "Library and Information Center Management." *Annual Review of Information Science and Technology* 7 (1972): 499–533.

Includes sections on planning, programming, and budgeting systems; operations research and systems analysis; modeling; and cost-effectiveness. Cites 163 items published during 1967–1972.

9. Mick, Colin K. "Cost Analysis of Information Systems and Services." *Annual Review of Information Science and Technology* 14 (1979): 37–64.

Describes a representative sample of key studies. Focus is on the literature from 1975 to 1979. The bibliographic essay includes previous reviews and bibliographies then is divided by levels: function/service, organization and other.

The areas of interest in terms of functions or services are acquisitions and cataloging. The organization section covers staff time, academic libraries and technical libraries.

Contains over 175 references.

10. Olsen, Harold A. "The Economics of Information: Bibliography and Commentary on the Literature." 2nd ed. *Information, Part 2: Reports-Bibliographies* 1 (March/April 1972): 1–26.

Includes citations from the information literature and the economics literature.

Most relevant to costs of technical services are the sub- categories labeled "Access (Libraries, Information Services, Abstract and Index, etc." under the topics section 11: "Information: Surveys/User Studies"; section 12: "Information: System Evaluation/Analysis/General Management Studies" and section 13: Information: System Development/Planning/Automation.

Also of interest is the "Bibliographic Supplement to the 1971 edition."

11. Penner, Rudolf J. "Practice of Charging Users for Information Services: A State of the Art Report." *Journal of the American Society of Information Science* 21 (January 1970): 67–74.

Reviews 50 documents published from 1959–1968 containing data on costs involved in information systems.

Divided into two sections: billing systems and cost accounting systems. Published data on costs of unit operations for sixteen tasks are summarized in a three page table.

12. Reynolds, Rose. *A Selective Bibliography on Measurement in Library and Information Services.* London, England: Aslib, 1970.

Includes only those works held by the Aslib Library. The sections on cost and time cover much of the same ground as Dougherty and Leonard. However, there are some citations not found in that earlier work.

13. Stenstrom, Patricia F. "Current Management Literature for Technical Services." *Illinois Libraries* 69 (February, 1987): 96–103.

Reviews management literature relevant to library technical services operations published since 1980 under general headings of "Budget and Finance", "People", "Machines", "Space", and "Time".

14. Tesovnik, Mary E. and DeHart, Florence E. "Unpublished Studies of Technical Service Time and Costs: A Selected Bibliography." *Library Resources & Technical Services* 14 (Winter 1970): 56–67.

A bibliography of 15 unpublished studies identified through a survey. The studies cited cover unit times and costs in academic, public and special libraries. Arrangement is by type of operation: ordering; ordering and preparation; card production; cataloging and preparation; ordering, cataloging and preparation; and reclassification to LC.

Each entry includes, in addition to the bibliographic citation, summary demographic data in the areas of work activities, size of collection, sample size, and duration. Methods of determining direct costs—labor and materials—and indirect costs are given. Cost figures for each activity are also given when available.

15. Wessel, Carl J., et al. *Criteria for Evaluating the Effectiveness of Library Operations and Services. Phase 1: Literature Search and State of the Art.* ATLIS report no. 10. Washington, DC: J.I. Thomas and Co., 1967.

Describes the ways in which evaluation can be done: system analysis, cost effectiveness, queuing theory, value analysis, break-even analysis and others.

Abstracts for 472 items make up the major part of this volume. There is a subject index to the abstracts. They are supplemented by 15 citations from library science and by 268 citations from management science.

16. West, Martha W. and Baxter, Barbara A. "Unpublished Studies of Technical Services Time and Costs: A Supplement." *Library Resources & Technical Services* 20 (Fall 1976): 326–333.

Includes citations and annotations for 19 studies done since the 1970 article by Tesovnik and DeHart. Nine of the studies are available as ERIC documents. Academic, public and special libraries are represented. About half of the studies are in the area of cataloging and half cover several areas of technical services.

17. Wilson, John H. "Costing for Libraries: A Summary Review of the Recent Literature." In *Cost Reduction for Special Libraries and Information Centers,* edited by Frank Slater, pp. 2–9. New York: American Society for Information Science, 1973.

Reviews the literature in the areas of cost-effectiveness analysis; planning, programming and budgeting systems; marketing of information; cost benefits of library services. Cites over 100 items published from 1937–1971. A shorter version of the review in *ARIST* (1972).

18. Wilson, John H. "Costs, Budgeting, and Economics of Information Processing." *Annual Review of Information Science and Technology* 7 (1972): 39–67.

Cost reporting and accounting, cost-effectiveness analysis, computers and improved cost-effectiveness, cost-effectiveness analysis of libraries, and cost benefits are some of the topics covered in this bibliographic essay. Covers the literature published from 1936–1971.

## BACKGROUND

19. Anthony, Robert N. and Heizlinger, Regina E. *Management Control in Nonprofit Organizations.* Rev. ed. Homewood, Ill.: Richard D. Irwin, 1980.

Provides a brief description of cost accounting, standard costs and cost analysis; and discusses full versus direct costs, opportunity and imputed costs and capital costs.

Looks at selected analytical techniques of benefit/cost analysis.

20. Atkinson, Hugh C. "Personnel Savings Through Computerized Library Systems." *Library Trends* 23 (1975): 587–594.

Personnel costs are among the highest of all the factors making up the total cost of any operation. They are also often understated by concealing unreported expenses such as fringe benefits, administration, and overhead.

Personnel budget costs are rising while computer technology costs are falling. Any personnel savings which can accrue on the professional level through automation will be done through shared-intellectual activities. The elimination of routine and repetitive tasks with computer systems results in clear and identifiable time-savings of library personnel.

Hidden motivations may prevent the transfer of monies from personnel to other expenses. Personnel policies may not allow the free elimination of positions.

The most likely spheres for personnel savings are those which contain the elimination of redundancy—on a local, regional, or national level.

21. Baumol, William J. and Marcus, Matityuahu. *Economics of Academic Libraries.* (Prepared for Council on Library Resources by Mathematica, Inc.) Washington, D.C.: American Council On Education, 1973. [excerpted as "The Costs of Library and Informational Services" in *Libraries at Large: Tradition, Innovation and the National Interest,* edited by Douglas M. Knight and E. Shepley Nourse, pp. 168–192. New York & London: Bowker, 1969.]

An analysis of available statistical data on college and university libraries. Growth rates of 58 large academic libraries over two decades, the 1950s and the 1960s, are reviewed. The data examined are total investment, volumes held, personnel, professional and nonprofessional staff, total expenditures, and combinations of subdivisions of those categories.

Library costs in almost 700 private and public college and universities for 1967 and 1968 are analyzed using regression analysis of explanatory variables—volumes held, expenditure per student, volumes added 1967/68, college enrollment, and number of professional librarians—in relation to dependent variables—number of professional librarians, total library staff, volumes added 1967–68, cost of volumes added and total library operating costs.

Trends relevant to changing costs are the development of a standard format for bibliographic records in machine-readable form; a continuing decrease in the cost of computers; increases in the capacity and reliability of channels and [then] decreases in unit costs; and the creation of modular, computer-based library systems.

Other factors affecting cost trends in libraries are increasing labor costs, book production, and price of books and journals.

22. Baumol, William J. [and] Blackman, Sue Ann Batey. "Electronics, the Cost Disease, and the Operation of Libraries." *Journal of the American Society of Information Science* 34 (May 1983): 181–191.

Describes some alternative scenarios for the use of computerized facilities by libraries. Examines trends in the costs of conventional library operations and trends in the costs of electronic devices.

Library costs rise far more rapidly than costs in the rest of the economy because certain services are directly dependent on the amount of labor expended per unit of production. During the 1950s and 1960s library cost per student and cost per volume held rose significantly. Those same decades computational power and memory costs declined. Library unit costs fell because of the rise in real costs per volume and student.

Significant developments in library automation can be attributed to affordability of mini- and micro-computer systems and the emergence of online bibliographic activities. Motivation of libraries to automate has been "not financial but service oriented and designed to obtain better control over the library collection." Although hardware costs may decrease library personnel costs will increase thus resulting in greater total costs.

23. Bickner, R.E. "Concepts of Economic Cost" In *Key Papers in the Design and Evaluation of Information Systems,* edited by Donald W. King, pp. 107–146. White Plains, N.Y.: published for the American Society of Information Science by Knowledge Industry Publications, 1978. [reprinted from *Cost Considerations in Systems Analysis,* Gene A. Fisher, ed. New York: American Elsevier, 1971.]

Defines economic cost and relates cost to benefits.

Identifying, measuring, and evaluating are steps in the analysis process. This can be done by estimating and listing resources required, identifying and describing alternative uses of the resources, estimating the value of the alternatives and estimating the dollar expenditures involved.

Various costs must be identified as relevant. Future, fixed and variable, internal and external costs are all considered as appropriate. Minimizing costs or maximizing benefits is of concern also. However costs should not be minimized because of oversight. Dollar expenditures and total costs must both be considered. Costs are consequences of decisions; they depend upon the choice and the chooser.

Cost analysis considers three components of alternatives: common components, specified differences, and unspecified differences. Dollar costs must be related to other costs and the value of time considered. Discounting of future dollars is explained. Macro- and micro-cost analysis are compared.

24. Bookstein, Abraham, "An Economic Model of Library Service," In *Costing and The Economics of Library and Information Services*, edited by Stephen A. Roberts, pp. 305–323. Aslib Reader Series, vol. 5. London: Aslib, 1984.

Describes the classic economic model and relates it to libraries. Differentiates library output from products of traditional businesses.

Presents a model of library activity based on output as an abstract variable, the capacity to provide service, combined with an intermediary variable, service capability. The size of the output variable is influenced by the amount and type of inputs a library receives. Inputs can be book, equipment and personnel. When a second component of the model, the budget, is combined with the inputs, one gets the potential for service.

Bookstein presents three mathematical models of library budgets based on public finance, free-market or fee-for-service, and a mixed economy with partial subsidy.

25. Bregzis, Ritvars. "Technical Services Budget—1980 and Beyond." In American Library Association. Association of College and Research Libraries. *New Horizons for Academic Libraries*, pp. 160–169. New York: Saur Verlag, 1979.

The general economic situation of the 1970's introduces budget cuts in technical services. The need for traditional cataloging and rising salaries keeps costs up even though cooperative cataloging has reduced numbers of staff necessary for that function. Serials and binding requirements have increased while one-fifth of cataloging costs is absorbed in pre-order and pre-cataloging verification. One-third of costs can be attributed to subject analysis. Alternatives for the implementation of *AACR2* are described in terms of benefits. Findability of sources and correlation of sources bearing some relationship could be dealt with separately by applying new technologies to catalogs. The application of computers to the question of linking records has great potential.

Library expenditures, average technical services salaries, staff attrition and cataloging costs are graphically presented.

26. Brown, Eleanor Frances. *Cutting Library Costs: Increasing Productivity and Raising Revenues*. Metuchen, N.J.: Scarecrow, 1979.

A how-to book on reducing costs. The first six chapters are general. Chapters 3 and 4 include the roles of all levels of staff. Chapters 5 and 6 describe processes to use and give general guidelines. Chapter 9 addresses "Saving Costs in Technical Services" and the last chapter addresses research and future trends.

27. *Cost Reduction for Special Libraries and Information Centers*, Frank Slater, ed. New York: American Society for Information Science, 1973.

A collection of 20 papers from the ASIS 1972 mid-year regional conference is presented. The papers fall into four categories: review of the literature, general background and theory, case studies, and theoretical studies.

The papers of R. Bregzis, R.P. Palmer, D.S. Price, E.A. Maas, and J.H. Wilson are entered separately in this bibliography.

28. "Costs of Bibliographic Control: Continuing Concerns." *Journal of Academic Librarianship* 12 (July 1986): 140–146.

Two papers delivered at the 1985 IFLA conference focus on cataloging (Geoffrey G. Allen, "Change in the Catalog in the Context of Library Management") and authority control (Martin Runkle, "Authority Control: A Library Director's View").

Allen first examines the historical view of cataloging costs then dissects the current environment. Coping with changes in cataloging codes, filing rules, classification, machine readable formats, and short entry or minimal level cataloging are endemic to the cataloging world. These changes, which continue indefinitely, have obvious cost implications. It is suggested that mechanisms be developed so that library administrators, who have to meet the costs, can exert some control over the extent, direction and timing of future changes and revisions to cataloging practices.

Runkle states the need to continue authority control in library catalogs. The ways to accomplish this at least cost are to follow Library of Congress cataloging practices, help determine costs and feasibility of converting LC's catalog, and be less sensitive to the idea of LC practice as a standard.

29. English, J. Morley. *Cost Effectiveness: The Economic Evaluation of Engineered Systems*. New York: Wiley, 1960.

Topics of interest are the concepts of system resource requirements, standardized costing, and fallacies and misconceptions.

Resource requirements include these types of costs: allocated, sunk, opportunity, time, inflexibility, risk, etc.

The standard approach is a ten step process beginning with definition of goals, including establishing evaluation criteria, and ending with analysis.

30. Ford, Geoffrey. *Library Automation: Guidelines for Costing*. London: Office for Scientific and Technical Information, 1973.

Ford's costing methodology is based on a system model and a formula (total costs = direct costs and indirect costs). He defines direct costs as labor and discusses work measurement and time study for labor.

The pros and cons of self-recording and observation are presented. Costs of materials and devices are included along with labor as a part of direct costs. Indirect costs cover administration, building, utilities, and equipment. Those costs are figured based on life span and applicability to the department (acquisition, processing, etc.). Estimating costs of automation can be done in part from the existing system. Design, machines, programming, materials, supplies, procedures and conversion costs are input/output elements unique to automation implementation. Personnel and building costs may vary because of staff and environmental needs.

Appendices are included to assist in analyzing costs. They list the areas, procedures and functions comprising library systems (acquisitions, processing) and provide a classification scheme for operations (processes, items and things). Coding sheet used in self-observation and diary forms for recording activities and time expended are provided.

Formulae for activity sampling are described. A list of cost headings used by the British Library is presented.

31. Gilchrist, Alan. "Cost-Effectiveness." *Aslib Proceedings* 23 (September 1971): 455–64.

Provides background information on the application of cost-benefit analysis and cost effectiveness to libraries. Relates resources expended in producing output. Cost-effectiveness analysis is "a method of finding either the cheapest means of accomplishing a defined objective or the maximum value from a given expenditure."

*Costs* can be classified into direct expenditures for documents, labor and overhead. Cost-effectiveness analysis needs to include variable costs. *Effectiveness* is measurable based on objectives and whether they have been met. *Benefits* are difficult to quantify.

The relationship between costs and effectiveness may be difficult to distinguish from the relationship between costs and benefits. Trade off and diminishing returns are concepts important in this regard.

32. Gilchrist, Alan. "Work Study in Libraries." *Journal of Librarianship* 2 (April 1970): 126–138.

Reviews method study and work measurement. A discussion of the usefulness of these two procedures in libraries.

33. *Handbook of System Analysis: Overview of Uses, Procedures, Applications, and Practice,* edited by Hugh J. Miser and Edward S. Quade. New York: North-Holland, 1985.

Explains the context, nature and use of systems analysis and provides an overview of the methodology.

Formulating the problem; considering objectives, constraints and alternatives; and predicting the consequences through models are completed. Then decisions, based in part on cost-benefit and cost-effectiveness analysis, are made and implementation occurs.

34. Heinritz, Fred J. "Quantitative Management in Libraries." *College & Research Libraries* 31 (July 1970): 232–238.

Discusses elements of management: motion, time, and cost studies; operations research; other mathematical techniques; and computers.

Sees motion study as the prerequisite to time study. Process and decision charts are used for motion studies. Record the present method, analyze it, and develop an improved method.

The time study is reliable for determining performance standards using stop watches or work sampling to collect time data.

Since cost is a function of time, the times must be known before costs can be computed. It is necessary to relate cost to depreciation, and supply costs can be included or excluded as desired.

Operations research problems can be classified as allocation, sequencing, inventory, replacement, queuing theory, and competitive strategies. Other mathematical techniques may be useful, including the traditional statistical procedure of random sampling. Computers provide the calculation facilities needed for data analysis.

35. Hewgill, J.C.R. "Management Accounting and Library Activities," [paper presented at a one-day conference, "Value for Money: Costing and Some Aspects of Cost Effectiveness in the Library/Information Unit," held at Gregory House, the Thomas Caram Foundation, Brunswick Square, London on 8th March 1977] In *Costing and The Economics of Library and Information Services,* edited by Stephen A. Roberts, pp. 87–92. Aslib Reader Series, vol. 5. London: Aslib, 1984.

Three ways to present costs are based on inputs-labor, material, expenses, and capital assets; organization-departments plus overhead; or outputs-products and services. Fixed, variable, direct and indirect costs must be identified.

Cost/output or cost/activity ratios are easy to find by adding direct to indirect costs and dividing by number of units. Management determines whether this is the right cost by internal and/or external comparisons and cost through commercial concerns. Benefits are also examined in terms of customers' satisfaction, cost/benefit analysis, cost-effectiveness analysis, etc.

The effective use of accounting data means assessing future workloads, setting performance targets, and deciding on staffing levels and processes.

36. Keller, John E. "Program Budgeting and Cost Benefit Analysis in Libraries," *College & Research Libraries* 30 (March 1969): 156–160.

A general discussion of program budgeting and cost benefit analysis. Offers definitions and some situations where applying these might be useful.

37. Kelly, Joseph T. *Costing Government Services: A Guide for Decision Making.* Washington, D.C: Government Finance Research Center of the Government Finance Offices Association, 1984.

Provides an overview of cost analysis. Describes the process, how it can be used, and the relationship between budgeting and cost analysis. Explains different types of costs and defines cost concepts. A checklist of direct and indirect costs, a matrix of management options, and a costing matrix are included.

Examines the costs of contracting out services or goods. The make or buy decision process is to perform an in-house cost analysis, determine the cost of contracting out, evaluate cost and quality issues and monitor the results.

The appendix is a discussion of "Life-Cycle Cost Procurement" by Stanley D. Zemansky.

38. King, Donald Ward and Bryant, E.C. *Evaluation of Information Services and Products.* Washington, D.C.: Information Resources Press, 1971.

Although this work is focused on information storage and retrieval systems, the discussions of evaluation and measurement (p. 1–18) are of general interest.

Evaluation is based on some objective(s) such as modifying an existing system or procedure. Determining what to measure and how to go about it are the next steps in the process.

A model for evaluation relies on the concepts of cost- effectiveness and benefits. The resources used, performance, and benefits are all measured and compared. Fixed and variable costs are related to the benefits gained.

39. Koel, Ake I. "Bibliographic Control at the Crossroads: Do We Get Our Money's Worth?" *Journal of Academic Librarianship* 7 (September 1981): 220–222.

Raises interesting questions about how little economic efficiency libraries exercise in bibliographic control.

40. Lancaster, F. Wilfrid. "Evaluation of Technical Services." In his *The Meas-*

*urement and Evaluation of Library Services,* pp. 264–271. Washington, D.C.: Information Resources Press, 1977.

Technical services cannot be evaluated directly in terms of user satisfaction. They can be evaluated by looking at their internal efficiency and their long-range effect on public service.

Cost and productivity factors are important in measuring the efficiency of an operation. Unit cost figures have limited value for comparison since they may be attained using different methods. The technical services cost ratios (TSCORE) relates the cost of technical processing to the costs of purchasing library materials. Like unit costs it may be used for internal and external comparisons if the same materials are used.

The efficiency of library operations can be improved by using techniques from industrial engineering, operations research, and management services.

"Attempts to analyse the quality of technical services are almost nonexistent, and very little has been done to evaluate the operations of a technical services department to determine the effect these operations will have on the public services provided by the library."

41. Leimkuhler, Ferdinand F. "Library Operations Research: A Process of Discovery and Justification." *Library Quarterly* 42 (January 1972): 84–96.

Operations research can be used to look at new technologies and their consequent environments. Operations research must be supported by management since it is a long term and high risk investment.

Five criteria for good models, from William Morris' *Management Science: A Bayesian Approach* (Prentice-Hall, 1968), are relatedness, transparency, robustness, fertility, and ease of enrichment. Choice of models can also be done according to their realism, flexibility, capability, usefulness and cost. Criteria for each feature are listed.

Libraries have been the targets of several operations research multidisciplinary team projects. Leimkuhler describes bibliographic control generally and storage models specifically as areas in libraries which have been studied through operations research.

42. Line, Maurice B. "The Psychopathology of Uneconomics." In *Costing and The Economics of Library and Information Services,* edited by Stephen A. Roberts, pp. 324–336. Aslib Reader Series, vol. 5. London: Aslib, 1984.

Increased publishing and the resultant acquisition/processing and storage of materials by libraries in concert with reduced resources have demanded increased fiscal responsibility.

Economics are directly related to the objectives of the institution. Examples of economics by reducing existing costs are given in the areas of cataloging, classification, subject analysis, book selection, acquisitions, and storage costs.

Resistance by librarians to economic pressures is characterized as the traditional which may encompass perfectionist, cultural or passive reactions. Other responses may be political, psychological or pseudo-altruistic, or economic. The latter can be mini-economic, pseudo-economic, or marginal economic. The false economy or overkill responses are also possible. Other attitudes come from those who encourage excessive change and the hypereconomist.

Faculty attitudes can be ambivalent—there is competition for funds, need for a strong collection to support research. Student reactions are less easily characterized. The university administration applies the pressures to economize yet may support the concept of a strong library.

These conflicting attitudes and values have to be balanced by the library director. Analyzing the problem, identifying possible solutions, and comparing options for costs and effectiveness must be combined with cultural and humanistic values. The end result is a library run economically and effectively which provides the best possible service with the resources available.

43. Mahapatra, M. "Systems Analysis as a Tool for Research in Scientific Management of Libraries: A State of the Art Review." In *Costing and The Economics of Library and Information Services,* edited by Stephen A. Roberts, pp. 37–45. Aslib Reader Series, vol. 5. London: Aslib, 1984.

Briefly reviews systems and system characteristics; systems analysis applications; phases, techniques and future prospects of systems of study.

Includes the formula developed by Carol Slaverson ("Relevance of Statistics to Library Evaluation," *College & Research Libraries* 30 (1969): 352–361) and refined by Lipetz:

$$\frac{\text{Useful results}}{\text{costs involved}} = \frac{0}{I} \text{ efficiency} = \frac{\text{output}}{\text{input}}$$

44. Malinconico, S.M. "Technology and Productivity [in the Library]." *Library Journal* 108 (15 May 1983): 978–80.

The pitfalls of attempting to cost automated systems are postulated. Unrealistic expectations, minimal staffing patterns, and the service deficit make it difficult to appropriately assess the costs of automation. The economic investment must be examined in light of expected benefits and accurate costs. Clear objectives which can be achieved at acceptable costs must be based on adequate implementation plans. Benefits, instead of economic arguments, are used for justification of automated systems.

45. Marron, Harvey. "On Costing Information Services." In American Society of Information Science. Conference, 1969, San Francisco. *Proceedings: Cooperating Information Societies,* pp. 515–20. Westport, Conn.: Greenwood Press, 1969.

Reviews the reasons for cost accounting: intellectual curiosity, budgeting, allocation of resources, long range planning, and profit or loss.

Standard methods of cost accounting are presented and examples of budgets are given. Unit cost computation is then tackled.

One of the differences between information centers and businesses is that the former cannot precisely categorize its output. As an example, Marron asks how depreciation can be applied to a document collection.

One approach to costing information is suggested, although it does not account for input costs.

46. Martin, Murray S. "Cost-Benefit Analysis for Austerity." In *Austerity Management in Academic Libraries,* edited by John F. Harvey and Peter

Spyers-Duran, pp. 236 +. Metuchen, N.J. and London: Scarecrow Press, 1984.

Defines cost effectiveness analysis and cost-benefit analysis and gives examples of when each is used. Describes the preparations necessary for self-study.

A detailed explanation of cost-benefit analysis covers listing activities, cost calculation, cost quantification, identification of benefits in terms of quality and user satisfaction.

The nature of benefits and a way of quantifying them must be established before a cost-benefit analysis. Space considerations should be part of any such analysis.

An area where cost-benefit analysis is paramount is automation. It should determine not only the kind of system needed but how it should be deployed and exploited.

Factors affecting costs are centralization versus decentralization, access to versus ownership of collections, success rate, service elimination, cost recovery, and income generation.

47. Martyn, John [and] Lancaster, F. Wilfrid. "Cost Analysis." In their *Investigative Methods in Library and Information Science: An Introduction,* pp. 175–192. Arlington, Virginia: Information Resources Press, 1981.

Defines benefit evaluation, cost-effectiveness evaluation, and cost benefit studies.

Costing is discussed in general terms. Direct, indirect and overhead costs must all be considered. Data required for costing can be gathered task by task or by staff diaries.

Cost-effectiveness analysis may be either explicit or implicit. Operating systems are examined with a view to improving their cost-effectiveness; or calculations are applied in choosing between systems or services. Before one can evaluate a system's effectiveness the objective of the system must be clear. System evaluation can be viewed by the operators (staff) or the users. Effectiveness criteria can be used by adding a cost per element.

Cost benefit analysis should include costs that come from outside the system being evaluated. There is a balance between total incurred costs and total benefits. Each situation has its own benefits and the effects of a cost-benefit study cannot be transferred from one situation or location to another. Cost-benefit studies reveal the uses actually made of a system and the benefits that users expect.

48. Mason, Robert M. "The Economics and Cost Benefit of Analysis Services— The Case of Information Analysis Centers." In *Evaluating New Telecommunications Services,* pp. 303–324. Martin C.J. Elton, William A. Lucas, David W. Conrath, eds. New York: Plenum Press, 1978.

An overview of the products/services of information analysis centers. Includes factors affecting demand and model criteria of services.

Two models, one based on objectives and cost categories and one on benefits to users are presented.

Mason concludes with a discussion of conceptual issues, the impacts of technology and research needs.

49. Price, Douglas, S. "Cost Analysis and Reporting as a Basis for Decisions." In

Clinic on Library Applications of Data Processing University of Illinois, 1976. *Proceedings: The Economics of Library Automation,* pp. 83–106. Urbana-Champaign: University of Illinois, Graduate School of Library Science, 1977.

Examines the characteristics of available cost data. Points out the problems of using gross numbers, data from sample time periods, and the stopwatch technique. Unit costs are useless, and even dangerous, unless they include all costs and are interpreted. Usable cost information requirements are listed.

Describes the building block concept of costing which begins with the systems analysis technique of flow charting. Next is the identification of components that can be costed. The collection of cost data must include direct and indirect costs and detailed production counts.

The data are used for monitoring budgets and performance. Pitfalls of cost studies are also addressed.

50. Raffel, J.A. "From Economic to Political Analysis of Library Decision Making." *College & Research Libraries* 35 (November 1974): 412–23. Comment by R.L. Hadlock, with rejoinder. 36 (March 1975): 154.

Includes a definition and critique of cost-benefit analysis. Addresses the politics of economic analysis and discusses political analysis in libraries.

Concludes with some hypotheses and lessons on the politics of cost-benefit analysis in library decision making.

51. Roberts, Stephen A. *Cost Management for Library and Information Services.* London; Boston: Butterworths, 1985.

The managerial, economic, and financial environments of libraries require management information. The needs and requirements of cost data are explained and a schema for management information presented. Performance measures and their relationships to cost measures and accounting procedures are examined.

Methods and types of cost studies include service cost structures, cost analysis, cost distribution or allocation, unit costing and timing, cost-effectiveness, and cost-benefit. All of these depend on categorization and calculation of costs for capital charges, current costs and overhead, and labor time. The desirability of generalized cost measurement models is stated and further discussed.

The step for implementing a cost study are outlined: checklist of needs, study design, system description, data collection, work measurement, analysis of results, and interpretation of data.

An integrated approach to budgeting, accounting, costing and performance measurement is necessary. Sources of statistics, performance measures, and management data are summarized as is the application of management information systems in libraries. The development of managerial and economic models in libraries is suggested.

A case study illustrates the applications from the text. Many bibliographical references appear throughout. There is a glossary and an index. Appendices include descriptive lists, terms, account codes, tasks, and sample data collection forms.

52. Sassone, Peter G. and Schaffer, William A. *Cost-Benefit Analysis: A Handbook*. New York: Academic Press, 1978.

Introduces cost-benefit analysis with a brief history and economic basis. Decision criteria are surveyed: net present value, cutoff period, pay-back period, net average rate of return, internal rate of return, annual value, benefit-cost ration, minimum average cost, and equity.

Identifying costs and benefits can be done with classifacatory schemes such as internal versus external effects, invommensurables and intangibles, or direct versus indirect effects.

53. Schabel, Donald. "Performance Standards and Cost Analysis." *Illinois Libraries* 64 (September 1982): 874–880

Basic, general description of performance standards in technical services. Provides formulas for determining unit costs and shows how fringes and non-productive time increase costs. Includes figures from Ken Bierman's study at the Tucson (Az.) Public Library.

54. Schauer, Bruce P. *The Economics of Managing Library Service*. Chicago: American Library Association, 1986.

Presents the basic principles of microeconomics as applied to library services. Library decisions are characterized as economic problems based on consumer behavior and demand. Consumer preferences and choices are examined in terms of library materials and budget constraints. The model of consumer choice is applied to changes in income, price of services, individual demand, market demand, and time price of library use.

Production theory can analyze inputs and physical outputs such as number of items processed, cataloged, used, number of patrons served, etc. Inputs include physical facilities; staff, equipment and information within the library; access to documents and information external to the library; and administration. There are several examples of relationships between inputs and output in the library. These are followed by a discussion of the nature of production costs in the short run (marginal cost) and long run (average cost). The balance between consumer choice and production provides the library with a way to examine services in terms of price and quantity. Changes in supply—inventory control, delivery policy and market price—and changes in demand—shift in taste, seasonal variations—affect this balance.

Applications of microeconomic theories is done by using quantitative methods such as probability, breakeven analysis, inventory control, and queuing theory. Other approaches include information economics (payoff tables and decision trees), cost-benefit analysis, and public finance theory.

55. Shillingham, Gordon. *Managerial Cost Accounting*. Homewood, Illinois: Richard D. Irwin, Inc., 1977.

Topics addressed are the role of cost accounting, the costing structure, cost behavior and decisions, variable costing, standard costing, controlling overhead costs, and interdepartmental cost allocation. The decision of costing by organization segment, by object of expenditure, and by activity is useful. Factors of activity costing include materials, labor and overhead.

56. Shoffner, Ralph M. "Comparative Cost Analysis." In *Information Roundup; A Continuing Education Session on Microforms and Data Processing in the*

*Library Information Center: Costs/Benefits/History/Trends;* Proceedings of the 4th Mid-Year Meeting of the American Society for Information Science (ASIS); 1975 May 15–17; Portland, OR, edited by Frances G. Spigai, Theodore C.W. Graws and Julie Kawabata, pp. 1–32. Washington, D.C.: ASIS, 1975.

The principles of cost analysis which are presented are 1) measurements almost always contain error, 2) use only the precision needed, 3) relate the measurements to each other, 4) subject the results to tests of reasonableness, and 5) having identified unreasonable measurements, guess the possible sources and retest.

Shoffner uses these principles to examine summary data from the Office of Education and circulation in an individual library.

57. Sowell, Ellis Mast. *The Evolution of the Theories and Techniques of Standard Costs.* Huntsville: University of Alabama Press, 1973.

Reviews cost estimates and variations which preceded standard costs. Gives the historical background and development of standard costs which are predetermined costs of raw materials, labor, and overhead. They are compared with actual or historical costs.

Discusses in detail accounting for materials, direct labor and burden in standard costs.

58. Stitleman, Leonard. *Cost Utility Analysis Applied to Library Budgeting: A Paper Presented at the Institute on Program Planning and Budgeting Systems for Libraries, Wayne State University, Detroit, Michigan, Spring 1968.* Detroit, Mich.: Wayne State University, Department of Library Science, 1968. (ED 045 126)

Describes cost utility analysis as a tool in decision making. Emphasizes quantification and draws on analytical tools. States that cost analysis applications should compare inputs to outputs. The utility or benefit aspects must be included even if not quantifiable.

59. Tuttle, Helen M. Welch. "Standards for Technical Service Cost Studies," In *Advances in Librarianship,* vol. 1, ed. by Melvin John Voigt, pp. 95–111. New York: Academic Press, 1970,

Describes the lack of standards for units of measurement in libraries generally and in the technical services specifically and summarizes the existing standards used by libraries. Promotes the definition and use of standards in technical services for management purposes. Reviews existing cost studies and attempts at developing cost standards. Promotes development of standards for obvious costs before those for more complex areas such as values. Restates the need for standardized terminology and statistics used and suggests agencies to promote, implement, and coordinate standards divisions and committees of ALA as appropriate.

60. Vickers, Peter H. "Ground Rules for Cost-Effectiveness." *Aslib Proceedings* 28 (June-July 1976): 224–29.

A brief overview of the systems approach in providing cost effective information services: defining objectives, examining information needs, determining existing information resources, designing services and systems appropriate to objectives and resources.

Pitfalls include lack of communication, current needs, and devoting time/effort to activities not visibly useful.

The information service can be clearly defined according to the objectives, can provide services needed and can provide maximum output.

61. Vickery, B.C. "Research by Aslib into Costing of Information Services." *Aslib Proceedings* 24 (June 1972): 337–341.

Provides a general discussion of costs and benefits. Costs are classified into labor, materials, equipment and overhead.

Measuring the time expended on a job and translating that into cost is the problem. Estimates of time spent are obtained using existing records such as schedules, interviews, work diaries, activity sampling and time study or observations using a stop watch. After establishing times for activities, the next step is to get an average cost based on productive hours per year. Standard unit times are useful for comparing performances and for predicting numbers of staff needed.

Other parts of the full cost include materials, machines, and maintenance. Overhead encompasses administrative and service costs. The latter are such things as rent, insurance, heating, lighting, etc. There are many alternative ways of calculating and allocating overhead costs.

Effectiveness is defined as "how well a service to users achieves its objectives." Benefit is a "monetary measure of the value to the user of the service received." The purpose of cost effectiveness studies is to see what changes can be made in service to increase effectiveness without increasing costs or to reduce costs without reducing effectiveness.

62. Washington Operations Research Council. *Cost-Effectiveness Analysis: New Approaches in Decision-Making,* edited by Thomas A. Goldman. New York: Praeger, 1967.

A basic description of cost-effectiveness analysis. Chapters of interest are those on "Measures of Effectiveness," A. William Niskamer; "The Choice of Analytic Techniques," Alfred Blumstein; "The Use of Cost Estimates," Harry P. Hatry; and "Estimating Systems Costs," James D. McCullough.

Defines cost-effectiveness analysis in terms of its steps, virtues, and limitations.

Describes models for use in determining a systems' effectiveness: real world, gaming, simulation and analytical modes. Considerations in model selection are addressed.

63. White, H.S. "Cost Benefit Analysis and Other Fun and Games." *Library Journal* 110 (15 February 1985): 118–21.

Discusses the current interest in cost benefit analysis. Differentiates among cost efficiency, cost effectiveness, and cost benefit analysis (CBA). Believes generalization of CBA to libraries will not work—that it is pointless and dangerous. Distribution of library costs to user groups should be done on the basis of presumed or expected use, not actual use.

Establish ground rules to limit information seeking behavior of persons or groups external to the library. Those include limiting their ability to spend organizational funds for library materials, establishing rules for the use and retention of materials purchased with library funds, and insisting that justifications for trips to gather information include notes on information sources already consulted.

Monitoring of expenditures to determine their usefulness is not at issue. Rather, propose alternatives designed to demonstrate that these alternatives will do the job more simply, more accurately, and with greater efficiency and effectiveness overall. Libraries must propose realistic and meaningful alternatives to meaningless and unrealistic techniques of measurement.

64. Wilson, John H., Jr. "Improved Costing Techniques and Cost-Effective Operations for Technical Libraries and Information Centers." In *Contemporary Problems in Technical Library and Information Center Management: A State-of-the-Art*, Alan Rees, editor, pp. 177–199. Washington, [D.C.]: American Society for Information Science, 1974.

An overview of the literature as well as general discussions of cost effectiveness, PPBS, the value of information, and cost benefits.

Problem areas and proposed projects are presented.

Recommends production of guides and handbooks on costs, cost-benefit analysis, charging for library services, and budgeting.

Good bibliography.

65. Alfano, Vicki Ann. "Cutting Costs: Establishing Library Automation Goals." *Bottom Line* 1 (no. 1, 1987): 45–47.

Explains the use of a variety of analysis charts as a method to identify program priorities (functional analysis chart), activities to be automated (decision analysis chart), and areas which are the most costly to automate (time management chart). Specimens of the charts are provided and what they measure is described.


METHODOLOGIES


66. Armstrong, Alan. "Analysing Industrial Information Service Costs: A Simple Check List." In *Costing and The Economics of Library and Information Services*, edited by Stephen A. Roberts, pp. 107–111. Aslib Reader Series, vol. 5. London: Aslib, 1984.

Enumerates all the elements to be taken into account when doing cost analysis: salaries, including overtime; fringe benefits such as health insurance, pension, training, holidays, sick leaves, group insurance, professional fees, and conferences; recruitment; temporary staff; subsidies, for example, the cafeteria; overhead items like rent, heating, lighting, cleaning, maintenance, stationery, postage, furniture, telephone, professional tools, travel, and consultants.

67. Armstrong, Alan. "Cost-determining Formula for Library Staff." *Library Association Record* 74 (May 1972): 85–86.
—Comment by J.L. Bate [letter]. 74 (August 1972): 156.

Provides a formula for determining the full operational cost per hour for each librarian employed.

The formula takes the annual salary and divides it by the average number of hours a worker is paid per year, 1950 (or 260 days) multiplied by 7 1/2 hours per day. (This does not include hours paid but not worked, e.g., vacation and holidays). Then add 26% for fringe benefits such as insurance, sick leave, vacation and holidays. Next, add to the total 175–225% for overhead and profit. This includes departmental costs for equipment and supplies; occupancy costs of rent, lighting, maintenance; and 10% for profit. The latter figure is applicable to special libraries which sell services to other departments or divisions. The price per hour worked is finally multiplied times the hours worked to yield the total cost of employing one person for a year, about three to four times the annual salary.

68. Aslib Research Department. "The Analysis of Library Processes." *Journal of Documentation* 26 (March 1970): 30–45.

Focuses on analyzing activities in technical services by using a modification of the Lehigh technique developed by R.S. Taylor and C.E. Hieber. This is done by first examining all forms used and recording the purpose, name, size, characteristics, points of origin and disposal, frequency of use, etc.

Activities are described in terms of personnel, department, regularity, description by code, and information transferred.

All data are coded on punched cards and reports generated. Printouts are translated into flow charts for further analysis. Sorting of the card decks allow for data on personnel levels, duplication of information on forms, etc.

Weaknesses identified are: lack of use of files; limitations of the printouts; and the data are for tasks, not general processes. Although no data is gathered on costs, the methodology is useful for the intermediate stages of a cost study—after tasks have been identified. If the information collected is expanded to include time spent on tasks, then costs can be determined.

69. Barnes, Ralph H. *Motion and Time Study: Design and Measurement of Work.* 7th ed. New York: Wiley, 1980.

Provides detailed description and examples of work measurement. Topics of greatest interest are process analysis, time study, and work sampling.

Process analysis includes flow diagrams and process charts. Time studies utilize a stop watch, electronic timer, motion picture camera, or observation. A formula for determining the number of observations is given. Rating factors and time standards result from the time study.

Work sampling involves selecting a confidence level and using random times.

Fatigue, human factors and motivation and work are also addressed.

70. Beecher, John W.; Self, Phyllis C.; Stenson, E. Roy; and Anderson, Nancy D. "Use of Random Alarm Mechanisms for Analyzing Professional and Support Staff Activities in Science Libraries: Part I: Methodology." *Library Research* 4 (Summer 1982): 137–146.

Describes the planning for gathering empirical evidence about staffing in departmental libraries. The project is designed to study possible relationships between staff activities and computer literature searching, budget and the automated circulation system; the relationship between staff size and research and publication activities; and the level of public and technical service activities in decentralized departmental libraries.

The sampling technique chosen is the random alarm mechanism (RAM) because of its accuracy, objectivity, and cost effectiveness. A basic list of activity categories and their definition is generated. Summary sheets are developed for use in data collection.

A sample data collection form and definitions of categories are included. Results of the study are reported by Anstine in another article.

71. Bierman, Kenneth J. "Technical Services Cost Studies: A Cookbook Approach." *Illinois Libraries* 65 (May 1983): 306–310.

Underscores the importance of planning for cost studies. Methodology, data gathering, analysis, presentation and decision making are the ingredients of the recipe Bierman gives.

Methodology depends on the data needed and the appropriate process for gathering them. The proper approach to data gathering is described. Analysis should be timely and provide results as soon as possible. Either a formal presentation or brief report may be called for. Using the results to aid in decision making is, of course, the culmination of the cost analysis.

72. California State Universities and Colleges (Los Angeles). Office of the Chancellor. *Report on a Cost Study of Specific Technical Processing Activities of the California State University and College Libraries.* Los Angeles, [Calif.]: CSUC, Office of the Chancellor, 1973. (ED 973 779)

Provides raw data for unit costs, bibliographic searching and production units. Most useful are the appendices which provide descriptions of activities in acquisitions, cataloging, and administrative functions; instructions for completing function worksheets and production unit summary reports; formulas used to determine summary and unit costs; and samples of the data collection forms themselves.

73. Churchman, C. West. "Operations Research Prospects for Libraries in the Realities and Ideals." *Library Quarterly* 42 (January 1972): 6–14.

The author provides an overview of operations research in terms of its strategies.

The resources of operational research include values such as purposes expressed quantitatively or benefit minus cost subject to policy. Models and computer simulation techniques are available, too.

The support systems to be utilized are existing data; the purposes, policies, characteristics, environment, and problems of the system; and funding.

Churchman then presents the first steps of operational research: understanding the system, identifying critical problems, and matching the latter to possible solutions. Testing the solutions, making and implementing recommendations conclude the process.

74. Clements, D.W.G. "The Cost of Library Systems." *Aslib proceedings* 27 (March 1975): 98–111.

Costing is done routinely to provide regular financial and management information or as a special exercise to deal with a particular procedure.

Standards must be used in all costing exercises. These standards include the headings used on data collection forms, methods for apportioning costs such as overhead, lists of library operations, and units of measurement of output or service.

Methodologies for routine costing include allocating expenditures and revenues to sections for producing sectional cost accounts and analyzing sectional costs by activities and associating them with units of output or service.

Special exercise costing is based on work diaries for recording time spent on main and/or secondary tasks. Number of units completed by individuals or groups is used to estimate labor costs per unit.

Descriptions of procedures for either type of costing can be presented in flow charts.

The exact methodology used for recording work and analyzing the data is given. Clements provides an overview of the entire process from preliminary discussions through report writing.

75. Dougherty, Richard M. and Heinritz, F.J. *Scientific Management of Library Operations*. Metuchen, N.J.: Scarecrow, 1966 & (2nd ed.) 1982.

Both editions have a chapter on "Time Study" which describes how to conduct time studies with a timing device and how to use the data gathered to rate workers. The second edition includes system throughput/ delay analysis, diaries, and work sampling as well.

Each has a chapter on "Costs" which shows how to determine unit, labor, depreciation, supply and general costs. The second edition has some formulas for these and includes overhead and total costs. The latter also discusses break-even analysis.

Other chapters of interest are "The Flow Process Chart, Flow Diagram" and "Decision Flow Charting" (1st ed.) or "Flow Charting and Other Techniques . . ." (2nd ed.); Sampling (both eds.); and "Tools of Analysis" (2nd ed.).

76. Drake, Miriam A. "Attribution of Library Costs." *College & Research Libraries* 38 (November 1977): 514–519.

Describes four methods for attributing costs of library services: divide costs according to the proportion of faculty in each department, distribute indirect costs based on faculty salaries, examine intended use or direct cost, or allocate costs based on actual use.

Choice of cost allocation methods depends on the size of the library budget relative to the institution's total budget, diversity of instruction programs, availability of data, and philosophy of university management.

Reviews the results of library cost studies at Columbia, Stanford and Purdue.

77. DuBois, Dan. *Library Labor Cost Accounting System*. Los Angeles, [Calif.]: California State Universities and Colleges, Office of the Chancellor, 1972. (ED 075 063)

Discusses a system developed for use at libraries on all campuses. Encompasses activities in technical services functional areas of acquisitions, cataloging and administration. Attempts to determine hours spent and hourly rate, level of skill, media handled, average unit cost and total cost.

Much of this report is coding used, layout of the coding program and sample printouts. The most useful sections are the production unit summary form and function worksheets.

Includes descriptions of the functions in acquisitions, cataloging and related administrative tasks.

78. Duchesne, Roderick M. "Analysis of Costs and Performance." *Library Trends* 21 (April 1973): 587–603.

Proposes a library management information system which provides budget, cost and performance data in addition to conventional financial and statistical statements.

The data needed for such a system include budget and actual expenditures, process and program parameters, and basic performance data.

Output may include process, program, capital, revenue or output budget statements. Another potentially useful method is discounted cost-flow analysis. Tables provide illustrations of the different budget statements.

79. Evans, G.E. "Work Analysis." In his *Management Techniques for Librarians*. New York: Academic Press, 1976 &(2nd ed.) 1983.

Operations research; systems analysis; block and flow diagrams, flow process charts, decision flow charts, Gantt charts and PERT techniques are described as methods of work analysis.

Electronic data processing and quantitative techniques are suggested for increasing output and aiding in decision making respectively.

80. Gilder, Lesley and Schofield, James Leonard. *Work Measurement Techniques and Library Management: Methods of Data Collection*. LMRU Report n.2. [Leicestershire]: Loughborough University of Technology, Library Management Research Unit, c1978, 1976.

Presents the principles and techniques of work measurement and their application to library management.

Methods for and results of a time/cost study for acquisitions and cataloging are given. The most useful parts are the forms used for collecting the data.

81. Goodell, John S. *Libraries and Work Sampling*. Challenge to Change: Library Applications of New Concepts, no. 1. Littleton, Colo.: Libraries Unlimited, 1975.

A general discussion of work sampling followed by procedures, calculations and uses. Several useful forms are given. Briefly reviews a dozen studies dealing with work sampling.

82. Hayes, Sherman and Klein, Lawrence A. "On Account: Cost Accounting Basics: When (or) Do They Apply to Libraries?" *Bottom Line* 2 (no. 1, 1988): 29–30.

Outlines the advantages for libraries in employing cost accounting as a systematic approach to budgeting, pricing, performance evaluation, costing inventory or services, and reaching special decisions.

83. Hines, Theodore C. "Evaluation of Processing Services." *Library Trends* 22 (January 1974): 305–314.

Processing services are defined as acquisition, cataloging, and physical preparation and servicing of library materials. Evaluation of these are to determine whether materials are acquired rapidly and whether appropriate access, both intellectual and physical, is provided, all at reasonable cost.

General techniques for evaluating and improving services are named. Hines then suggests a technique for evaluating processing services by determining "areas in which there is such a broad professional consensus as to methods, procedures, concepts, and goals and to examine the extent to which a given library is applying them." Pros and cons of this technique are discussed. Examples are drawn from the use of standardized cataloging information; centralized or cooperative acquisition, cataloging or processing; acquisition of materials in all formats; appropriate use of different levels of personnel; and networking for resource sharing.

84. Jacob, Mary Ellen L. "Standardized Costs for Automated Library Systems." *Journal of Library Automation* 3 (September 1970): 207–217.

Advocates using standardized methods for giving costs and attempts to define cost criteria. Providing a clear definition of "cost" and what things are included is essential. Personnel costs should clarify skill and experience levels. Problems of performance evaluation for both personnel and programs are delineated. A sample job description is presented.

Equipment costs may include computers, input devices, and supplies. Equally important are program compilation time and maintenance costs. Conversion, too, may be of significance. A format for presenting costs is suggested.

85. Kountz, John C. "Library Cost Analysis: A Recipe." *Library Journal* 97 (1 February 1972): 459–64.

The steps in cost analysis are to: identify and quantify the function; determine the component parts; look at resource requirements such as staff, supplies, equipment, supervision, space, and overhead; identify times and volumes in relation to cost; cost alternate methods; and repeat the process for other alternatives.

86. LARC Association. *Proceedings of the LARC Computer-Based Unit Cost Studies Institute, September 16–17, 1971, Austin, Texas.* Edited by H. William Axford. Tempe, Az.: LARC Association, 1972.

The institute proceedings is a presentation by H.W. Axford on "A Unit Cost Study of Technical Services." He provides an overview of the study conducted at Florida Atlantic University and then describes, step by step, how to carry out such a study.

First is the decision to perform cost studies and getting staff support. Then the specific steps of the study are carried out: assigning codes to each department, diary studies for determining percentage of time spent on each assigned responsibility, data forms for recording salary functions and time spent for each position, coding data for computer processing, and interpreting the results.

Problem areas identified are original cataloging and acquisition by approval plan. Included is the Fortran program used to analyze the data.

87. Leimkuhler, Ferdinand F. and Cooper, Michael D. "Analytical Models for Library Planning." *Journal of the American Society for Information Science* 22 (November 1971): 390–398.

—Comment by A.G. Mackenzie [letter]. 23 (May 1972): 222.

Examines the growth and obsolescence of a collection of materials and their effect on acquisition, storage and circulation.

Models for the cost of storing items held indefinitely or held a limited time are developed. Included are models for minimizing average cost per use and for acquisition and processing delays in relation to item use. A generalized model of library costs and benefits is presented.

88. Losee, Robert M. "A Decision Theoretic Model of Materials Selection for Acquisition." *Library Quarterly* 57 (July, 1987): 269–283.

Presents a decision theoretic model designed to minimize costs of the materials selection process. The model suggests formal methods for ranking books for selection using binary, Poisson, and normally distributed features. The system using the proposed model is most easily implemented where large numbers of retrospective machine-readable catalog records are available so that they may be used to establish a set of features for the use of the model and to estimate parameter values for each feature.

89. Magson, M.S. "Techniques for the Measurement of Cost Benefits in Information Centres." *Aslib Proceedings* 25 (May 1973): 164–85.

—Comment by F.H. Ayres [letter]. 25 (September 1973): 349.

The application of management by objective, work measurement, activity sampling and critical examination are used to determine cost benefit activities.

Activity function tables are generated to indicate the time spent on different activities by which staff. Times are converted into cost figures (based on salaries), other costs added and cost activity analysis performed. The same steps are applied to alternative methods of producing the work. Alternatives include using commercial services, different levels of staff, and not performing the work.

Cost related benefits are calculated for each alternative and comparisons made. Where they are developed, better methods of quantifying benefits can be used in the model.

90. Marcotie, F.A. "Operational Audit and Library Staffing [in a U.S. Air Force Technical Library]." *Special Libraries* 73 (January 1982): 39–45.

The use of operational audit provides objective, quantitative and verifiable workload information only for work currently being performed. It can be used to improve work flow and identify unnecessary work through use of a task list.

Description of a work center contains a task list of activities performed with definitions for each task. The operational audit itself uses four techniques: good operator, historical performance, technical estimate, and directed requirement.

Through sampling and observation of several workers, time values for each task are determined. Production/statistical records reveal historical performance data. Technical estimates of the auditor, the worker, and the supervisor may be used for tasks not measurable in other ways. Directed requirements cover areas such as staffing of a catalog information desk where not all time expended is production.

A combination of the four techniques should be selected according to local needs. There are suggestions for recording task frequencies and time values.

91. Martin, Murray S. "Financing Library Automation: Selling the Benefits and the Budget." *Bottom Line* Charter Issue (1986): 11–16.

Based on experience at Tufts University, outlines methods used in development of generalized cost statements to determine the feasibility of proposed turnkey automated systems. Key elements to be considered are capital, maintenance, and preparation costs. After the statement is developed it is presented in a cost-benefit package to decision makers in a way which will point to added value of automation represented by time savings, added productivity, better record control, etc.. Strategies for fund raising, rallying internal support, and allocating costs are also examined.

92. Mason, D. "Programmed Budgeting and Cost Effectiveness [with discussion]." *Aslib Proceedings* 25 (March 1973): 100–110.

Promotes Planning-Programming-Budgeting System (PPBS) as a technique for demonstrating cost effectiveness.

PPBS is based on analyzing expenditures in relation to purpose and the results achieved. The objectives of the organization, the activities contributing to achieving the objectives, the resources devoted to the activities and what is being achieved must be determined.

93. Mitchell, Betty Jo; Tanis, Norman E.; and Jaffe, Jack. *Cost Analysis of Library Functions: A Total System Approach.* Greenwich, Conn.: JAI Press, 1978.

Describes the cost accounting system for labor costs, in time and money, at California State University, Northridge. The introduction sets forth the assumptions and guidelines followed.

First, production units are defined in volume equivalents and a conversion factor for some areas is explained. Technical service functions of processing and circulation are in this section. Second are activity, task, and function relationships. Activities are grouped into tasks which are assigned to functions and are then allocated to the appropriate organizational unit(s). Third, organizational units rather than departments are utilized in function allocation.

Data collection involves time spent on the job recorded in quarter hour increments, production statistics, and salary information. Reports generated from the data analysis do not include task cost information. They give costs per task (unit) but no cost benefit analysis.

Time sheets and instructions plus descriptions of tasks; the procedures manual and workload statistical forms are the most useful of the appendices, which comprise over half of the text.

94. Mlynarczyk, Frank, Jr. *Measuring Library Costs: A Paper Presented at the Institute on Program Planning and Budgeting Systems for Libraries, Wayne State University, Detroit, Michigan, Spring 1968.* Detroit, Mich.: Wayne State Univ., Dept. of Library Science, 1968. (ED 045 120)

Describes five steps in the process: break down budget figures by department and by function and get total direct costs; study relationships and reach conclusions about the order of allocation; identify meaningful measures of output of service departments in operation terms, i.e. the allocation basis; allocate costs to each department; and determine unit cost figures.

95. Nachlas, Joel A. and Pierce, Anton R. "Determination of Unit Costs for Library Services." *College & Research Libraries* 40 (March 1979): 240–247.

Explains macrocosting and microcosting techniques of cost analysis. Categories of costs examined are: direct labor, indirect labor, materials and equipment, and overhead.

Flowcharting and work sampling are major tools used to determine labor expended. Work sampling is based on random observations where data are recorded for specific task categories.

Describes microcosting as applied to tracking overdue materials at Virginia Tech. Available data are for percentages of employee time expended on direct labor and on indirect labor activities.

96. Niebel, Benjamin W. *Motion and Time Study*. 4th ed. Irwin Series in Management. Homewood, IL: Richard D. Irwin, Inc., 1967.

Covers numerous aspects of motion and time studies. Chapters of interest are those on the construction and use of operation and flow process charts; time study requirements, equipment and elements; allowances for personal delays, machine interferences, etc.; and work sampling by observation.

97. Plate, Kenneth. *Cost Justification of Information Services*. Studio City, CA: Cibbarelli, 1983.

Intends to provide "approaches and techniques [for justification of] costs of information services." Approaches include examining client needs, use and satisfaction. Both direct, public services, and indirect, technical services, functions are used to determine final costs and benefits.

Examples of six general techniques are included in the chapter on "Comprehensive Cost Benefit."

The chapter on "Indirect Functions" covers three areas of interest to technical services: collection support, circulation, and centralized processing. Provides formulas for costs of collection support: periodical routing and items per use; circulation: total number of items circulated, number of items circulated per department, number of periodicals routed; and document purchasing: verification time and tools, duplicate avoidance, and orders to those who offer discounts.

Lists accounting and cost analysis software packages for CP/M, Apple, TRS (Radio Shack), and IBM microcomputers.

"Cost Data" provides two published sources of comparative data for each area: books, salaries and serials lists.

The bibliography is comprised of over fifty items from the library and information science and business literature.

98. Price, Douglas S. "Rational Cost Information: Necessary and Obtainable." *Special Libraries* 65 (February 1974): 49–57. [summarizes a longer paper: *Collecting and Reporting Real Costs of Information Systems*. Washington, DC: American Society for Information Science, 1971. (ED 055 592)]

Techniques of interviewing, sampling, time studies and unit costs are briefly examined. The system of building-block costing is described. Units must be valid measures of activities, readily countable, verifiable and documented. Costs include overhead and must be detailed and extensive enough for statistical analysis. Costs can be characterized as direct, allocation, and burdens.

99. Price, Douglas S. "Real Costs for Information Managers." In *Cost Reduc-*

*tion for Special Libraries and Information Centers,* edited by Frank Slater, pp. 156–176. New York: American Society for Information Science, 1973.

Presents building-block costing which is based on sub-unit costs. Data collection covers number of units, direct costs (including fringes), internal allocations and transfers (or costs not directly associated with production), and external burdens. Each of these is sub-categorized by general costs (overhead and operation), ad hoc efforts, input activities, output activities, and collateral services. Examples used to illustrate building-block costing are acquisitions and cataloging.

100. Prosser, Carolyn. "Cost Analysis Without Tears: Some Hints for Librarians." *New Library World* 75 (1974): 163–65.

The determination of costs can be achieved by following the steps given in this article: identify the activities of the job; identify the staff involved; determine salary for each person; figure in fringe benefits and overhead and equipment costs; calculate an hourly rate based on work days less holidays and vacation and non-productive time (coffee breaks, etc.); and multiply hourly rate by time spent on each activity. Arriving at appropriate time figures may be done through various techniques; but the author recommends approximation using an inventory of activities.

101. Reilly, Catherine R. "Productivity Measurement for Fiscal Control." *The Bottom Line* 1 (1986): 2–28.

Asserts the need for productivity measurement in libraries. Gives an overview of a study of functions such as cataloging, research inquiry, routing, circulation, orders processed, and subscriptions renewed. Each function is broken down into processes; and each time a process is performed, it is recorded. Staff also record how they spend their time each day, using codes assigned to each activity. Work effort is compared against previously estimated volume, staff, and productivity levels for each task. Productivity standards can be used to justify automation or new equipment.

A method of measuring quality of work is described for information or research requests, orders, credit agency reports, circulation, and routing. Quality measurement criteria include timeliness, completeness, and accuracy. Tracking of service quality is accomplished through recording time spent and by a quarterly questionnaire completed by users.

Sample forms included are a time ladder, reporting forms, standard hours worksheet, and user questionnaire.

102. Rosenberg, Philip. *Cost Finding for Public Libraries: A Manager's Handbook.* Chicago & London: American Library Association, 1985.

Provides an overview of cost concepts, introduces the methodologies used in cost finding, and discusses the rationale for applying cost funding techniques to library expenditures and outputs.

Defines costs as direct—personnel, equipment, materials and supplies; and indirect—support services and operating expenses. Cost information can be collected from the annual budget, financial reports, and expenses based on the relative cost of an item or service as it is used or provided.

Methods utilized are cost accounting and cost finding.

Selecting activities and unit cost measures appropriate for cost finding are crucial. The steps are: identify the cost center; determine activities and tasks within a cost center; select units of measure; capture unit cost information; and analyze the data.

Provides a workbook approach to calculating the full cost of the library activities identified by the library manager. Theses steps include the data collection process; classifying expenditures; coding personnel costs and outputs; and determining and allocating costs of materials, supplies and capital outlays. Sample worksheets are provided within each category.

Use of these data can be in cost comparisons, budget preparation and contracting for services. There is a glossary of terms and appendices which include further discussions, guidelines for costing, and blank worksheet forms.

103. Schwachow, Werner. "The Economic Analysis and Evaluation of Information and Documentation Systems." In *Costing and the Economics of Library and Information Services,* edited by Stephen A. Roberts, pp. 26–31. Aslib Reader Series, vol. 5. London: Aslib, 1984.

Presents the results of a West German study to test standard systems and methods for cost accounting; to establish indices for the cost of individual activities; and to develop approaches to and methods of determining levels of performance, efficiency, and usefulness. Lack of standardized cost accounting methods and difficulties of applying them in libraries are recognized.

General surveys examine the costs and factors involved in information and documentation systems and case studies test detailed procedures for cost accounting.

Criteria for evaluation of performance include amount of services, revenue per unit, speed, currency, completeness, effort, etc. Analysis of efficiency examines the relationship between performance and resources. Systems parameters which affect costs are environmental, institutional, and functional. Analysis and evaluation of the benefits consider individual and social benefits.

104. Smith, G.C.K. and Schofield, J.L. "Administrative Effectiveness: Times and Costs of Library Operations." *Journal of Librarianship* 3 (October 1971): 245–266.

Describes a project to determine necessary management information on operations and staff of the library. Self-recording of less regular or unusual activities by staff is suggested.

Records of productivity, units of work accomplished, as well as work being taken on and work waiting are all important. Data on hours worked and lost by staff is also utilized.

To facilitate interlibrary comparisons, a list of task elements and statistical units for recording work created and completed is developed.

To collect appropriate data, a simple reporting form asks for the gross hours staff are available and not available. Another form asks for details on secondary tasks which do not contribute directly to productivity or output.

Two studies conducted at university libraries (600,000–700,000 volumes) generate personnel and departmental time and task data. Using average salary figures, costs within departments for each task are shown. Related tasks and procedures are costed and combined. The authors conclude that unit costs from one library at one time are not helpful. Comparisons with different time periods or libraries can suggest improvements.

Tables show unit times and costs for book acquisitions, cataloging, catalog revision, and binding.

A brief review of other costing methods in the literature is included.

Proposes a package to be offered to libraries: instructions on flow charting; checklist of tasks; list of units of output, input and service given; form specifications for diaries; general instructions for the study; specifications of tables for analysis and notes on the method.

105. Smith, George L., Jr. *Work Measurement: A Systems Approach*. Grid Series in Industrial Engineering. Columbus, Ohio: Grid Publ., 1978.

Describes the background and issues of work measurement. Summarizes the procedures utilized for five methods: work sampling, multiple regression, time study, standard data, and predetermined times. Each follows the process of stating objectives, establishing activity elements, determining scope, scheduling observations, designing forms, notifying workers, and conducting the study.

Any work measurement process must be based on objectives, environment, selection of the appropriate measurement technique, measurement, introducing results and follow up.

106. Thomas, Pauline A. *Task Analysis of Library Operations*. Aslib Occasional Publication, no. 8. London: Aslib, 1971.

Takes the operational subsystems of acquisitions, processing, use and maintenance and presents procedures and flow charts for each. A model based on initiating, authorizing, activating, recording, reporting and canceling activities is given.

Within acquisitions system the procedures are select, order and receive. For processing there are five activities: accession, catalogue, classify, label and shelve. Maintenance encompasses binding, replacing and withdrawal.

Each procedure is explained with a short narrative and then presented visually in a flowchart. Definitions and forms used are given in appendices.

107. Vinson, Michael. "Cost Finding: A Step-by-Step Guide." *Bottom Line* 2 (no. 3, 1988): 15–19.

Reports on a study conducted at DeGolyer Library to determine the actual costs involved in ordering a book in order to better assess possible adoption of a vendor approval plan. Major steps were identifying cost centers and their activities, tasks, and cost units; compiling a daily log summary for each activity; calculating employee cost per productive hour; summarizing the output; preparing a materials and use report; figuring the depreciation of major equipment; computing the direct costs; combining the figures for each activity; and concluding the cost analysis.

108. Waldhart, Thomas J. and Marcus, Thomas P. "Productivity Measurement in Academic Libraries." In *Advances in Librarianship* 6 (1976): 53–78.

Begins with a general discussion of growth and productivity. The

measurement of productivity can be achieved by examining labor expended in relation to products or services yielded and capital investment in
relation to overall production yield. Another approach is to use weighted
values for input—labor, capital and/or materials—to determine *total*
productivity. There is a formula provided for the latter.

Libraries must decide the level at which productivity measurement is
to be accomplished, (system versus institutional), and the type of measurement to be used (partial versus total). Input and output must be identified
and expressed as common units and any weighting determined. The
authors go through the steps using a hypothetical cataloging system.

109. Wessel, Carl J., et al. *Criteria for Evaluating the Effectiveness of Library
Operations and Services. Phase 2: Data Gathering and Evaluation* [and]
*Phase 3: Recommended Criteria and Methods for Their Utilization.* ATLIS
reports no. 19 & 21. Washington, DC: J.I. Thomas & Co., 1968–1969.

Documents the application of evaluation tools and techniques in technical libraries. Activities and costs in technical services and other areas
are subjected to cost-effectiveness analysis as well as group attainment
program and PPBS (planning-programming-budgeting system) for developing criteria.

Assesses and recommends criteria and methods for evaluating the
effectiveness and efficiency of library operations and services. The techniques presented are: SCORE analysis (measures the effectiveness of a
service and the associated change in effectiveness due to a change in
operations or costs); SCOUT analysis (determines the optimum balance
between operations which yield maximum effectiveness within budget
constraints); CORE analysis (derives unit cost standards for given operations which produce a given quality of output); and GAME analysis
(eliminates unnecessary work or excessive delays, arranges work in the
best order, standardizes usage of proper work methods, and develops time
standards to accomplish essential events).

110. Wilkin, A.P.; Reynolds, Rose and Robertson, Stephen E. "Standard Times
for Information Systems: A Method for Data Collection and Analysis."
*Journal of Documentation* 28 (June 1972): 131–150.

Describes how to conduct both the systems analysis and data collection
(via a diary) phases. Accessions lists and abstracts bulletins are used as
examples. Analysis of the data using multiple regression is explained.
Includes forms and formulas.

MULTIPLE

111. Anstine, Frances A.; Davis, Elisabeth B.; Hulsizer, Bernice; and Williams,
Mitusko. "Use of Random Alarm Mechanisms for Analyzing Professional
and Support Staff Activities in Science Libraries: Part II: Data Analysis
and Discussion." *Library Research* 4 (1982): 147–161.

Provides the summary data and analysis resulting from the study
described by Beecher. The libraries studied are grouped together to

analyze the effect of constraints of budget size, staff size (full-time equivalents or FTE) and collection size on the library staff's activities.

The relationship of staff activities to computer literature searching, budget and the automated circulation system are examined in terms of the library's total time in the activities and by the individual's time in them. No inverse relationship holds between computer search activities and other reference activities. An inverse relationship does appear for those librarians without assistants.

No relationship is seen between the size of the acquisition budget and the total percentage of time spent in acquisition activities such as selection, ordering, and de-acquisition.

A slight relationship can be made between increases in circulation statistics and percentage of time spent in automated circulation activities.

There is a tendency for librarians in larger-staffed libraries to spend more time in research activities than do librarians in smaller-staffed libraries.

There appears to be no apparent relationship between the number of FTE and the percentage of time spent in public technical services activities by professional and nonacademic staff. It is found that departmental staff are spending up to one-third of their time in technical services activities although all technical services functions are centralized in the main library.

The highest areas of activities for professional staff focus on eight categories: acquisitions, administration, committees, computer literature searching, personal, professional, and research and publishing.

Support staff spends more of their time in circulation activities than in any other area. Other top categories include administration, cataloging, acquisition, other automated system, shelving, serial check-in, and personal.

112. Arcari, Ralph D. "A Cost-Sharing Formula for Online Circulation and a Union Catalog through a Regional, Multi-type Library Cooperative." *Bulletin of the Medical Library Association* 75 (July, 1987): 245–247.

Describes the development of a cost-sharing formula for an online circulation and union catalog system shared by 29 libraries of Capitol Region Library Council in Connecticut. Each library was assessed a basic unit cost, and remaining costs were allocated according to additional ports and terminals, and to circulation volume.

113. Aro, Barbara. *Cost Analysis Study*. Denver, Colorado: University of Denver Library, Technical Services Division, 1965.

Determines the average cost, exclusive of purchase price, of placing a non-fiction title in the library ready for circulation. The major operations are acquisition, cataloging, and mechanical preparation. The costs of depreciation, plant and equipment improvements, and utilities are not included.

Procedures and definition of work activities are given for acquisition (selecting, ordering, and accounting), out-of-print materials, gifts, cataloging (description, classification, and subject headings), and mechanical procedures (marking, binding, mending, and supplies). In each area work activities are identified as being performed by professional or support staff.

Data are collected using daily record forms, for each task performed by each staff member, and monthly reports showing the work activities of one day for each participant.

Appendices include the guidelines for supervisors, guide for participants, instructions, sample data collection forms, and classification and descriptions of technical services activities.

Results are reported as time (in minutes and seconds) spent on each activity and costs (in cents and hundredths of cents).

114. Association of New York Libraries for Technical Services. *ANYLTS Cost Projections and Suggested Phase-In Schedules: A Report to the Board of Trustees*. [Rochester, NY: The Association], 1969. (ED 039 007)

Presents data on the costs of operating a processing center or centers. Divides operating costs into fixed (overhead, rental and some salary) and variable (labor and supply) costs. Projects unit costs in relation to volume of activities.

The center(s) will handle entry and receipt of orders as well as cataloging, card production, physical processing of materials and maintenance of a union list. Cost figures for all of the above areas are presented in tabular form.

115. Association of Research Libraries. Systems and Procedures Exchange Center. *Technical Services Cost Studies in ARL Libraries*. SPEC Kit 125. Washington, DC: ARL, 1986.

The questionnaire for the study, "Technical Services Costs Survey (Three-Year Update) February 3, 1986," and the summary data from seventy-six respondents are presented.

The four procedures consist of a survey form (including guide and definitions) used by Canadian libraries; an outline of the methodology used, summary of unit cost data, cataloging workflow description and flowchart, and card catalog maintenance cost study; an overview of a planned technical services review; and the results of a technical services study.

Reports from four libraries cover technical services processing costs, manual versus automated costs for technical services, costs associated with production and maintenance of a card catalog, and detailed costs of an in-house retrospective conversion project utilizing OCLC.

116. Association of Research Libraries. Systems and Procedures Exchange Center. *Technical Services Cost Studies in ARL Libraries*. SPEC Kit 89. Washington, DC: ARL, 1982.

A collection of seven cost studies representing both top-down and bottom-up approaches.

Top-down studies assign categories of known expenditure to categories of known product over a period of time. Bottom-up studies rely on analysis of specific functions.

Areas covered in the reports are cataloging, binding, and processing; cataloging and receipt of serials; acquisition, cataloging, and binding; catalog work assignments and staffing; receipt of serials; and acquisitions.

Also included are the summary data of the ARL Technical Services Cost Studies Survey (1982) which reveal that 24 libraries had conducted cost studies in the last three years.

117. Axford, H. William. "An Approach to Performance Budgeting at the Florida Atlantic University Library." *College & Research Libraries* 32 (March 1971): 87–104.

Elements used to lower costs in technical services operations are described. Catalog preparation costs are reduced by color highlighting of data on catalog cards, extensive use of guide cards in the catalog, and not transfering LC class numbers to the upper left corner of cards. Acquisitions functions are computerized for fiscal control of the book budget and for status reports on orders, funds and approval plan materials.

Efficiency and effectiveness of these systems are tested using a cost study. Each position is analyzed to determine functions performed. A diary study reveals the times expended for functions performed. These two elements yield a cost per volume. Each function is analyzed to ascertain total time and percent of salaries consumed. This also reveals how many staff are involved in each function and leads to some reassignments.

Descriptions of using the Clapp-Jordan and University of Washington formulas to examine staff positions are included but not relevant to technical services costs.

Includes data analysis results.

118. Axford, H. William. "Performance Measurement Revisited." *College & Research Libraries* 34 (September 1973): 249–257.

Describes the usefulness of performance measurement in technical services. The method developed at Florida Atlantic University is to have each department define its functions, establish its own productivity goals and measure achievements in terms of goals. Establishing a base year for comparative purposes is necessary. Also important is determining the volume to title ratio.

Application of the methodology at Arizona State University causes procedural and system changes to have a positive affect on productivity. Minor changes include not penciling the call number or underlining the first letter of the main entry on the title page of the book. Major changes instituted are: (1) not establishing the main entry before ordering an item, (2) dividing the catalog into three parts—author, title and subject, (3) color highlighting and using guide cards for added entries, (4) leaving the call number in the lower left corner of the card and (5) using the title catalog as the "on order" file. Savings amount to a 45 to 50 percent decrease in time expended. This enables the catalog department to do more complex cataloging and to eliminate a large backlog.

Unit cost study programs have a tolerable margin of error and, when properly used, can enhance staff development and staff self-esteem.

119. Bayunus, Owain. *A Cost Analysis of the Automated Systems Control Group, the Acquisition Department and the Catalog Department of the Central Technical Services.* Ithaca, N.Y.: Cornell University Libraries, 1975. (ED 102 996)

Describes a time and cost study and a work sampling study. Methods of taking observations for both studies are given.

Acquisition includes receipt of orders, bibliographic searching and receipt of books. Cataloging encompasses copy and original cataloging using OCLC.

Makes recommendations within the three departments in areas such as combining all bibliographic searching.

Appendices include results of the studies, comparison of results, and floor plan.

120. Benson, Nancy Dollahite. *A Study of Acquisitions and processing Costs in a Small Public Library.* Denver, Colorado: University of Denver, General Services Librarianship, 1978. (ED 165 723)

Analyzes current procedures for acquisition and processing. Speed, cost and quality are compared with a centralized system, the Washington Library Network (WLN). Overhead and administration are omitted because they are the same for local or centralized processing. Examines costs of manual acquisition and processing.

Reviews the literature of bibliographic automation, scientific management in libraries, and networks and centralized processing.

The study itself begins with flowcharting of acquisition and processing. Eleven steps are identified as being affected by adoption of network processing. Data for time and costs are obtained from work studies.

Current acquisition and processing tasks are listed. Number and length of interruptions to those tasks are recorded and the effect of interruptions on cataloging efficiency are calculated in terms of time and cost. Data for acquisition and processing tasks are reported on a work distribution sheet listing each task and amount of time spent on each by various staff.

Summary costs to acquire and process a book are given. Percentages are calculated for books received with CIP data, CIP and cards from a vendor, cards from a vendor, and no cataloging data from either CIP or the vendor.

Time elapsed from receipt of book until it is ready for circulation is also recorded and analyzed. Time and cost comparisons of in-house processing network processing are made.

The appendices provide flow charts for ordering and processing, sample forms for the work study, and information from WLN.

121. Bierman, Kenneth J. *Overview of the Cost of Acquiring, Cataloging, and Processing Materials at the Tucson, Public Library.* Tucson, Ariz.: Tucson Public Library, 1980. (ED 194 092)

Takes costs from the acquisitions, cataloging and processing studies to get total average cost per copy including staff and cost per copy for staff.

Examples are for single copies of new titles with cataloging copy available and those needing original cataloging, multiple copies, added copies and media.

Appendixes include the organizational chart showing staff numbers, levels and functions for technical services; major activities or tasks performed in the acquisitions, cataloging and processing units; and a description of the use of automated systems in the three functional areas.

122. Bierman, Kenneth J. *Unit Time/Cost Study of the Processing Unit, Technical Services Division, Tucson, Public Library*. Revised ed. Tucson, Ariz.: Tucson Public Library, 1980. (ED 194 092)

Daily log sheets are used to record time spent and quantities of materials handled. Salary figures reflect direct personnel costs, plus thirty percent in fringe benefits, and adjusted salaries include overhead costs. Statistics are recorded on a per item rather than per title basis.

Details the procedures for processing materials. Summarizes unit times and costs, personnel costs, and cost by type of material. Does not include a sample of the data collection form used.

123. Bills, Linda B. "Cost and Benefits of OCLC Use in Small and Medium Size Public Libraries." *Resource Sharing and Information Networks* 3 (Spring/Summer, 1986): 9–34.

Describes an experimental project in OCLC use conducted by the Illinois Valley Library System from 1980 through 1982. The costs of OCLC are explored in terms of absolute costs (which for cataloging were average increases of $1.95 to $2.06 per item), justification of these costs to governing boards and communities, and the intangible aspects of automation. Various factors influencing the decision to keep or drop OCLC at the end of the project are listed. Conclusions reached from the survey include the finding that increased quality of cataloging through OCLC was more appreciated than improved efficiency. The most important benefit of OCLC, however, was viewed as the increased resource sharing and ILL activity it made possible, prompting a large number of libraries to retain OCLC at the project's completion.

124. Boice, Eugene T.; Noble, Richard G.; and Smith, Faye. *The Medical Library Center of New York: A Cost Study*. METRO Miscellaneous Publication no. 6. New York: New York Metropolitan Reference and Research Agency, 1970. (ED 043 357)

Provides flow charts of technical services operations: current serials check-in and claiming, gift serials, transfer serials, monograph processing and dissertations. These are followed by cost estimates and cost calculations per transaction.

Cost estimates include an administrative cost ($2.059) and building cost ($.207) per technical services employee plus personnel overhead costs ($3.028). Methods for arriving at these figures are given.

Technical services per transaction costs are calculated by multiplying time expended by hourly wage. How the time expended is arrived at is not explained.

125. Bolef, Doris. "Cost Considerations in Automating the Library." *Bulletin of the Medical Library Association* 75 (April, 1987): 109–113.

Investigates many of the cost elements in an automated system: hardware, maintenance contracts, software, telecommunication, circulation, retrospective conversion, implementation, training and personnel, consultants, furniture, supplies, security, lighting, public relations, and miscellaneous and unexpected expenses. Costs are derived from estimates for a Midwestern medical school library in 1985/1986.

126. Bourne, Charles P. *Summary Cost Data from 300 Reports of Library Technical Processing Activities.* Berkeley, Calif.: University of California, Institute of Library Research, 1977. (ED 140 871)

Summarizes cost studies reported in over 300 publications up through the early 1970's. The 12 broad areas include total processing, selection and acquisitions, cataloging, card set production, card sorting and filing, physical processing, recataloging, circulation, interlibrary loan, serials conversion and maintenance, catalog file conversion, and abstracting and indexing.

Results are presented in 62 graphs with costs and date of data forming the X and Y axes. In most cases there is a legend for public, academic and other libraries. A useful addition would be a bibliography of the reports from which these summary data are taken.

127. Brinker, Eugene B. "Non-OCLC Processing Costs: St. Norbert College Library Reports a Study." *Wisconsin Library Bulletin* 75 (July/August 1980): 155–156

Examines the ordering, receiving and cataloging processes. Developed a form (not included) listing 14 operations and 41 steps with space for recording time started and ended, number of items and other comments.

Multiplies the time required and the hourly rate of workers to yield a per volume labor cost of $3.20. Materials costs for the *NUC*, a cassette power typewriter, typewriter and labeling unit, cards, detection strips, labeling tape and date due slips are $.93 per volume. The total cost per volume is $4.15.

Includes a chart showing the 14 operations and times expended for a 100 book sample.

128. Brown, Maryann Kevin and McHugh, Anita L. *Survey of Costs in Technical Processing and Interlibrary Loan: Summary.* Boulder, Colo.: Western Interstate Commission for Higher Education, Western Interstate Library Coordinating Center, 1976. (ED 148 358)

Summarizes the results of cost data collected in 76 public, academic, and state libraries. Details the methodology used including sample selection and survey data collection.

Acquisition cataloging and serials throughput and budgeting data include expenditures, staffing patterns, and function patterns.

Appendices give glossary to terms and activity sheets and task definitions. Related documents are the *Data Processing Users Manual* (ED 148 357) and *Survey Tables & Results of Case Studies* (ED 148 359).

129. Burgis, Grover C. and Buchinski, Edwin J. "MARC at the University of Saskatchewan, Saskatoon." In C.A.C.U.L. Workshop on Library Automation: 4th: 1970: Hamilton, Ont. *Automation in Libraries,* pp. 69–119. Ottawa: Canadian Library Association, 1970.

Describes the use of the LC MARC tapes for producing catalog cards and an in process file for acquisitions.

The section on costs includes figures for development and maintenance of computer programs, computer time, and leasing of a print train. Costs are less than that previously spent on purchasing LC printed cards.

Also discusses costs of updating the format and suggests ways to reduce costs via sharing a database and reducing the size of local storage of MARC data.

130. Campbell, Brian. "Whither the White Knight: CD ROM in Technical Services." *Database* 22 (August, 1987): 22–40.

Evaluates the latest "white knight" technology (CD ROM) in technical services applications: the provision of bibliographic records for cataloging, source records for cataloging, and public access catalogs. Investigates factors affecting price such as public domain vs. proprietary databases, frequency, bundled or unbundled. Interfaces, maintenance, retrieval software, and contractual protection are discussed as well. The article summarizes major features, specifications, and prices of CD ROM products which provide technical services functions.

131. Cart, Michael. "Caveats, Qualms, and Quibbles: A Revisionist View of Library Automation." *Library Journal* 112 (February 1, 1987): 38–41.

Contends that costs of automating libraries have been excessive, pointing to turnkey vendor gross profits in 1985 of $88,587,000. Interprets headlong rush to automate as evidence of librarians' lack of confidence in their professional selves and in the enduring importance of libraries.

132. Cohen, Jacob. "Cost Benefit Model of Library Operations." in Allen Kent, et al. *Use of Library Materials: The University of Pittsburgh Study,* pp. 161–187. New York: M. Dekker, 1979. [also available as *A Cost-Benefit Model of Some Critical Library Operations in Terms of Use of Materials* from NTIS, 1978.]

An expansion of his "Book Cost and Book Use: The Economics of a University Library." Adds new sections on *The Economics of Increased Book Use* and *Measuring Cost-Benefit Over Time.* The former refers back to his discussion on economics in the earlier chapter and looks at books as an investment. The latter traces the decay rate in book use with acquisitions age. That is, the book transactions in a given year are related to acquisitions of the same or previous years. Patterns of use are shown to increase in the second year after acquisition, then to decrease steadily for three to five years and finally slow down.

133. Cohen, Jacob. "Economics of Materials' Use." in Allen Kent, et al. *Use of Library Materials: The University of Pittsburgh Study,* pp.195–159. New York: M. Dekker, 1979.

Variable costs cover acquisitions and circulation and depend on use. Fixed costs include administration, maintenance and depreciation of other costs and are independent of use of materials.

Data on acquisition costs as either fixed or variable costs are included. Examines the total cost per item circulated and per transaction. Those costs, respectively, range from $16.02–71.48 and $28.56–128.20 over a five year period. Journals in six branches are analyzed for subscription cost per use.

A library decision model for book purchase is presented by Chen and James R. Kern. They use LC classes in relation to cost per item and cost per transaction. Risks inherent in using the model are described. This is followed by substituting cost centers (specific subject areas, such as Latin America) in place of the LC class in the model and analyzing those results. Appendices give variable, fixed, and excluded cost data for the study.

134. Cox, Nigel S.M. "On the Introduction of Machine-Processable Centralized Cataloguing Services to Libraries." In *Interface: Library Automation with Special Reference to Computing Activity*, edited by C.K. Balmforth and N.S.M. Cox, pp. 146–178. Cambridge, Mass.: MIT Press; [Newcastle-Upon-Tyne]: Oriel Press, 1971.

Includes cost estimates in pounds, rather than dollars, for data entry and printing a catalog. Also addresses the percentage of BNB MARC records with errors.

Formulas are given for costs of recataloging, physical handling, withdrawing and storing materials.

Promotes a central retrospective bibliographic file as cost benefiting libraries.

135. Dougherty, Richard M. and Maier, J.M. *Centralized Processing for Academic Libraries: The Final Report (phase III, January 1–June 30, 1969) of the Colorado Academic Libraries Book Processing Center: The First Six Months of Operation*. Metuchen, N.J.: Scarecrow, 1971.

Unit costs are determined for books with copy available and with original cataloging. The analysis indicates that the cost of acquiring and cataloging is reduced from $3.10 to $2.63 per volume.

The section on cost analysis (p. 34–69) explains how labor costs of acquisitions and processing are calculated. Labor charts are used to record the standard time, frequency, level, wage, and to determine the overall cost of each activity.

Formulas for standard times, unit overhead costs, transportation costs and total unit processing times are given.

136. Getz, Malcolm and Phelps, Doug, "Labor Costs in the Technical Operation of Three Research Libraries." *Journal of Academic Librarianship* 10 (September 1984): 209–219.

A look at three libraries, each with some automation. Costs are gathered in six areas: acquisitions, cataloging, end processing, binding of monographs, binding of serials, and serials.

Labor costs are given for librarians (omitting managerial time), support staff and student workers to get an average wage. Comparisons show that labor costs per volume vary among the three libraries by more than fifty (50) percent. This can be partially attributed to wage differences. quality of labor, and organizational structure.

137. Havlik, Robert J. "Program Analysis and Planning for a Project to Complete Current Library Backlogs in a Five Year Period Utilizing the INCOLSA/OCLC Cataloging System," pp. 45–66. In Association of Research Libraries. Systems and Procedures Exchange Center. *Cost Studies and Fiscal Planning in Research Libraries*. SPEC Kit 52. Washington, D.C.: ARL, 1979.

Identifies acquisition and cataloging backlogs in six specific areas which include serials and media. Cost projections for each area are based on the steps involved.

Labor and material costs per unit for acquisition and cataloging using automation are presented. Unit costs are given for each step in these areas of activity: pre-order/order, acquisition/receiving, cataloging, card production, book preparation, and catalog edit. The methodology used in determining costs is not explained although all activities or steps needed for each of the six areas are listed.

138. Hayes, Robert M. and Becker, Joseph. *Handbook of Data Processing for Libraries.* New York: Wiley, 1970 or (2nd ed.) 1974.

General discussion covering purpose, principles and issues of cost accounting in libraries. Covers a variety of ways to analyze a system. Includes formulas, charts and interview questions.

Specific chapters focus on the formulas and forms to use in arriving at costs of catalog production, circulation, ordering, administration, and serials.

139. Horney, Karen L. "Fifteen Years of Automation: Evolution of Technical Services Staffing." *Library Resources and Technical Services* 31 (January/March, 1987): 69–76.

Examines the question of whether automating saves money in technical services through reductions in staffing. Findings indicate that, at Northwestern University Library, staffing reallocations linked to automation in the period between 1970 and 1985 allowed a reduction of 2.5 librarian and 5.5 support staff positions, resulting in savings of $86,393 per year. Other results were improvement in the quality of work plus quicker and more comprehensive access to bibliographic information as well as to the materials themselves.

140. Kantor, Paul B. *Remarks on the Economics of Academic Libraries.* Research Report: Tantalus/PR-85/02. Cleveland Heights, Ohio: Tantalus, Inc., 1985.

Summarizes the findings of three studies of library econometrics, unit costs, and technical costs. The unit cost study focus is circulation ($3.72 per loan), in-house reading ($7.70 per hour) and reference service ($11.93 per query). Also costed are data on interlibrary loans ($13 per loan).

The econometric study attempts to model the total operating budget of a library based on three principal services performed. Results suggest that unit costs increase by 4.2% with each doubling in library size.

The study on technical costs examine the transformation of money into monographs. Average copy cataloging acquisition costs $15.34 per item and takes 38.3 days. Original cataloging acquisition averages $33.01 and takes 85.3 working days. Hidden and direct costs of consortium membership are discussed as are general benefits.

141. Knoblauch, Mark. "Budgeting for Technical Services in the Public Library: Some Considerations." *Illinois Libraries* 69 (February,1987): 104–106.

Discusses complexities of cost accounting as they relate to public library technical services' operations. Treats cost considerations of foreign language materials, specialized materials, non-print materials, capital budgeting, editing of original cataloging, processing, binding, and personnel. Examines advantages of program planning budget system.

142. Kantor, Paul B. *Three studies of Costs and Services at Academic Libraries.* Research Report: Tantalus/PR-85/1. Cleveland, Ohio: Tantalus, Inc., 1985.

Introduces the studies through a discussion of three approaches to library economics: econometric studies comparing cost and service statistics, functional or unit cost analysis and detailed cost analysis of specific processes.

Technical processes are selecting a book, ordering it, and providing access to it. Data collection analysis yields average cost data on ten tasks: book selection ($1.43), searching ($1.77), ordering ($1.70), receiving ($0.16), accounting ($1.76), holding (no figure given), copy cataloging ($6.94), original cataloging ($22.46), marking ($0.62), and card handling ($0.18). A sample data collection form is provided.

The second study uses a technique for determining unit cost which is outlined in seven steps (p. 19). Results allocate average costs of services for four activities: in-house use (50% at $7.70 per hour), circulation (27% at $3.72 per loan), reference (30% at $11.93 per query), and interlibrary loan (3% at $13.00 per loan).

An average budget formula for use by academic libraries is reported in the third study. The model centers around a presumed relationship between costs and services (in-house use, circulations, and reference queries). Kantor asserts that library budgets are not in accord with accurate cost functions. Budgets are not based on levels of service given, efficient procedures, or service loads that are commensurate with capacity. Use of collection size as the basis for library budgets may not be suitable as the nature of services offered changes. Budgets linked to levels of service delivered are based on service incentives.

The methodology, forms used, raw data collected, and participants list comprise the last half of the report.

143. Leimkuhler, Ferdinand F. and Cooper, Michael D. *Analytical Planning for University Libraries.* Berkeley: Office of the Vice President—Planning, University of California, 1970.

Focuses on the problems of measuring library costs and how such costs might be reduced by the choice of an operating policy. The methodology is a cost-benefit ratio based on decision rules for minimizing average cost per unit of service.

Reviews library storage models found in the literature. Looks at the exponential growth obsolescence in library materials and their effect on acquisition, storage and circulation. Suggests that policies for limiting the retention time of an item should be based on a consideration of both the costs and the benefits incurred or avoided by the policy.

Mathematical models for storing both single and many items are given. Leimkuhler provides formulas for determining cost of providing users of an item, minimizing the average costs of usage, exponential obsolescence and circulation, cost when all items are held for a limited time, storage of older items, acquisition delays and item usage, and circulation interference and usage.

Finally the author presents a generalized model of library costs and benefits. This model is based on options of scale of an activity and those related to how the activity is performed. The general model ties together the scale variables and technology variables with acquisition, storage, and usage functions.

144. Leimkuhler, Ferdinand F.; Cooper, Michael D. "Cost Accounting and Analysis for University Libraries." *College & Research Libraries* 32 (November 1971): 449–464. [the full report is available as *Cost Accounting and Analysis for University Libraries*. Berkeley: Univ. of California, 1970. (ED 040 728)]

Processing centers and service centers are the two types of cost centers found in libraries. The flow of costs through libraries can be based on standard costs as a measure of performance. Standard costs are determined by number of items processed, acquired or held.

A cost model is applied to the University of California, Berkeley library using materials, processing labor, facilities, and service labor as starting points. Direct costs for materials and labor and indirect costs for space and overhead are presented. Unit costs combine purchase price, selection costs, acquisitions labor and space, cataloging labor and space, serials check-in labor and space, and miscellaneous costs to arrive at total cost per monograph and serial in branches and in the main library. Circulation, holding and acquisitions costs are compared for each branch library. Cost per item held, circulated or acquired and staff and space is plotted to show differences among the branches.

145. Leonard, Lawrence E.; Maier, Joan M.; Dougherty, Richard M. *Centralized Book Processing, a Feasibility Study Based on Colorado Academic Libraries*. Metuchen, N.J.: Scarecrow Press, 1969. [summarized in "The Colorado Academic Library Book Processing Center Study," edited by Richard M. Dougherty. *Library Resources & Technical Services* 13 (1969): 115–141.]

Reports on a study to determine whether a centralized processing operation can perform more effectively and economically than each library processing its own material. Data are gathered on ordering patterns, title duplication, cataloging modification, processing time lags, processing time, unit processing costs, and business office procedures and costs.

Flow process charting, diary studies, time observations and standardized lists of technical processing activities are used in the data collection phase.

Data are analyzed to identify operating requirements for the proposed processing center and to design a prototype system. Decision flow charts, work flow diagrams and flow process charts are developed. Organizational patterns and space requirements are recommended and unit processing charges determined.

A study of approval plans and centralized processing is also conducted. Faculty at each of the institutions are surveyed to determine their attitudes toward library resources and services, to assess the impact of services introduced as part of a proposed bibliographic network, and to gain insight as to the level of faculty awareness of library services. Areas covered by the survey are adequacy of library book collections, the card catalog, rush requests, interlibrary loan, inter-institutional courier, services offered (photocopying, SDI, demand bibliographies), and possible library services.

Concludes that a centralized book processing center would offer these benefits: cost savings in acquiring and processing materials, reduce acquisition/cataloging time lags, enable better utilization of librarians, be cost effective and provide automation.

Appendices include sample work diary and time observation forms, list and description of standardized technical processing activities, frequency percentage formulas for activities performed, standard time summaries, unit cost calculations for personnel in each library, overall standard times for each library, the attitude questionnaire and phone interview checklist, and tabular data on faculty responses.

146. Marsterson, W.A.J. "Work Study in a Polytechnic Library." *Aslib Proceedings* 28 (September 1976): 288–304.

Describes a study conducted at Newcastle-Upon-Tyne Polytechnic Library to show the proportion of time spent on various activities by different levels of staff and to give unit times for operations.

Staff are interviewed for descriptions of library operations and identification of tasks and task elements . Work diaries are used to record time spent on tasks. Movement from one part of the library to another is also recorded. These time data are analyzed by staff level and by library site. Available working time and primary task time are calculated. Technical service departments involved in the study are acquisition, overall technical services, and cataloging.

Results are used to estimate the number and levels of staff needed in each department.

147. Mason, Ellsworth. "Automation, or Russian Roulette?" In Clinic on Library Application of Data Processing, 1972, University of Illinois. *Proceedings: Application of On-Line Computers to Library Problems,* edited by F. Wilfrid Lancaster, pp. 138–156. Champlain-Urbana: University of illinois, Graduate School of Library Science, 1972.

Points out the lack of cost available for operational automated systems. Discusses problems related to costs of automating library functions which include a "lack of easily available information on costs of competitive manual or manual-machine methods."

Most cost figures included are incomplete. For automated circulation and acquisitions they do not include salaries, data collection or preparation, and steps in the operations. One good cost analysis for the production of a COM catalog is given.

Mason concludes that whether computers do libraries any good will depend on their being treated like all other components in determining valid operation costs.

148. Montague, Eleanor. *Summary of a Feasibility Study on the Participation*

*of Four Colleges and Universities in a Stanford University Automation Project.* Stanford, California: Stanford University, 1971.

The cost analysis undertaken by five libraries is examined. The methodology uses existing statistics for all calculations.

Manual costs are determined for 13 major library technical services functions which consist of various activities. Personnel times are assigned to each activity and costs are calculated according to level of staff, annual productive working hours, and salaries. Equipment and supply costs are allocated for the functions. Function worksheets and function summary forms are designed for collection of times and calculation of costs for each activity and function. Flow charts are prepared for each function.

The functions are then flow charted for the automated environment. The volume of transactions is established and online activities are assigned standard times per unit. Then online and batch processing costs are calculated. Equipment and computing overhead costs for the automated system are determined. Costs of each function affected by automation are re-calculated and compared to the manual costs. Some activities are not affected by automation.

The appendices contain examples of the data collection forms for manual functions and online/batch transactions.

149. Mount, Ellis and Fasana, Paul. "An Approach to the Measurement and Use and Cost of a Large Academic Research Library System: A Report of a Study done at Columbia University Libraries." *College & Research Libraries* 33 (May 1972): 199–211

An overview of the process of measuring and evaluating users, services and materials for research and instruction. Categories for data gathering include (1) salaries and wages, (2) space, (3) supplies and equipment, (4) bibliographic materials and (5) user services. The first three categories are applicable to technical services costs.

Unit costs for activities within the Catalog Department are calculated. These figures, when compared to earlier studies, reveal an increase of six percent per year. Space allocations for library staff were established. Expendable supplies, furnishings, etc. are inventoried and reviewed then allocated using data from the salary survey.

Details of the user and materials and procedures and data are provided in the appendices. Data from the three areas directly relating to technical services are not provided.

150. Murphy, Marcy and Johns, Claude J., Jr. "Financial Data for Future Planning at the U.S. Air Force Academic Library." *Special Libraries* 65 (January 1974): 4–11.

Administrative and technical services (acquisitions, cataloging and serials) functions are surveyed over ten days using work diaries. These are supplemented by operational audits for tasks performed at other times during the year.

A job profile for each employee is generated. This lists each task performed, amount and percent of time, frequency, salary and cost per occurrence. Tasks are ranked according to cost per occurrence. Standardized activities, tasks and forms from the Leonard, Maier and Dougherty study are used (*Centralized Book Processing,* 1969).

151. Nash, Mary and Hession, Sandra. "Justifying an Automated Library System—A Case Study." In American Society for Information Science. Conference. Anaheim, California, 1980. *Communicating Information.* Proceedings, v. 17. White Plains, NY: Knowledge Industry Publications for ASIS, 1980.

This study determines that automation of acquisition, cataloging and circulation functions can save money.

Historical data for the three areas are examined to project work loads for the next five years. Labor costs are calculated and time savings for each area are predicted. The latter figures are based on a benchmark study done in 1979.

Staff needs are predicted to decrease 19% in acquisition and, 32% in cataloging with the introduction of automation. The largest reductions in circulation will come about through avoiding replacing lost books if overdue items are recalled using automation.

Additional benefits of automation include increased budget and accounting information; tracking acquisition trends; and reducing or eliminating error-prone, labor intensive and duplicate activities.

152. Price, Douglas S. *Collecting and Reporting Real Costs of Information Systems.* Washington, D.C.: American Society for Information Science, Special Interest Group on Costs, Budgeting and Economics, 1971. (ED 055 592)

Explains the philosophy, development and practice of a building-block system of unit costing. Elements for costing include the project, product (activity), accounts or classes such as direct labor and materials and indirect costs, and organization.

Design of a cost system is based on the general accounting system; detailed data from the operational level; collection, analysis and reporting of unit costs; and knowing the system.

Tools used in developing the unit cost system are materials balance charts and tables of input and output; process flow charts; standardized report forms or formats; functional analysis; production counts (of what, where, how and when); non-production costs such as system development and burdens; allocations of costs; and coding cost elements.

Implementation of a cost collection and reporting system is outlined in terms of human limitations, error detection and control, staff education and assistance, and staff orientation. Limitations of using the data collected for forecasting are addressed as are the fringe benefits.

Appendices are extensive and provide definitions, codes, functions, flow charts, formats, numbering schemes, production reports, validity lists, input forms, and cost and volume projections.

153. Raffel, Jeffrey A. [and] Shishko, Robert. *Systematic Analysis of University Libraries: An Application of Cost-Benefit Analysis to the M.I.T. Libraries.* Cambridge, Mass.: M.I.T. Press, 1969.

This case study begins with the mission statements of the M.I.T.

Libraries. The allocation of the budget in relation to those missions then allows the examination of benefits in relation to costs.

Major areas of analysis are collection storage; study space and reserve materials; and cataloging, ordering and interloan.

The chapter on "Storing the Collection" provides a model for determining book storage costs based on three variables: location of the storage facility, type of storage, and degree of user access. Maintenance and perhaps building costs can also be determined. A table summarizes the cost per volume of ten different storage alternatives. Costs of alternative storage systems, including remote storage and microfilms, are compared with weeding costs.

Ordering and cataloging processes are examined along with messenger service, interloans, use of other collections, and collection development (based in part on cooperative acquisitions) in the chapter on "Fulfilling Research Requirements." Alternative cataloging schemes, including limited and temporary cataloging, are costed. Also mentioned is the possible use of the LC MARC tapes. Costs of acquiring journals on microfilm, messenger service, transportation to other collections and union catalogs are briefly mentioned. Plans for improving selection and acquisitions based on number of potential uses per item are discussed.

"Benefit Evaluation" presents the goals and problems of measurement. Survey research methodologies used are described and results given. Conclusions are drawn and future research questions presented.

Appendices include a "Personnel Time Survey" of functions and data from the areas studied.

154. Revill, D.H. "Unit Times in Study of Academic Library Operations." *Aslib Proceedings* 29 (October 1977): 363–80.

A report of studies done in the Liverpool Polytechnic Library Service to determine activities performed, unit times and costs. The 1972 study uses work sheets for recording descriptions of tasks, procedures used, time spent and quantities involved. The 1974 study uses coded tasks which are discontinued and the 1975 study analyzes the proportions of each task which is performed by professional staff.

Weaknesses of the studies which are discussed include lack of availability of unit times, general areas, and the use of "average" times.

Nonproductive time is 23.5 percent. This includes "relaxation allowances" for fatigue as well as physiological, psychological and environmental factors.

Of particular interest are the tables comparing the results of the Liverpool studies to five other British studies.

155. Richmond, Elizabeth. "Cost-Finding: The Wisconsin Experience." *Bottom Line* 2 (no. 1, 1988): 23–28.

Presents results of a 1984–85 study to develop full costs by focusing on three levels: direct library costs to the service; indirect library costs to the service; and indirect government, municipal, or agency costs to the service. Concludes that a successful cost finding study requires that hard decisions be made on desired project goals, units of measure, and tasks to be counted.

156. Rocke, Hans Joachim. *Analysis of the Data From a Technical Processing Cost Study: A Research Paper.* (Master's thesis, California State University, San Jose, 1974.) (ED 140 795)

Attempts to spot trends or other factors affecting costs in technical services from a study done for the California State College system. Includes a report of the literature on costs in technical services, mostly limited to the ten years preceding 1974. The review covers cost analysis, standardization and optimization. Methodologies employed are sorting operations, mathematical percentages and averages and graphic histograms.

The study is limited to costs of staff time per unit for fourteen activities in ordering, cataloging and processing. Concludes that the productive times used are reliable and that task allocation among levels of staff is appropriately related to costs in most of the libraries. Physical arrangement of work space, planning and organizing procedures and skill or efficiency of staff may be contributing factors.

Calls for standardization of criteria, units and methods to ensure truly comparative data while realizing that it may not be possible because of human elements affecting processes.

Appendices include descriptions of activities covered and formulas used in the original study, statistical output and flowcharts of activities.

157. Ross, Ryburn M. "Cost Analysis of Automation in Technical Services," In Clinic on Library Applications of Data Processing. University of Illinois, 1976. *Proceedings: The Economics of Library Automation,* pp. 10–27. Champaign-Urbana: University of Illinois, Graduate School of Library Science, 1977.

Examines the relationship of costs of library automation to total library costs.

Describes a mathematical model incorporating direct and indirect costs of the existing system, an improved manual system, and proposed automated systems.

The processes under discussion are acquisition of monographs, serials control, and circulation and inventory control.

Provides manual processing costs for social science monographs, presents the minutes per title for items searched and cataloged through the OCLC automated cataloging system, and shows the technical services cost ratio (TSCOR) for salaries in relation to the amount spent for library materials.

158. Schmidt, C. James; Rast, Elaine K.; and Linford, John S. "Library Services to University Branch Compuses: The Ohio State Experience," *Library Resources & Technical Services* 14 (Fall 1970): 562–573.

The main technical service department begins processing materials for branch campuses. They order, receive, catalog and process monographs and order serials.

Initial operations are costly and take longer than anticipated; so a separate unit is established to handle only the branch materials.

Procedures are based on acceptance of available LC and OSU cataloging, combining the requisition and order forms into one, and pre-cataloging materials while they are on order. Processing time is reduced by about 50 percent.

The method of estimating staffing levels is based on number of books to be purchased, by average net purchase price per volumes, and annual production rate.

Production rates and comparative data for copy and original cataloging are presented. Flow charts for the total process, searching and card production, and invoice processing are include.

159. Sheahan (Drake)-Stewart Dougall, Marketing and Physical Distribution Consultants, New York. *Book Processing Facility Design,* sponsored by the Association of New York Libraries for Technical Services. Garden City, NY: ANYLTS, 1969. (ED 038 992)

Methods of processing begin with receipt of materials and encompasses 21 steps including computer-printing of cards, packing, and delivering boxes to the shipping dock.

Processing costs are summarized in the report. The methods and costs for physically processing books for public libraries in New York State are detailed. Costs are divided into labor, processing materials, equipment, and building rental. Appendices give data used in determining new book cost figures.

160. Stanfield, Karen L. "What Price Technical Services? A Survey of Libraries in Illinois." *Illinois Libraries* 65 (May 1983): 310–313.

Attempts to draw relationships between technical services allocations and total library budgets. Technical services is defined as acquisitions, cataloging, binding and circulation.

Only four questions were asked: percentage of total budget allocated to technical services; percentage of work area assigned to technical services; percentage of staff time spent in technical services activities, with a break down by level of staff; and number of volumes in the library.

The sampling and distribution procedures are described. Data analysis reveals some difficulties with questions two and three. Analysis of each question is presented in graphic form.

161. University of California, Santa Barbara. Library Systems Development Project. *Background for the Cost Analysis of the Order and Standard Loan Library Operations.* Santa Barbara: UCSB, 1970. (ED 061 970)

Report of a cost study of 3000 + employees throughout the University of California library system.

Procedures for weekly timekeeping include a list of tasks and assign responsibility to each person or category (eg. supervisor, systems analyst). Includes explanation and illustrations of the time sheets used.

Defines measureable tasks in terms of quantities for acquisitions (12) and circulation (19) activities. Also provides definitions for major tasks performed in the two areas. These are presented together on worksheets which are divided into major groups of tasks such as order initiation, claims processing, vendor file maintenance, book charging, patron registry, supporting (administrative) tasks and non-production oriented activities. The latter includes vacations, breaks, etc.

162. University of California Santa Barbara. Library Systems Development

Project. *Conceptual Replaceability Analysis for Order and Standard Loan Tasks*. Santa Barbara: UCSB, 1971. (ED 061 972)

Examines how the manual tasks delineated in earlier studies will change when automation is implemented in each of the two areas: acquisition and circulation. Estimates of increase or decrease in personnel costs for main and secondary operations are given by percentages based on three possible levels of confidence: low (low estimate, 95% level of confidence), best (executed value), high (high estimate, 20 to 1 odds.).

These percentages are based on "educated guesses," not actual automated systems.

163. University of California Santa Barbara. Library Systems Development Project. *Library System Definition: Functions and Interfaces*. Santa Barbara: UCSB, (ED 061 971)

Provides definitions for all the activities within the University of California library system: collection development, acquisitions, cataloging, binding, loans (including interlibrary loans), reference services, circulation, administration, personnel, equipment and facilities. These are divided into 71 modules, each of which is clearly defined.

The report also shows how each module interacts with others in terms of input processed and output created.


CATALOGING


164. Allen, Chris Willig [and] Branson, Judy Rose. "OCLC for the Hospital Library: The Justification Plan for Hospital Administration." *Bulletin of the Medical Library Association* (July 1982): 293–297.

A cost study at a hospital library designed to identify unit costs for cataloging, determine if automation would be cost effective, and provide documentation and statistics for a proposal to the administration.

The study was conducted over three months. Statistics are kept on (1) searching the printed *CATLINE* for NLM cataloging records, (2) professional time spent editing cataloging copy or doing original cataloging, (3) processing of materials—labeling typing book cards, pasting in pockets, and stamping, (4) producing catalog cards via a duplicator and (5) filing.

Cost of the current manual system were compared to costs of using OCLC. Figures for the latter were estimated based on price schedules for OCLC and a study done by J. Raper. Analysis revealed a savings in staff time of 200 hours per year with the automated system. It was determined that start up and operating costs could be shared with another institution rather than carrying all those costs alone. The proposal to the administration included all these figures as well as projections of workload, based on staff time and volume of work, for the next year.

165. Anderson, James F. "Break-Even Point for a Proof Slip Operation." *College & Research Libraries* 33 (March 1972): 119–121. —Comment by C.O. Landram. 33 (July 1972): 329–330.

The economics of using Library of Congress (LC) proof slips to Xerox cards are compared to purchasing LC printed cards. Costs examined include buying LC cards sets, Xeroxing a set of cards, proof slip subscription, filing, and number of titles ordered per year.

Presents a formula for the break-even point where the proof slip operation equals the cost of ordering LC cards for each title.

The later comment points out that Anderson did not include labor costs for operations other than filing proof slips. Landram also questions the costs of Xerox rental as being a constant.

166. Angold, Linda. *Cost and Time Analysis of Monograph Cataloging in Hospital Libraries.* Detroit: Wayne State University, School of Medicine, Library and Biomedical Information Service Center, 1969.

Five possible models of cataloging are analyzed for cost and time involved. Precataloging, cataloging, and post-cataloging work units are defined. Each model is discussed in terms of materials used and time expended. Very useful are the tables of all work units comparing time and cost for alternative procedures within each model. The methodology is fairly simple: a librarian with no cataloging experience performed each task. Salary figures are outdated but the time expended for each work unit may be useful.

167. Axford, Lavonne. "Toward a Functional, Multidimensional Catalog." *Southeastern Librarian* 21 (Summer 1971): 101–9.—Comment by Beatrice Montgomery. 21 (Summer 1971): 110–12.

Advocates a three way split catalog (author, title, subject) to better serve the user, eliminate the backlog of untyped catalog cards and to reduce costs.

Guide cards are used in the subject catalog to eliminate typing of headings on purchased Library of Congress cards. The printed *Library of Congress Subject Headings* is used as an index, thus avoiding typing of cross reference cards. Subject heading changes are dealt with by simply moving the card to the correct location behind the appropriate guide card.

The title catalog can make use of shortcuts by underlining the title in red or highlighting with a colored marker. Added titles (and added authors in the author catalog) are highlighted in the tracings area with a diagonal line drawing the users eye from the upper left corner. Estimates for 25,000 titles per year averaging eight cards per title would save 1666 hours of filing and 1538 hours of typing. Adjust that figure by 25% to allow for less than 100% efficiency.

The comment by Montgomery points out the lack of time and cost data for providing the guide cards and splitting the catalog.

168. Bednar, Marie. "Automation of Cataloging: Effects on Use of Staff, Efficiency, and Service to Patrons." *Journal of Academic Librarianship* 14 (July 1988): 145–149.

Overview of changes which have taken place at Penn State University Library since its library cataloging operation was automated in 1981. Points to the centralizing of some functions and decentralizing of others with the attendant impact on staffing which included a reduction in the cataloging workforce. Problems concerning quality of cataloging, adjustment of staff, and establishing and maintaining lines of communication are discussed.

169. Bock, Rochelle; Braude, Robert M.; Butkovich, Margaret. "Cataloging Costs with *CATLINE:* A Follow-up Study." *Bulletin of the Medical Library Association* 63 (October 1975): 414–415.

Replicates the earlier study by Butkovich and Braude to determine costs of using the NLM *CATLINE* online database for cataloging copy.

Unit costs are greater although percentages of original cataloging drops and NLM copy goes up. The rise in unit costs can be partially attributed to downtime, delayed updates of the database, change in cataloging personnel and absence of a printer for recording copy found online. Other factors to be considered are access points other than the main entry, the cumulative nature of the database, and potential currency of the database.

170. Bongiorno, Mary E., "On the Way to An Online Catalog," *Productivity in the Information Age,* edited by Raymond F. Vondran et al., pp. 172–176. ASIS Conference Proceedings, v. 20. White Plains, NY: Knowledge Industry, 1983.

Describes a work and cost benefit analysis to justify an online catalog.

Goals of the online catalog are provided as are factors determining the choice of a commercial vendor when lack of funds rules out other options.

Charts comparing staff time per record and computer costs per record for card and online catalog support activities.

171. Bregzis, Ritvars. "Some Cost Aspects of On-Line Input of Bibliographic Records." *Cost Reduction for Special Libraries and Information Centers,* edited by Frank Slater, pp. 85–94. New York: American Society for Information Science, 1973.

The conversion of bibliographic records for 300,000 monographs is described. Monitoring staff time expended reveals these activities: securing, editing, source documents revising, and keyboarding source documents, proofreading, file maintenance, supervision, overhead.

Production is quantified in terms of number of records edited, keyboarded and damaged or lost through unacceptable computer performance. Over nineteen months 126,000 records are converted. The 74,000 done in a calendar year took 22,000 staff hours and cost $70,000 in salary expenditures.

Editing the source record, keyboarding it and proofreading the results accounts for 71.4% of the total time expended. The average time per bibliographic record is 18 staff minutes. Records requiring no correction range from 26% to 80%. Factors contributing to the fluctuation of work effectiveness, and thus to unit costs, are staff characteristics and computer systems support.

172. Bryant, Philip [and] Needham, Angela. *Costing Different Forms of Library Catalogs.* Bath University Comparative Catalogue Study Final Report, Paper No. 7. Bath University Library, 1975.

Considerations in costing of catalogs include kinds of catalogs, methods used, sequences, number of copies, and type of output. A large part of the cost is for staff time. These figures can be obtained through work study or activity sampling. Equipment and overhead costs must be determined on a percentage basis. In comparing costs for different forms produced from the same machine-readable file, staff time is not considered since it would be the same for all. The production costs and necessary equipment and furniture are where the differences will result.

Costs for card, computer printout, and roll film catalogs are presented, with a summary comparison showing costs of one, three, and ten copies of the applicable forms.

173. Butkovich, Margaret and Braude, Robert. "Cost-Performance Analysis of Cataloging and Card Production in a Medical Center Library." *Bulletin of the Medical Library Association* 63 (January 1975): 29–34.

Examines cataloging copy received on commercially provided cards extracted from NLM copy and local cataloging and card production using stencils. Four areas are studied: bibliographic searching, cataloging, card production and book preparation.

Studies a sample of ten percent of annual acquisitions which are English language and requires original cataloging. Excludes added copies or volumes and new editions. All items included are recorded. Data are collected for time and supplies for card production and book preparation, time and count for bibliographic searching, and time and data information for cataloging. Overhead costs are not included as it is felt they will be constant for any method used.

Cataloging costs with commercially available cards involve checking call numbers, making necessary changes, and doing original cataloging for the 42 percent not provided. Local card production costs include time spent in typing stencils, printing and proofing, and supplies used. Purchased card costs include extra cards (1.5 per title), typing headings on extra cards and local production for the 42 percent of items still requiring original cataloging and card production. Data on time spent receiving and processing commercially available cards are omitted for lack of information. Possible factors in purchasing cards are storing new acquisitions waiting for cards and a system for temporary cataloging.

Times are recorded for all activities to determine unit times and costs. Analysis gives time in minutes, item counts and time span data. Unit costs for supplies, equipment maintenance, and salaries including fringe benefits are determined. An important part of the study is examining turnaround, or throughput, time: 27.97 days for local production and 34.11 days for externally obtained cards.

174. Butler, B.B. and others. "Conversion of Manual Catalogs to Collection Data Bases." *Library Technology Reports* 14 (March 1978)—Erratum. 14 (July 1978): 303.

This comprehensive discussion of data conversion included tables showing yearly and cumulative costs over ten years. Costs of creation/conversion, display and storage are estimated.

The section on procedures and costs of conversion relates hit rates to factors governing costs. Those factors include size of collection, age/currency of items, language, amount of information to be converted, conformance to standards, etc. Each factor is graphed to show relationship to cost per title converted.

Tables present cost data for record extraction, keyboarding, online entry, editing, and catalog production for records of 200, 400, and 600 characters.

Although the actual cost figures are dated, the elements and methods of comparison will be useful to any library planning for conversion.

175. Chapin, Richard E., and Pretzer, Dale H. "Comparative Costs of Converting Shelf List Records to Machine-Readable Form." *Journal of Library Automation* 1 (1968): 66–74.

Describes three methods of converting bibliographic records: keypunching, paper-tape typewriting and optical scanning. Data transcribed are 1) call number, 2) author, 3) title (sometimes truncated), 4) date and 5) copy numbers.

Cost data for each method are broken down into labor (salaries and fringe benefits), equipment (rental of computer), supplies (overhead) and contracted services, where appropriate. Explanations for salary differences are given. Stop watches are used to obtain average times for some operations but methods of ascertaining overall times are not included.

176. Christian, Roger L. and Steele, Martha. "Little Things Can Mean a Lot — ... Microfiche Catalog." *Library Scene* 3 (December 1974): 14–15.

Compares the costs of maintaining one union card catalog with those of providing microfiche union catalogs for four locations.

Filming of the catalog is done by renting a microfilmer. Equipment, supplies and labor costs are calculated to determine one-time costs and recurring costs. A twice a year re-filming schedule, with weekly paper supplements, is proposed. There will be continuing costs for maintaining the "master" catalog to use for each re-filming.

177. Cloud, Patricia. "The Cost of Converting MARC AMC: Some Early Observations." *Library Trends* 36 (Winter 1988): 573–583.

Reports on a project conducted by 12 major research libraries retrospectively converting 21,000 data records describing archival and manuscript to the MARC Archival and Control (AMC) format. Factors which slowed creation time of AMC records were problems with existing finding aids, authority work, cataloging problems, and staff turnover.

178. "Cost-Effective Participation in a Bibliographic Utility by a Small Library [panel discussion at 1980 AALL Conference]." *Law Library Journal* 73 (Fall 1980): 908–928.

Three presentations cover overview of costs for different methods of using the bibliographic utilities and examples of OCLC and RLIN use.

The experiences of a consortium of small libraries using OCLC via a shared dedicated terminal are described. Cataloging costs for each member is provided in tabular form. A breakdown of the consortium budget is also given.

Costs for cataloging via dial access to RLIN are compared to those for manual cataloging.

179. "Cost of Conversion." In RECON Working Task Force. *Conversion of Retrospective Catalog Records to Machine-readable Form: A Study of the Feasibility of a National Bibliographical Service,* edited by John C. Rather, pp. 97–101. Washington, D.C.: Library of Congress, 1969.

Presents costs per record for four methods of conversion. Costs for those alternatives include editing, input devices, sorting and printing, computer equipment for storing the database, and design and programming costs. Personnel costs include a director, editors, data entry, catalog comparison and quality control.

180. Divilbiss, J.L. and Self, Phyllis C. "Work Analysis by Random Sampling." *Medical Library Association Bulletin* 66 (1978): 77–81. [also In *Costing and The Economics of Library and Information Services,* edited by Stephen A. Roberts, pp. 77–81. Aslib Reader Series, vol. 5. London: Aslib, 1984.]

The amount of time spent in various activities can be determined through diaries, observation, or self-observation. For a workday fragmented into numerous activities, self observation at the times an electronic random alarm mechanism (RAM) beeped is selected.

To achieve a three percent accuracy level, 500 samples are required. One month is selected as the time period for recording the sample activities of a librarian with responsibility for cataloging audiovisual materials.

Categories chosen for the study are drawn from the subjects' job description and from a prestudy of activities. Predefined categories include MEDLINE, cataloging, reference, supervision of staff, administration meetings and professional meetings.

Problems of this type of study include missing samples through failure to have the beeper close at hand and the distraction of recording data in the middle of an activity.

Data analysis involves counting the number of samples for each of the predefined categories and assigning the others to existing or new categories. Diary samples from data recorded in the absence of the beeper are converted to synthetic beeps. Although one quarter of the librarians' time is to be devoted to cataloging audiovisual materials, the study revealed that only 4.2% of her time is spent on that activity. Other analyses resulted in reallocation of work and additional staff.

181. Dolby, J.L. and Forsyth, V.L. "Analysis of Cost Factors in Maintaining and Updating Card Catalogues". *Journal of Library Automation* 2 (1969): 218–41. [A condensed version of ED 035 432.]

Compares costs of manual and computerized catalogs. Problems of cost comparisons and uses of cost information are discussed. The costs of cataloging are extracted from studies done at the New York Public Library, Columbia University and Lockheed Research Library Science libraries and are compared to cost studies in Colorado and Southern California.

Card processing cost data are extracted from studies at Columbia, the New York Public Library, Sacramento State, University of Toronto, Air Force Cambridge Research Laboratory, and Yale Medical Library. Costs of cabinets and space are discussed. Book and card catalogs are compared. Conversion costs at the Library of Congress, New York Public Library, Los Angeles Public Library, University of California at Berkeley and Stanford are presented. A number of tables compare costs from three different studies.

182. Dolby, J.L.; Forsyth, V.J.; and Resnikoff, H.L. *Computerized Library Catalogs: Their Growth, Cost, and Utility.* Cambridge, Mass.: MIT Press, 1969. [also published as Dolby, J.L. *An Evaluation of the Utility and Cost of Computerized Library Catalogs: Final Report* / J.L. Dolby, V. Forsyth, and H.L. Resnikoff (R & D Consultants Co.) Washington: US Dept. of Health, Education and Welfare, Office of Education, Bureau of Research, 1968. (ED 022 517)]

   The chapter on "Analysis of Cost Factors in the Automation of Library Catalogs" (pp. 23–52) is of special interest. Costs incurred in the production of printed catalogs are for: programming, which is dependent on the level and availability of language used; hardware, which include printing, storage, and searching; conversion; and input equipment.

   Tables of comparison are given. Includes an appendix on programming languages.

183. Dolby, J.L.; Forsyth, V.J.; and Resnikoff, H.L. *The Cost of Maintaining and Updating Library Card Catalogs: Final Report.* Los Altos, Calif.: R & D Consultants Co., 1969. (ED 035 432)

   Addresses the growth of knowledge and thus library collections and the impact on activities for ensuring access to that information.

   Analyzes costs incurred in maintaining and updating card catalogs. Problems in arriving at and using cost data are presented.

   The elements defined as making up the cost of cataloging in three studies (Lockheed, New York and Columbia) are compared as are costs determined in five studies (for the first three plus Colorado and South Carolina).

   Card processing costs as determined in studies at Sacramento State, New York Public Library, Stanford, Ontario, the Air Force and Yale Libraries are summarized.

   Maintenance, cabinets, and space contribute total costs. Catalog conversion costs are described too. Data on manual and computer processing are compared.

184. Druschel, Joselyn. "Cost Analysis of an Automated and Manual Cataloging and Book Processing System." *Journal of Library Automation* 14 (1981): 24–35.

   This study done at the Wayne State University Library compares manual and automated cataloging and processing costs. The method is a per-unit cost approach to the tasks: bibliographic verification, bibliographic record production, bibliographic record maintenance, physical processing and binding activities.

   The comparison, presented in tabular form for all processes, includes staff cost per item, database and/or miscellaneous costs per item, average number processed per month and total costs.

   An example of a work assignment/staffing profile is given for copy cataloging. A formula is given for determining staff costs. Database, subscriptions and materials, and equipment costs are presented.

   Conclusions drawn from the comparison are that automation of these processes saves the library about $67,000 per year, mostly in staff reductions.

185. Faust, Julia B. "Microcomputers as On-Line Catalogs in Special Libraries." *Special Libraries* 77 (Summer 1986): 133–139.

Uses *DB Master IV* to create an online catalog with an Apple IIe. The costs for hardware, software, and personnel are $14,000. About 400 hours are required for pulling 4000 books and cards, entering data and reshelving the materials.

On-order materials and audiovisual holdings are also entered into the database. Printed catalogs or lists for author, title and subject are generated every week or two. An audiovisual materials list is printed separately.

186. Folk, Clara A.; Campbell, Bill W.; and Bloomfield, Masse. "Microfilm Card Catalog at Work." *Special Libraries* 67 (July 1976): 316–18.

Book, card, and microfilm catalog costs are estimated for the first year of operation.

Considerations of user acceptance and updating of the microfilm catalog are discussed. Expansion of the microfilm catalog incorporates holdings for government documents, technical reports, patents, etc.

187. Fox, Mary Anne and Chervinko, James K., "Cost of AACR2 at Morris Library (SIU-C)." *Illinois Libraries* 65 (May 1983): 314–15.

Results of studies on building and maintaining a card catalog and on implementing *AACR2* in an academic library. The latter is to be accomplished via a single card catalog with headings interfiled, split or changed and numerous cross references.

Establishing a new name authority file and procedures for verifying *AACR2* headings are described.

Statistics for pre-*AACR2* and *AACR2* cataloging are compared. Analysis of staffing changes and associated costs yield former and current personnel costs per title.

188. Friedman, Joan and Jeffreys, Alan. "Cataloging and Classification in British University Libraries. Part 2: The Labor Force." *Journal of Documentation* 25 (March 1969): 43–51.

A cost analysis of cataloging and classification is achieved by gathering data on each staff member involved.

Of particular interest is the data collection form which lists 22 activities (including assistance to readers and interlibrary loans, which are not technical services tasks) and ranges of time, e.g. 5–8 hours, along with salary ranges specified.

Results do not reveal professional versus paraprofessional staffing patterns. Data analysis reveals that the three or four hour span used was too large for meaningful times.

No attempt is made to determine quality of the cataloging and classification done.

189. Gains, James E. "The Financial Aspects of Reclassification." In Conference on Reclassification, University of Maryland, 1968. *Reclassification: Rationale and Problems: Proceedings*. Edited by Jean M. Perreault, pp. 116–138. College Park, Md.: School of Library and Information Services, University of Maryland, 1968.

Identifies elements that make up costs of reclassification. Suggests that the catalog department estimate costs based on procedures and standards. Meanwhile other departments can examine their policies. Some of these may be changed before beginning reclassification. Reclassification *should* be treated as a capital expenditure and funded independently of the regular operating budget. The project *should* be in an autonomous unit of people. Funds support direct costs: salaries, wages and supplies but cover equipment and furniture only if necessary. Unit costs should be calculated only from direct costs.

Efficient operations can be achieved by a mixture of experienced full-time and part-time workers and some students. Appropriate use of clerks and paraprofessionals who are supervised and assisted by catalogers on an "as needed" basis will keep costs down. Costs of shifting the collection may be absorbed as stack maintenance and not as part of the project. Reclassification costs according to the standards the library adopts for the new collection, that is the quality of classification. (Gaines also brings descriptive cataloging standards into the discussion here.) Screening numbers for correctness or obsolescence is necessary. Overlap of reclassification activities and regular cataloging operations can make it difficult to accurately determine reclassification costs. Lists the options for changing cards by (1) purchasing LC cards, (2) commercial copying, (3) multilith, (4) local copying, (5) use of labels and (6) computer printed cards.

Details some arguments against reclassification. Concludes that reclassification to LC is well worth the money as in time reduced cataloging expenses will occur. Also advocates using LC as a standard.

190. Ghika, Mary W. "Cost Assignment in Implementation of Online Catalogs." In *Online Catalogs, Online Reference Converging Trends,* edited by Brian Aveney and Brett Butler, pp. 134–152. Chicago: ALA, 1984.

Describes a survey of cost data used in decision making for online catalogs. Results show that installation and maintenance of hardware and telecommunications are subsumed in the large institutions' computer center budgets, personnel costs are not significantly assigned, and online cataloging components of previously installed systems are not assigned appropriately.

Installation and cost figures do not show incremented cost of increased use or any clear relationship between collection cost and collection access cost.

The management issues of online catalog costs are value of increased access, costs of greater collection utilization, the price of longer and more catalog use, cost control in terms of users, and budgets or funding for online catalogs.

Planning for costs of online catalogs must include full system costs: investment, operation, maintenance; fixed and variable incremental costs; costs elements incurred by any department or paid from a different funding source; future costs; financial repercussions in other areas, and the cost of solving this problem.

Tools available are current data, local estimates, vendor estimates, cost estimating relationship statistics, and institutional cost factors. The questionnaire is reproduced in the appendix.

191. Goodell, John Silas. *A Case Study of Catalogs in Three University Librar-*

*ies Using Work Sampling.* (Ph.D. dissertation, Florida State University. Tallahassee, Florida, 1971.)

Categorizes the activities of catalogers and describes the procedures used in collecting data in three libraries.

Data analysis reveals that percentages of time spent on activities by the catalogers in the libraries are different but similar. Thus work sampling may not be the best method for comparing times among libraries. Individual differences, the physical environment, and work cycles will also affect comparisons. Neither the directors nor the catalogers themselves estimated correctly the amount of time spent by catalogers on various activities.

Appendices include lists of activities found in other studies, sample tally form, initial and revised list of activities used in this study, instructions and form used in estimating time, and floor plans.

192.   Gorman, Michael. "Implementing Changes in Cataloging Rules." *Library Journal* 112 (February 15, 1987): 110–112.

Examines the internationalizing of cataloging theory and changes in the bibliographic universe in terms of costs and benefits. One side is characterized as believing that the cost of change is less important than the benefit and the other as looking at changes only from an economic standpoint.

The alternative to change in cataloging rules is stagnation and thus a diminishing of cooperation. The American reaction of superimposition to the *Anglo American Cataloging Rules* (1967) resulted in bibliographic anarchy and schizophrenic practices. *AACR 2* resolves differences in cataloging practices; leads, in some cases, to the demise of the card catalog; and enhances the success of machine readable formats.

The cost of implementing a new cataloging code are for educating the creators and users of the catalog and paying organizations to change their cataloging practices. The benefits of new rules are providing a basis for cooperation in the technological age and presenting a more user-oriented bibliographic system. They also allow for bibliographic control to proceed efficiently and to deal reasonably with continuing changes.

193.   Grosch, Audrey N. *Current and Retrospective Sources of Machine Readable Monograph Cataloging Records: A Study of their Potential Cost and Utility in Automated System Development at the University of Minnesota.* Rev. ed. Minneapolis, MN: University of Minnesota Library, 1975. (ED 112 859)

Investigates the utility, availability and costs of sources of MARC II monograph cataloging records for current and retrospective titles.

Six sources of bibliographic data are estimated in terms of components required, total costs, five year costs and cost per year. All alternatives are based on maintaining a file locally, but acquiring the data from various sources, acquiring another library's file, maintaining a gradually decreasing file locally, purchasing a vendor file, or obtaining only records matching local holdings from two possible sources. For each alternative, costs are further broken down per record and per usable record.

Detailed analyses of each alternative are presented in narrative form, and other possible sources for retrospective data are examined in terms of acquisition costs, programming costs, and temporary storage costs. Equipment; training and documentation; supervision and editorial work, and data entry costs of conversion are also calculated.

194. Hamann, Edmund G. "Expansion of the Public Card Catalog in a Large Library." *Library Resources & Technical Services* 16 (Fall 1972): 488–496.

The project of expanding the public catalog is divided into six phases: determine average number of cards for each drawer, mark the new divisions, list labels to be made, type temporary labels, shift the cards using temporary labels, and prepare permanent labels.

A sampling technique measures current drawer capacity and those data are used to determine optimum capacity in the expanded catalog. Division of the drawers at average intervals is done with guidelines of a minimum of five inches and a maximum of twelve inches of cards per drawer.

Listing, editing and typing of temporary labels is done prior to the actual shifting of cards. It is later determined that typing of temporary labels could be omitted.

The nine activities comprising the expansion are listed along with hours, cost, and levels of staff involved in each. Staff expenditure by level, hours, cost and percentages are also given.

195. Hitchcock, Jennette E. "Cost Estimates and Time Schedules in Reclassification." In *Institute on the Use of the Library of Congress Classification System: Proceedings of the Institute on the Use of the Library of Congress Classification Sponsored by the American Library Association, Resources and Technical Services Division Cataloging and Classification Section, New York City, July 7–9, 1966*, edited by Richard H. Schimmelpfeng and C. Donald Cook, pp. 192–208. Chicago: American Library Association, 1968.

Presents kinds of costs involved in changing classification systems. Reviews costs derived from other libraries' projects. Steps in the reclassification process are described and costs given. Changing the call number on the book spine and title page plus revision and supervision times are estimated. Options for changing the number on cards are specified, then times and costs given.

Assigning of classification numbers using the Library of Congress schedules is described as encompassing numbers available from external sources (i.e. copy cataloging) plus original classification. Classification is assumed to take 30 percent of total cataloging time. Assigning classification numbers from a local, former scheme, the Library of Congress schedules, and copy cataloging varies from five to twenty minutes on the average. Comparing the time needed for classification by Library of Congress with classification by the former scheme yields time, and thus money, saved. Costs of maintaining a classification scheme and salaries are variables which may affect possible savings.

Examples of other procedures and overhead are factors affecting the total reclassification costs are given. Staff, tools, and supplies needed for the task must also be included. Physical handling of the collection must be planned and supervised.

196. Hobrock, Brice G.; Bierman, J.; and Beverly, H.W. *Cost and Cost-Effective Studies in Libraries: 1. A Working Model. 2. Cost Analysis of the Preparations Divisions at VPI (Virginia Polytechnic Institutes) and SU (State University).* Blacksburg, VA: Virginia Polytechnic Institute and State University, University Libraries, 1975. (ED 108 698)

Discusses cost effective studies and presents a model for cost-analysis. The steps in cost analysis are to identify and define the specific operation being analyzed, break the specific area into its component parts, quantify the processes identified, document each component in terms of steps, determine resources required for each step, identify times and quantities related to costs, calculate unit costs, identify alternatives, and cost the alternatives.

The second part details the cost analysis of monographic cataloging of new materials with the current manual system and alternative systems. Flowcharts document the processes and costs and times are given for the activities in the categories of searching and filing, speed and original cataloging, master card processing and end processing.

Unit direct costs, direct costs, and adjusted costs are summarized for staff and materials. Average costs per title and administrative cost allocations are also noted.

197. Hoffman, Herbert H. and Magner, Jeruel L. "Future Outlook: Better Retrieval Through Analytic Catalogs." *Journal of Academic Librarianship* 11 (July 1985): 151–153.

Discusses the Santa Ana College Library's consideration of an enhanced catalog that would list not only books, but also all of the bibliographically separate works contained in collections and anthologies. Costs of such a project are examined and found modest if done cooperatively, especially when one considers reference search time which is expended on alternative means of retrieval.

198. Horney, Karen L., et. al. "Minimal Level Cataloging: A Look at the Issues—A Symposium." *Journal of Academic Librarianship* 11 (January 1986): 332–342.

Includes views of six symposium participants regarding the pros and cons of minimal level cataloging (MLC), including cost considerations. While it is obvious that creation of MLC records is less costly than original cataloging, the costs of increased time for reference librarians, interlibrary loan staff, and researchers to find items with one access point must be considered as well. Moreover, not all materials will produce great savings when given the MLC treatment.

199. Jaroff, Grazia. "RLIN/OCLC Cataloging Costs Study in the Health Sciences Library." In *Advances in Library Administration and Organization* 1 (1982): 69–125.

Selected elements of the cataloging process are studied: processing time per unit of work, cost per unit processed, processing time, staff utilization, direct costs, and hit rates.

Techniques employed are identification of functions, tasks and activities; workload sampling; and a diary of times and units processed. Only direct costs are determined. Personnel costs include 30 percent for fringe and nonproductive time.

Time, units and personnel are charted for pre-order searching, precataloging searching, copy cataloging, full (original) cataloging, and post cataloging activities.

Analysis of the data reveal average times and costs for each system: RLIN and OCLC. There are also frequency distributions for tasks and a breakdown of costs by cataloging activity. Employee levels and times for each system are determined and then broken down by task. Hit rates for both systems are recorded and the time lag for processing on RLIN is charted.

The conclusions drawn are probably influenced by lack of experience with one system and by technical factors over which the library has no control.

200. Johnson, Carolyn A. "Retrospective Conversion of Three Library Collections." *Information Technology and Libraries* 1 (June 1982): 133–39.

Describes the collections, procedures, staff and standards for a conversion project.

The rate of conversion is determined by library characteristics: 1) cataloging standards, 2) quality of part cataloging, 3) quality of the databases, 4) degree of uniqueness or the hit rate, 5) special needs and problems, and 6) available staff.

Cataloging standards, hit rates, special needs and staff considerations are delineated. Statistics include the amount of editing of available records, original cataloging entered, and conversion rate per terminal hour and per staff hour.

General cost factors discussed are online time, overhead, equipment and supplies, and staff. No specific cost data are given.

201. Kantor, Paul B. "QUBMIS: A Quantitatively Based Management Information System for Libraries." In American Society for Information Science. Conference. 41st. *The Information Age in Perspective,* compiled by Everett H. Brenner, pp. 174–176. Proceedings, vol. 15. White Plains, NY: Knowledge Industry Publications, 1978.

This management information system is developed to measure the cost effectiveness of the card catalog.

Costs of overhead (furniture, space, supplies, light, etc.) can be calculated by applying appropriate records and formulae.

Staff costs are more difficult to estimate. Diaries, work logs or work samplings can be used in this process. These data can be used to establish norms or standards for the labor necessary to perform catalog maintenance (adding or removing cards). The quality of the catalog can be estimated using two samples—one drawn from the shelf list and another drawn from items recently returned from circulation. Each item is checked for under appropriate author, title, subject headings. The percentage of cards where they should be is a simple measure of catalog quality. Querying patrons about their use of the catalog can be done at the time they check out items and by observing patron use of the catalog. Also libraries who refer to the catalog when assisting patrons can tally the number of times. Unit costs are calculated using the formula:

$$\text{Unit Cost} \quad = \quad \frac{\text{total cost including labor}}{\text{patron uses} + \text{librarian uses}}$$

Other analyses can yield the average cost of circulating items, stack maintenance, and staffing the circulation desk, plus keeping circulation records.

202. Kayner, Nedra L. *Unit Time/Cost Study of the Cataloging Unit, Technical Services Division, Tucson, Public Library.* Tucson, Ariz: Tucson Public Library, 1978. (ED 194 091)

Daily log sheets are used to record time spent and quantities handled. Salary figures reflect direct personnel costs plus 30 percent in fringe benefits and adjusted salaries include overhead costs. Statistics are recorded on a per title basis.

Procedures are described for: new titles needing original cataloging; new titles having cataloging copy available; added titles; media; transfers; withdrawals; and related tasks such as receipt of cards, filing, subject authority work, cataloging maintenance, bar coding for the automated circulation system.

Summarizes staff and total costs per title and per volume as well as staff and total costs for media, transfers and withdrawals. Tables give unit times in minutes for major cataloging processes, costs per title and volume, and personnel costs per title and volume. Appendices detail processes and time data, title and volume ratios, and OCLC estimates plus give sample daily log sheets.

203. Kazlauskas, Edward John. "A Shelf List Conversion for Multi-Library Uses." *Library Resources & Technical Services* 15 (Spring 1971): 229–240.

Conversion of limited bibliographic records using three punched cards per title is described. The library of Congress (LC) card number, LC classification number, brief main entry, brief title, and serial record indicators are the data elements included. The cards are read to tape for creation of the bibliographic file in classification number order.

Cost of keyboarding, visual proofing, correction, supervision, supplies, and equipment rental averages $.1162/title.

Preparation, data entry, proofreading, and file creation/maintenance are flowcharted.

204. Kennedy, Joseph P. "File Size and the Cost of Processing MARC Records." *Journal of Library Automation* 4 (March 19710: 1–12.

Describes the costs of using the MARC tapes for catalog card production over three years. A formula for determining costs of computer time for processing a record is given. The formula is based on a number of records in the MARC file, number of records selected, reading and processing the record.

Cumulating the MARC II tapes can be done while selecting records, thus keeping costs down. Controlling the size of the cumulative file can be accomplished through deleting records not used or in subject areas not supported by the library. Older records may also be purged if materials are acquired rapidly. Some difficulties are likely to be encountered as the MARC coverage expands. Cooperative efforts may provide a workable solution for most libraries.

205. Kilgour, Frederick G. "Evolving, Computerizing, Personalizing." *American Libraries* 3 (February 1972): 141–147.

Discusses use of the computer in providing information to the user. Examples of computer applications for online catalogs. For SDI services, and for catalog card production are presented. The author reviews Baumol's economic analysis of libraries in a 1969 article, "The Costs of Library and Information Services." Kilgour's main thesis is that the high costs of cataloging are obvious targets for computerization. Costs, obtained from the literature and from research, of manual and computerized card production systems are compared.

206. Kochen, Manfred and Segur, A. Bertrand. "Effects of Cataloging Volume at the Library of Congress on the Total Cataloging Costs of American Research Libraries." *Journal of the American Society for Information Science* 21 (March/April 1970): 133–139.

Presents a mathematical model for determining the utility of Library of Congress (LC) cataloging by research libraries. This model is based on an optimal cataloging load by LC; the need for cataloging data by libraries; the cost of cataloging locally and with LC copy; and LC's cataloging costs. The authors estimate the number of items to be cataloged yearly and the corresponding costs if LC does all the cataloging or does none.

It is recommended that LC do as much of the cataloging as possible— about 820 titles per day. The use of a computer system will enable them to do so quickly at the appropriate quality level to suit most research libraries.

207. Lawrence, Gary S.; Matthews, Joseph R.; and Miller Charles. "Cost and Features of Online Catalogs: The State of the Art." *Information Technology and Libraries* 2 (1983): 409–449.

[also published as University of California Systemwide Administration. Library Research and Analysis Group and Division of Library Automation. *Costs and Features of Online Catalogs: The State of the Art,* with the assistance of Joseph Matthews. Berkeley, Calif.: University of California RLAG and DLA, 1982.]

[condensed version published as Lawrence, Gary G. and Matthews, Joseph R., "Financial Management of Online Catalogs," In *Academic Libraries: Myths and Realities: Proceedings of the Third National Conference of the Association of College and Research Libraries, April 4–7, 1984, Seattle, Washington,* edited by Suzanne C. Dodson and Gary L. Menges, pp. 187–199. Chicago: Association of College and Research Libraries, 1984.

Describes online catalogs in terms of the computer system and cost characteristics. The cost of computing equipment, the database and the telecommunication system are based on the size of the system and the features it provides.

Financial planning is based on initial and annual costs for hardware, software, and personnel. The source of the online catalog determines how much money is spent in each of those areas. Possible sources are the service bureau, turnkey vendors, local hardware and purchased software, local software and service bureau hardware, and the in-house.

Cost analysis for online catalogs can be done by examining actual experiences. Examples are given using the building block approach for a basic online catalog and for enhanced catalogs.

Cost management must deal with pressures for growth of the system and pressures arising from technological and economic change. Growth can be in the area of bibliographic records, terminals, access points, features, and function. Technological and economic change are based on computing capacity, storage capacity and cost, software and telecommunications.

The appendix provides a checklist of management issues and questions to assist in planning for installation, growth and change of the online catalog.

208. Lewis, Elizabeth Matthew. "Visual Indexing of Graphic Material." *Special Libraries* 67 (November 1976): 518–527.

Five methods of slide retrieval are created and tested for speed of retrieval and use of the indexes. Unit costs of the indexes—microfiche, super-8 cartridge, videotape, and card catalog—are compared. (The computer list is used as the primary entry to the visual indexes.) Components are stock (i.e. film, tape, cards), production, processing and labor. Retrieval costs incorporate the cost of the necessary playback devices.

User preference for each of the five indexes as well as advantages and disadvantages of each are noted. Choices for various local needs and other format alternatives are suggested.

209. Line, Maurice B. "Cost of Classification: A Note." *Catalogue & Index* no. 16 (October 1969): 4

Summarizes a study at Bath University which records the time spent by two catalogers in checking headings, cataloging and classifying 184 items.

Results show that classification with Universal Decimal Classification takes two and a half times as long as cataloging and twice as long as checking and cataloging together.

Line discusses types of classification schemes, use of para-professionals for descriptive cataloging, and centralized cataloging as factors which might reduce costs.

210. Linklater, W. "Catalogues in Book Form: Comparative Production Costs." *LASIE* 4 (November/December 1973): 16–24.

Lists three methods of producing book catalogs: impact printing, photo-reduced offset, and photocomposition. Specifications for two catalogs, author/title and subject, are set forth.

Cost per main entry, per entry, and per extra copy of the catalog (for 10, 20 and 50 copies) are compared for each of the three production methods.

Variables affecting costs include page and print size, print density, column format, and total copies. Costs given are for production of an initial cumulative catalog and do not include subsequent updating and cumulation.

An appendix gives detailed cost figures for each of the three production methods. Those costs include paper, computer time, machine collation, binding, and software (for the photocomposed catalog).

211. Lohman, Kathleen. "On-line Catalog vs the Card Catalog: A Cost-Effectiveness Comparison." *Illinois Libraries* 65 (May 1983): 316–319.

A feasibility study for an online catalog conducted by a public library. Costs used in comparing card and online catalogs are staffing, supplies, capital equipment and equipment maintenance.

Costs for the card catalog include supplies, equipment, filing, discarding, and typing. Actual cataloging costs are not included as it is felt they will remain constant. Online catalog costs cover terminals, maintenance, installation, and lines or telecommunications.

Five weighted criteria are used to judge the effectiveness of each form: user satisfaction, currency, resource sharing, reliability and work environment. Then costs and benefits over a six year period are compared.

Although the online catalog yields a better cost-effectiveness rating, that library's budget could not support its immediate implementation.

212. Maier, Joan M., et al. *The Bibliographical Center for Research, Rocky Mountain Region: A Cost Study of the Center's Present Operation.* Denver, Colo.: BCR, 1969. (ED 045 161)

Methodologies employed are interviews, flow process charts, time observation and sampling. The cost analysis methodology is reported in *Centralized Book Processing.*

Although the study's focus is on processing of interlibrary loan requests, it also covers union catalog maintenance activities.

Unit cost calculations for labor in areas of catalog maintenance are charted. Data for sorting, alphabetizing, blending and filing of cards are recorded in categories for observed mean time, frequency time, adjusted time, personal rating factor and standard time. Those data, along with category of worker and wage, yield cost of activity. Productive time and fringe benefits are presented in tabular form as are overhead costs.

Flow charts for current and proposed catalog searching sequences are included as is a sample data collection form. Appendices contain a description of the study—with a time schedule, forms inventory summary, list of files maintained, and size of card files.

213. Massonneau, Suzanne. "Bibliographic Control and Cataloging Cost Control: Interlocking Problems: A Plea for Standardization of Bibliographic Data by Publishers." *Library Journal* 98 (15 June 1973): 1890–93.
—Comment by N. Purcell [letter]. 98 (15 September 1973): 2489.
—Comment by R.V. Vaughn [letter]. 98 (15 October 1973): 2944.

Massonneau asks "What is it that makes cataloging costly?" and examines two causes. The first is the way bibliographic information is presented on titles pages: with incomplete authors' names and publication data. Her solution is to create guidelines or standards to be followed by the authors and publishers for title pages. The second reason cataloging costs are high is the complexity of cataloging rules, specifically *AACR,* first edition. Her resolution is to simplify the rules. These two steps would reveal lower cataloging costs and improved catalogs.

214. Matthews, Fred W. *Library Catalogue Automation: Cost-Benefit Factors.* Halifax, Nova Scotia: School of Library Science, Dalhousie University, 1979. (ED 180 485)

Presents a system developed as a catalog for the Dartmouth Regional Library, Dartmouth, Nova Scotia. Describes the MARC record format and the simplified fixed length format used in this system. Sort routines and page format of the microfiche catalog are explained.

Costs per title are derived from preparation of the machine readable input; computer processing and merging; creating new records; and printing. Nine copies each of author, title, and subject catalogs, one shelflist, and one master copy are printed.

Estimates costs at $1400 per year or $.11 per record or $.13 per title added and maintenance costs of $.019 per title. Does not include costs of input, estimated at 200 per year, or the process of classifying or assigning subject headings. Does include computer operating costs. Associated costs are those for MARC records, $.04 to $.07 per title. Admits that use of a simplified format reduces costs considerably.

215. Matthews, Fred W. "Library Catalogue Automation: Cost-Benefit Factors." In Canadian Conference on Information Science: 7th: 1979: Banff, Alberta. *Sharing Resources—Sharing Costs: Proceedings of the Seventh Canadian Conference on Information Science held at the Banff Springs Hotel, Banff, Alberta, May 12–15, 1979,* pp. 112–122. Ottawa: Canadian Association for Information Science, 1979.

The Dartmouth Regional Library, Nova Scotia, developed printed book catalogs using a fixed length record extracted from the MARC tapes.

Costs of computer charges for producing the printed catalogs (author, title, subject, and shelflist) are given. Not included are costs of classification (DDC) or assigning subject headings.

216. McCrank, Lawrence J. "The Bibliographic Control of Rare Books: Phased Cataloging, Descriptive Standards, and Costs." *Cataloging & Classification Quarterly* 5 (Fall 1984): 27–51.

Describes a study of 111 institutions in IRLA, ARL, and ACRL. Major issues addressed are size, acquisition, and personnel of rare book and special collections (RBSC); major characteristics of rare book catalogers; approaches to establishing bibliographical control; and costs of cataloging. The survey results for each of the areas are given in narrative form.

McCrank summarizes ten levels of cataloging for rare books and special collections. More than half of the libraries responding use *AACR 2* as the standard. One-third uses the Library of Congress or a similar standard and one-tenth combine *AACR 2,* LC and ACRL standards.

Costs for cataloging depend on these variables: salary, level of bibliographic description, rarity of the item, and the condition and presentation of bibliographic data in the original. The number of rare books cataloged per institution and cataloger varies greatly. Most (93.6%) rely on available copy when possible. The average cost to catalog a rare book is $34.37 +/-

$13.44; the range is $4.65 to $227. Unit costs are broken down by region, level of cataloging, and size of collection. Costs are higher in the Mid-Atlantic and lower in the Pacific Northwest; higher in large collections (more than 100,000 volumes) and lower in collections of 10,000–25,000 volumes.

An appendix summarizes the questionnaire used.

217. Morita, Ichiko T. [and] Gapen, D. Kaye. "A Cost Analysis of the Ohio College Library Center On-Line Shared Cataloging System in the Ohio State University Libraries." *Library Resources & Technical Services* 21 (Summer 1977): 286–302.

This description and analysis of a cost study is based on a comparison of production statistics and technical processing budgets over four six-month and one three-month periods.

Cost figures for departmental units and technical services functions are given. Pre-automation departmental units are cataloging, copy cataloging, and catalog maintenance and card production. After automation there are cataloging, quick editing (most copy cataloging), bibliographic records (input and maintenance), and photoduplication (local card production). Functions performed are editing card copy, computerized cataloging, original cataloging, and catalog maintenance. Tables present total units, basic unit cost, adjusted unit cost, additional unit cost, and OCLC assessment.

Basic unit costs are calculated per title and per volume by dividing salary costs by units produced. Adjusted unit costs include costs per production hour (salary plus fringes divided by productive time) times number of file times hours worked divided by units produced. Additional unit costs are for cards, equipment rental, and subscriptions. Variances in costs can be attributed to a number of factors, including changes in organization and work flow. Cost figures are more useful for comparison between periods than as absolute values.

218. New York Public Library. *Library Catalogs: Their Preservation and Maintenance by Photographic and Automated Techniques,* edited by James W. Henderson and Joseph A. Rosenthal. Cambridge: M.I.T. Press, 1968.

This classic work on book catalogs at the New York Public Library includes data for personnel and data processing costs associated with conversion for a computer-produced catalog.

Three alternate methods for determining total costs of the actual production of the catalog are given.

Descriptions of the current procedures and costs for searching, cataloging, card production, card preparation, and card filing are covered.

Personnel costs for new tasks associated with a computer produced catalog cover data entry and card filing.

A comparison of the catalog maintenance costs for the card catalog and various manifestations of the book catalog and supplements is in tabular form.

219. Nitecki, Joseph Z. *OCLC in Retrospect: A Review of the Impact of the OCLC System on the Administration of a Large University Technical Service*

*Operation.* Arlington, Va.: Eric Document Reproduction Service, 1984. (ED 087 482)

Describes the use of the OCLC for cataloging. Includes flow chart of the cataloging process using OCLC. Discusses advantages and disadvantages of shared cataloging systems.

Presents data in tabular form on times and costs of both manual and automated cataloging. Times for searching, cataloging, and card production are given. Costs include purchase of equipment and recurring charges for telecommunications as well as the physical cards.

Comparisons for costs of manual and automated card production are also presented.

220. Nitecki, Joseph Z. "Shared Cataloging; An Experiment in Cooperation Between University and Special Libraries." *Special Libraries* 61 (September 1970): 337–380.

A manual system of providing catalog copy is described. Searching of printed sources and local files based on data submitted (author, title, publisher, date) determines if cataloging copy is available. If no copy is available, original cataloging is done. Cards and book labels are prepared and delivered.

Costs include those for searching, cataloging, and card production. For the 30% of titles needing original cataloging, only limited cataloging (general classification numbers and one broad subject heading) is done. Average cost per title is $1.20 and average time per title is 27 minutes.

221. Overton, C. Mary and Seal, Alan. *Cataloguing Costs in the U.K.: An Analysis of the Market for Automated Cataloguing Services.* BLRD Report 5477. Bath: Bath University Library, 1979.

Details the results of a survey on cataloging costs. Those costs are based on salaries, commercial services and computer charges. Of greatest interest are the appendices which include papers by Alan Styles on a model for cataloging services and the economics of library automation as well as the questionnaire used in determining cataloging costs and detailed statistics generated from the analysis.

The model is based on network technology and cooperative cataloging. Library automation costs are determined by reviewing the costs of any service plus internal costs. Problems of work measurement techniques are circumvented by using a simple cost allocation method based on salary and percentage of time involved.

In analyzing cataloging, circulation and ordering systems data are required for: staff costs; material and equipment costs; volumes processed; annual rate of increase in volume processed; total collection size; and overlap in materials held/acquired with that held by other libraries.

The questionnaire on cataloging costs gathers information on computer policies, external sources and costs, number of titles and items processed, and number and salaries of personnel involved. Additionally, data on classification, subject analysis, catalog form and elements in cataloging records are gathered.

The statistical analysis reveals information on unit costs of cataloging, descriptive cataloging by type of library, and unit cost of subject processing as well as summary data on automation policies, external sources of cataloging, classification schemes used and forms of catalog.

222. Oxley, Anna. "Cataloging Costs in Atlantic Canada." *APLA Bulletin* 40 (Spring 1976): 19–20.

Reports the results of a survey on cataloging and card production in college and university libraries in the Atlantic Canada region. A questionnaire is developed to cover labor costs and duties; total production; supplies, equipment and cataloging services, overhead costs; and catalog card production. The instrument is distributed by mail and collected in person.

Difficulties are encountered in obtaining data on the amount of original, copy and added copy cataloging. Staff duties, overhead costs and supplies are other problem areas.

The results provide a range and average costs for five areas: production per card set, cataloging per title, cataloging per volume, cataloging per original, and copy cataloging.

223. Palmer, Richard Phillips. "Cost Reduction by Means of Computer Catalog Containing Fewer Bibliographic Elements." In *Cost Reduction for Special Libraries and Information Centers,* edited by Frank Slater, pp. 127–132. New York: American Society for Information Science, 1973.

A catalog study is conducted at the University of Michigan general library to determine whether a hypothetical five item computer catalog will meet user requirements. Over 90 percent of the respondents will be successful with the addition of the contents note.

General figures on start-up, conversion, storage and operating costs from several studies are reviewed. Palmer recommends that each area of the catalog record which is considered for inclusion in a computer-based catalog by subject to a rigorous cost/benefit analysis.

224. Peters, Stephen H. and Butler, Douglas J. "A Cost Model for Retrospective Conversion Alternatives." *Library Resources & Technical Services* 28 (April/June 1984): 149–162.

Provides a detailed model for determining the approximate cost of any method of conversion.

A basic step is establishing standards for the project. Next a random sample is taken from the shelflist areas to be converted, and then the sample is compared to the source database.

The comparison is made on the basis of defining matching records and the level of completeness.

Information on alternative methods of conversion can be obtained from vendors. Costs are determined from four activities: searching, verification and editing, coding and input of non-hits, and obtaining final records. Basic costs for each activity include labor, equipment and supplies, and vendor or bibliographic utility charges. Total cost for each alternative is determined then per item costs are calculated.

225. Pierce, Anton R. and Taylor, Joe K. "A Model for Cost Comparison of Automated Cataloging Systems." *Journal of Library Automation* 11 (March 1978): 6–23.

—Comment by C.H. Stevens [letter], with rejoinder. 11 (June 1978): 180–181.

One time, fixed recurring and use-sensitive costs are used to develop the model of expected costs. Performance of the system is also included in terms of overlap with existing items in a library's collection and the acceptability of cataloging copy in the automated system when compared to newly acquired items. Amount of original cataloging needed is also part of the model.

Additionally provides a formula for arriving at numbers of staff needed on both the professional and paraprofessional levels. From that figure costs can be determined. When these numbers are generated for different automated cataloging systems, cost comparisons can be made.

The authors apply the model and formulas to their manual system, OCLC (via SOLINET) and Ballots (non RLIN).

The comment questions the accuracy of the actual dollar figures used in the study.

226. Pieters, Donald L. "Magnetic Tape Typewriter Speeds Catalog Card Production in College Library." *Special Libraries* 61 (November 1970): 513–515.

—Comment by E. Love. 62 (May 1971): 242–244.

A sample of 100 books provides the basis for a time and cost study. Thirteen steps are involved in the ordering, receiving, cataloging, processing and shelving of materials. Average time per item is one hour. Average cost per title is $2.10 and costs do not include overhead or supplies. These costs compare favorably with earlier estimates of $5 to $10 per book when purchasing Library of Congress cards.

227. Ra, Marsha. "The Need for Costing in a Cooperative Retrospective Conversion Project." *Technical Services Quarterly* 4 (Summer 1987): 39–48.

Describes a regional database program in New York (METRO) which provides its members reimbursement for retrospective conversion in order to foster resource sharing, but has experienced a wide range of costs among libraries participating in this task. Suggests that the group of libraries should arrive at fair, standard reimbursement rates through defining project goals, setting standards, developing a workplan, investigating joint contracts, and considering a centralized project.

228. *RLMS Micro-file: Current State of Catalog Card Reproduction*, J.Z. Nietcki, compiler. Chicago: American Library Association, Resources and Technical Services Division, Reproduction of Library Materials Section, 1974.

Describes nine projects undertaken to experiment with different ways to produce cards for library catalogs.

The ITEL Automated Typing System report gives cost comparison for hand typing versus automated typing. Ohio State University compares the costs of manual production versus using OCLC for computer-printed cards. Also of interest is a description of costs incurred in using a card master enlarger.

229. Seal, Robert A., et al. *Report of the Task Force on Cost Analysis and*

*Technical Considerations.* Charlottesville, VA: Virginia University, Alderman Library, 1979. (ED 191 473)

Examines options for different catalog forms—card, computer output microform and online—in terms of technical feasibility and cost. Also compares costs of processing, especially cataloging, in the current system with the alternatives.

Equipment and production costs and technical feasibility of each optional form of the catalog are estimated. Equipment expenditures will be for cabinets, fiche or film readers, or computer terminals. Production costs include OCLC charges, card catalog maintenance, tape processing, etc. The production costs are charted based on frequency of cumulation and number of records for the first year and over five years.

The effects of each alternative on staffing and workloads are also considered. The methods of providing links via see and/or see also references are listed and task weighted in relation to each option. These are ranked according to workload.

Use of the catalog by staff is an important factor as is the catalog maintenance for each branch.

Staff use of the catalog is explored for each department: acquisitions, area collection development, rare books, manuscripts, reference, circulation. Branch libraries staff are also investigated.

Appendices include miscellaneous cataloging costs and statistics, cataloging wages and cost per hour, cataloging transactions, and "A Report on the Growth of the Card Catalog".

230. Schwarz, Philip J. "Management Decision and the COM Catalog." *Microform Review* 11 (Summer 1982): 156-171.

Reviews the history of catalog forms and discusses automated catalogs. Management decisions must be made in the areas of database scope, creation, maintenance and management; form and format of the catalog; and microform format utilized.

Costs of COM catalogs cover retrospective conversion and catalog production. Catalog production costs will include tape reformating, editing for duplicates, recording and processing the master microform, and producing duplicate microforms. (COM costs are detailed more fully in other articles.) Additional costs are incurred for reader stations and maintenance of film and readers.

Discusses the possible agencies involved in catalog production and gives criteria for selecting a catalog vendor.

231. Stecher, G. "Shared Cataloguing: An Exercise in Costing OCLC." *Australian Academic and Research Libraries* 7 (March 1976): 1–11.
—Addendum. 7 (September 1976): 200–201.
—Comment by A.D. Hogan [letter]. 8 (September 1977): 148.
—Rejoinder. 8 (December 1977): 206–207.

Reviews existing studies and reports on costs of cataloging activities, then examines the effects of an OCLC type system on a library.

Copy cataloging and original cataloging are differentiated in terms of staffing levels needed and cataloging copy available. Searching and card production are two additional areas affected by automation of the cataloging process.

Assuming that there is a 70% hit rate, the card production workload will be reduced by 31% or 5% of total costs. For both pre-order and pre-cataloging searching, a reduction of staff by 40%, or 7.2% of total costs, is assumed. Copy cataloging will increase so staff needs will decrease by about 2.7% of total costs.

Based on a manual cost of $13.00 for acquiring cataloging and processing a title, automation will reduce that cost by 15% or 20%. These are costs of using an automated service however. Those must be added to the savings per title to find the real net savings. Low unit costs of $12.00 in manual systems will not be reduced, and may even increase, with the introduction of automated systems. A unit cost of $15.00 would result in a net saving if the staff reduction were around 20%. However there may be other benefits from systems like OCLC that cannot be directly attributed to the cataloging process.

232. Taylor, Raymond G., Jr. "Incremental Costs of Library Services Policies for Online Catalog Access." *Information Technology and Libraries* 6 (December 1987): 305–309.

Reports on a study comparing the costs of various library service policies and the conditions under which a library may convert to an online catalog system which is highly service oriented. Explores the queuing model and its major variables—arrival rate, service rate, and service policy—to properly determine the number of terminals required to meet a given policy. Findings show that libraries will face only minor incremental costs when adopting strong service policies for online public access unless their high arrival rates (average number of patrons that can be expected to arrive at and use a catalog facility in a typical peak-use minute) are combined with low service rates (fractional number of patrons a single terminal can accommodate in one minute). Conducting a local arrival-service study and providing the associated queuing solutions will assure the meeting of service policies and the monitoring of system performance and adequacy, while also providing data for planning and budgeting.

233. Tucker, C.J. "Comparison of the Production of Different Physical Forms of Catalogue Output." *Program* 8 (April 1974): 59–74.

Five production methods for printed catalogs and five for microform catalogs are compared. Production costs are for processing entries to produce a magnetic tape properly formatted and to convert that data into its final form. Conversion costs will vary with the size of the catalog, number of copies produced, and frequency of cumulations. The physical form of output may require additional computer processing to produce the appropriate format.

Tables compare catalog production by: ALA line printer; ALA line printer and offset/lithography; 16mm microfilm and offset/lithograph; graphic arts 16mm microfilm and offset/lithograph; computer typesetting and offset/lithograph; microfiche; 16mm microfilm; graphic arts microfiche; graphic arts 16mm microfilm; and PCMI ultrafiche.

234. Turner, Ann Craig. "Comparative Card Production Methods." *Library Resources & Technical Services* 16 (Summer 1972): 347–358.

Seven methods of card production are used, analyzed and costed.

Card duplication of unit cards and completion or finishing of the set are the major components. Duplication methods used are flexowriter, ten-up masters run on offset press, eight-up masters photocopied, and four-up masters photocopied. Production of the masters are either typing or pasting stencils or producing flexowriter tapes.

Detailed data are given for times procedures and for labor costs per set of cards. Comparison of production costs for these seven methods are made.

235. Valentine, Phyllis A. "Increasing Production in Cataloging While Decreasing Cost." *Technicalities* 4 (July 1984): 10–13.

Describes the creation of an automation unit to deal with new monograph titles which have Library of Congress cataloging copy available. A major change involves doing authority checking at the end of the process rather than at the beginning. A flowchart provides the steps followed by the automation unit.

Statistics gathered show that conflicts in names are lower than and number of cards filed without needing authority work is larger than estimated. The quantity of materials processed by the types of materials handled in the automation unit increases. Overall cataloging production goes up although the personnel budget goes down.

236. Valentine, Phyllis A.; McDonald, David R. "Retrospective Conversion: A Question of Time, Standards, and Purpose." *Information Technology and Libraries* 5 (June 1986): 112–120.

Examines five factors determining retrospective conversion costs: definition of conversion, standards of acceptance, method of conversion, hit rate, and standards for the original creation of records.

The methodology of a time and cost study for converting monograph records using RLIN is detailed. A description of the step, whether it occurs always or sometimes, the method of measurement, and the level of staff performing it is recorded for each of ten steps. The time and cost for each step is given in tabular form: step, staff level, time, and cost (including benefits, sick time, vacations and holidays, etc.).

The amount of time required for RLIN processing is presented in six steps: searching, filling in fixed and variable fields, creating holdings, solving problems, and recording the RLIN identification number. Type of record being established effects the conversion time. The average times needed for original, LC and member copy cataloging, and LC and member derived records are given. Conversion is broken down into costs for staff, RLIN telecommunications and maintenance, RLIN communications and CPU time.

Suggestions for reducing conversion costs include selecting the resource file that has the greatest number of records, converting only a portion of the collection, streamlining the conversion process itself, choosing a cost-effective conversion process, and reducing the content of records converted.

237. Villwock, Klaus M. "Computer Produced Catalogues: Book or COM, and Emma Chisit?" *LASIE* 6 (May/June 1976): 2–22.

Examines costs of photocomposition and COM fiche for catalog production. Increases in costs of book catalogs is attributed to the fact that every entry is regenerated and reproduced for every cumulation in order to interfile all the entries.

Although COM is much cheaper than photocomposition, there are other factors to consider: convenience of use by patrons and staff, costs of equipment required for accessing COM, and the vulnerability of COM fiche.

For those wedded to the book form, Villwock suggests giving briefer entries in the public catalog as a way to reduce costs. Until online catalogs become a reality, a combination of book cumulations and COM supplements are likely. Proposes a gradual introduction of COM as supplements, then abandonment of the book catalog.

Costs for photocomposition and COM fiche are detailed in appendices. Data on the growth of COM catalogs, costs for COM supplements, and costs for total COM cumulations are provided.

238. Virginia Beach Department of Public Libraries and Virginia Beach Department of Data Processing. *Cost/Benefit Analysis of a Catalog System for the Virginia Beach Department of Public Libraries.* Virginia Beach, Va.: City of Virginia Beach, 1978. (ED 153 657)

Defines components of cost/benefit analysis as including personnel, equipment, space, support services from vendors, supplies, overhead and fringe benefits.

Determines cost estimates for three alternative catalog production systems: COM from outside, COM produced within the city, and the current card system.

Describes the current system of producing catalogs for the main library and four branches using stencils. Maintenance procedures are also discussed. Sets forth requirements for a new automated catalog production system. Determines work flow for the current and projected systems using a modified PERT chart and used time studies of operations to estimate costs. Projected growth rates are included for costs of new branch library sites, catalog cabinets, shifting and cards. Time lines for the three alternatives are presented.

Factors of the proposed system developed by the city are for computer time, program development, conversion and operations. A list details the tasks involved and time needed. The system produced by an outside vendor covers only costs of conversion and operations.

Benefits of a COM catalog include the availability of union catalogs in all locations and production of specialized catalogs as needed. Costs and times spent on reserving items are charted to show expenditures that would be reduced somewhat by the existence of a union catalog.

Appendices include all the PERT charts and forms used in data collection. Data are recorded for tasks and levels of staff involved in each category, evaluation of overall times and costs, personnel costs by level of staff for the main and branch libraries, equipment costs, space costs, support services such as outside maintenance, supplies, and overhead costs.

239. Waldron, Helen J. *Book Catalogs: A Survey of the Literature on Costs.* Santa Monica, Calif.: Rand Corp. Communications Dept., 1971. (ED 053 775)

Discusses specifications for book catalogs: number of entries, number of pages, number of copies, frequency of publications, and page reduction. Relevant costs include input method, content, programming, equipment, reproduction and binding, and cost per copy.

Compares computer printouts and typeset print for output.

Tables detail the specification costs and composition methods extracted from 12 articles along with composition and printing costs as determined by a LARC study.

Annotated references are provided for 22 articles which provide data on book catalog costs and for 25 articles which discuss book catalogs but give no real cost information.

240. Wheeler, Joseph L. "Top Priorities for Cataloging-in-Source." *Library Journal* 94 (15 September 1969): 3007–3013.

—Comment by C.W. Koch. [letter]. 94 (1 November 1969): 4074.

—Comment by E.A. Howard [letters]. 94 (1 December 1969): 4321.

—Comment by E.A. Howard [letter]. 95 (1 January 1970): 13.

[also in *Landmarks of Library Literature, 1876–1976,* pp. 400–419. Metuchen, NJ: Scarecrow, 1976.]

Proposes cataloging-in-source as a method of reducing local cataloging costs. Quotes the cost of cataloging a volume ranging from $1.25–$3.00. Printed cards distributed by the Library of Congress, books with cards, the *American Book Publishing Record,* and shared cataloging are examined for costs, availability, and effectiveness. Suggests a ten cent per book fee to be paid quarterly by every library as a way to underwrite the cataloging-in-service project.

241. Wiederkehr, Robert R.V. *Alternatives for Future Library Catalogs: A Cost Model: Final Report of the Library Catalog Cost Model Project,* prepared for the Association of Research Libraries. Rockville, MD: King Research, 1980.

The model presented here is based on identifying alternative forms of library catalogs, cost elements associated with each form, and characteristics of the library.

Twelve forms of catalogs are included in this cost model. These forms consist of card, microform and online catalogs with unified or split files.

Cost and output elements are grouped into ten categories: number and growth rate of titles and headings; costs of cataloging, editing and authority control; costs of implementing *AACR 2;* costs specific to card catalogs; costs of retrospective conversion; costs specific to microform catalogs; cost specific to online catalogs; costs of training and orientation; cost of catalog use by non-cataloging staff; and cost adjustments.

Each of the catalog alternatives are expressed in terms of the cost and output elements necessary or characteristic. The operation and costs of the library must also be estimated for inclusion in the model. Definition of the library parameters and cost model equations are presented.

Appendices include a background paper "The Future of the Catalog," by Richard W. Boss (1979), guidelines for estimating staff costs, and an input form.

The models were used by 68 ARL members to estimate costs of the various alternatives in their libraries. The FORTRAN software for implementing the model is available for interactive use at the local level.

## ACQUISITIONS

242. Allardyce, A. "Some Optional Costs of the Gift and Exchange Section of the British Library Lending Division [based on a presentation at the IFLA council in Strbske Plesco, 1978]." *Interlending Review* 7 (July 1979): 90–98.

Describes a diary survey used to cost activities of workers. Includes organizational charts and flow charts.

Costs of processing books and periodical issues are given in pence so must be converted to find dollars and cents.

The breakdown in the tables is by internal and external disposition for books, periodicals, and international offerings. Activities are unpacking, cataloging, listing, sorting, allocating, and dispatching.

243. Association of Research Libraries. Systems and Procedures Exchange Center. *Library Materials Cost Studies*. SPEC Kit 95. Washington, DC: ARL, 1983.

A collection of cost studies on library materials based on local receipts, total cost, average cost, and data from published indexes on inflation. The data from these studies are used in preparing and justifying library materials budgets and assisting in the distribution of funds among subjects.

The four categories for 13 studies included are: local data, local justification using national data, automated local cost studies, and vendor cost studies.

About two dozen items are listed in "Selected Sources of Published Library Materials Price Information."

244. Axford, H. William. "The Economics of a Domestic Approval Plan." *College & Research Libraries* 32 (September 1971): 368–375.

[similar article also in International Seminar on Approval and Gathering Plans in Large and Medium Size Academic Libraries, 3d, West Palm Beach, Florida, 1971. *Economics of Approval Plans,* pp. 3–23. Westport, Conn.: Greenwood Press, 1972.]

Identifies three functions which are not needed in approval plans: preorder searching, vendor selection, and typing purchase orders. Elimination of those functions reduces the time and money per volume significantly. Uses data for functions and times from the larger cost of technical service operations for the libraries in the Florida State University System.

Describes a University of Oklahoma study which analyzes titles from

*Publisher's Weekly* for relevance to the library's collection policies. Relevant titles are checked for presence in the collection. The 466 items not found are compared to the approval plan profile. Almost half (191) are not appropriate and over half (275) are approval plan materials. Of the latter, 111 match Oklahoma's profile and 133 do not. Thirty-three (33) items are unaccounted for.

A sample from the Florida Atlantic University approval plan books is compared to titles received by other libraries in the system. Thirty to sixty-five percent of the approval plan titles are not found in other libraries' catalogs. University press titles are extracted and checked again. The resulting data reveal that university press books are acquired much later when other acquisitions procedures are used.

Concludes that approval plans are more efficient and effective than traditional procedures.

245. Axford, H. William. "The Validity of Book Price Indexes for Budgetary Projections." *Library Resources & Technical Service* 19 (Winter 1975): 5–12.

Compares the average prices of books as listed in the *Bowker Annual* with the average prices of books received through approval plans.

Problems include comparing the Library of Congress classification numbers assigned to approval plan books with the subject categories used by Bowker, lack of Canadian data in Bowker, and difference in reporting years (calendar vs fiscal).

Figures from the University of Nebraska, Florida Atlantic University and Arizona State University are used to determine average price per approval plan title.

Comparisons are made for five years: 1966/67, 1967/68 and 1969/70, 1970/71 and 1971/72. Suggests that for scholarly books in English, approval plan average prices may be more valid than those reported by Bowker.

246. Bajema, Bruce D. "Marin County Free Library: Cost Effectiveness of a Dedicated Mini-Computer for Acquisition and Circulation." In *Information Roundup: A Continuing Education Session on Microforms and Data Processing in the Library Information Center: Costs/Benefits/History/ Trends; Proceedings of the 4th Mid-Year Meeting of the American Society for Information Science (ASIS); May 15–17, 1975; Portland, OR*, edited by Frances G. Spigai, Theodore C.W. Graws, and Julia Kawabata, pp. 57–61. Washington, DC.: ASIS, 1975.

Compares cost of manual and computer based acquisition procedures. Acquisition functions include ordering, claiming, fund accounting, pre-cataloging slip production, and spine label production. The costs of the manual system are for purchased processing, four levels of personnel, and supplies. The automated system costs are for lease of the system, four level of personnel, supplies and telephone. Major savings result from replacing purchased processing with the automated system.

Similar comparisons are done for the circulation function.

247. Baumol, William J. and Marcus, Matityahu. *Economics of Academic*

*Libraries*, prepared for the Council on Library Resources by Mathematica, Inc. Washington: American Council on Education, 1973.

A study of library costs which includes a section on acquisitions costs. Gives input and summary data. Methodologies are described and some formulas are presented.

248. Bierman, Kenneth J.; Kayner, Nedra L.; Mallon, Jane. *Unit Time/Cost Study of the Acquisitions Unit, Technical Services Division, Tucson, Public Library*. Tucson, Ariz.: Tucson Public Library, 1980. (ED 194 090)

Daily log sheets are used to record time spent and quantities handled. Salary figures reflect direct personnel costs plus 30 percent in fringe benefits and adjusted salaries include overhead costs. Gives an overview of activities within acquisitions. Summaries of unit costs are exemplified by single copy new titles not Baker & Taylor supplied, single copy new titles supplied by Baker & Taylor, multiple copies of new titles and multiple added copies.

Presents detailed explanations of: ordering procedures; accounting procedures; receiving procedures; periodical handling; labeling; and system reserves.

Tables show each task with time and staff allocations per week, estimated annual costs, unit time/personnel costs (including fringes) yielding cost per unit, and unit time/personnel costs (including fringes and overhead) yielding cost per unit. Includes the data collection form for recording time and number of items or transactions.

249. Bluh, Pamela and Haines, Virginia C. "The Exchange of Publication; An Alternative to Acquisitions." *Serials Review* 5 (April/June 1979): 103–108.

Provides a general discussion on the costs of exchange programs. Fiscal accountability of the 1970s included a review of acquisition policies and procedures, including exchange programs.

Hidden costs must be taken into account. Those costs are for purchases of some materials which are distributed, postage, and for processing of items received.

Escalating subscription prices for journals have precipitated the need to reassess exchange programs. Heavy use and relevance to current needs are obvious characteristics to be used in evaluation.

Inflation and fluctuating exchange rates for the dollar demand constant monitoring of costs. Formal agreements must be viewed as a fiscal concern as well as social or political one.

Use of the International Exchange Service may reduce shipping expenses although delivery time is slowed.

250. Cohen, Jacob. "Book Cost and Book Use: The Economics of a University Library." In Conference on Resource Sharing in Libraries: 1976: University of Pittsburgh. *Library Resource Sharing: Proceedings of the 1976 Conference on Resource Sharing in Libraries, Pittsburgh, Penn.*, edited by Allen Kent, Thomas Galvin, pp. 197–224. New York: M. Dekker, 1977.

Presents an economic model of book costs and circulation. Suggests interlibrary loan as a way to provide books for use at a lesser cost than acquiring and circulating them.

Formulas for (1) a cost/benefit analysis of acquisitions costs and book use and (2) costs of resource sharing in place of book purchases are given.

251. du Preez, M.H.C. "Purchase Costs and Budget Control." *Mousaion* 5 (1987): 66–74.

Describes acquisitions problems with regard to purchasing costs and budget control in a South African university library. Describes complexities of calculating encumbrances, foreign exchange rates, fees, etc., and surveys the impact upon budget control.

252. Ejlersen, Rita. "Economic Aspects of the Exchange of Duplicates: Time Studies on Books: A Case Study." In *Studies in the International Exchange of Publications*, edited by Peter Genzel, pp. 97–109. IFLA Publications, 18. New York: K.G. Saur, 1981.

Acquisitions, processing and distribution procedures for handling duplicate monographs are described. The tasks and activities involved in each stage are enumerated.

Summary data on the 15 activities are presented for number of items, time per minute, and number of staff categories involved. Although no cost data are included, if salaries are known, costs can be computed.

253. Futas, Elizabeth. "A Searching Sequence for College Libraries." *Collection Building* 1 (1979): 77–80.

A sample of 300 American books with a 1973 publication date is searched in six bibliographic tools (*BIP, PTLA, ABPR, NUC, PW*, and *CBI*). The comprehensiveness—author/title, publisher, date, and price—and timeliness of the trade bibliographies are determined. *BIP, ABPR* and *NUC* are the tools felt to be most useful.

The time, and thus cost, involved in searching trade bibliographies can be reduced by following the suggested sequence of searching.

254. Groot, Elizabeth H. "Comparison of Library Tools for Monograph Verification." *Library Resources & Technical Services* 25 (April 1981): 149–61. —Discussion 25 (October 1981): 408–409.

Preorder verification of books is studied for effectiveness and cost using six bibliographic tools. Forty monographs are selected from each of nine subjects areas. A small number of foreign imprints is included. Items, appearing in the review literature beginning in January 1976, are selected. Verification tools used are *ABPR, BIP, CBI, NUC, Micrographic Catalog Retrieval System,* and OCLC.

Each searcher records the time required for verification in each tool, the imprint year for each monograph verified, and the earliest issue date of each tool in which the item was listed. Inaccuracies found or discrepancies are noted. Each searcher uses all the print sources, but separate teams search each of the other tools, MCRS and OCLC. Data are also recorded for the performance of each tool in the imprint year plus the following year, and imprint year plus all succeeding years.

A cost analysis method to calculate the break-even point between any two tools in dollars per minute is: determine the cost of owning and maintaining each tool and add the labor cost of verifying monographs (number of items times minute). Plug those on each side of a formula to determine the break-even point. Results of the study are given in the areas of coverage (percentage of titles listed, foreign imprints listed, percentage by years searched, percentage of subject coverage); currency (imprint year and succeeding years); speed of searching (minutes per item); and cost analysis based on labor cost per item verified.

A computer analysis reveals the overlap among the tools and suggests that searching begin with the tools that performs the best in a particular subject area.

255. Hayes, Sherman. "On Account: Deposit Accounts for Monograph Acquisitions: A Budget Stretching Technique." *Bottom Line* 1 (no. 4, 1987): 28–29.

Explores the risks and advantages in establishing a deposit prepayment account with a book vendor to reduce costs by gaining discounts. Three types of accounts are discussed.

256. Kim, Ung Chon. "Purchasing Books From Publishers and Wholesalers." *Library Resources & Technical Services* 19 (Spring 1975): 133–147.

Requests for multiple copies of 32 titles are used as the basis for this study. Orders are placed simultaneously with four wholesalers (Richard Abel, Baker & Taylor, John Coutts, and Midwest Library Services) and with the publishers of the titles.

As copies are received, date of receipt, quoted list price, quoted discount rate, service charge, and net price are recorded. The number of days each title has been outstanding and the percentage of cost price against list price are calculated.

Average delivery time for publishers is much shorter than for wholesalers. Discount rates of the wholesalers are higher than the average discount rate of the publishers. Efficiency is calculated based on discount rate and delivery time. Use of the formula can assist librarians in determining which source to utilize.

257. Lee, Sul H., ed. *Acquisitions, Budgets and Material Costs: Issues and Approaches.* New York: Haworth Press, 1988.

Collection of papers delivered at a national conference focusing on acquisitions processes, material costs and library budgeting which was held under the sponsorship of the University of Oklahoma Libraries and the University of Oklahoma Foundation on February 26 and 27 of 1987. Four of the papers deal with approval plans; others treat materials costs and new technology.

258. McClelland, W.G. "Management in Service Environment." *Aslib Proceedings* 25 (March 1973): 93–99.

Economic reasoning and concepts such as the time value of money, the handling of uncertainty through probability theory, expected value, and analysis of cost are useful in management of libraries.

The example used is the decision to incur expenditures by acquiring an item in expectation of future benefits through use of the item. Number of uses per year for five years is divided into acquisition cost to yield a net value of each use. McClelland says this approach is unrealistic because it is based on only five years' usage or on estimates of value. It also assumes the values of an item independent of other items which is not necessarily so.

The difficulty is in determining the value of the use of the library. Use is low because it takes time, not because the value of information is low. There is some correlation however between low use and acquisition of less than optimum resources.

259.  Martin, Dohn H. "MARC Tape as a Selection Tool in the Medical Library." *Special Libraries* 61 (April 1970): 190–193.

Compares costs of manual and automated systems using Library of Congress (LC) data for collection development. The manual system is based on receiving and reviewing LC proof slips. Selected titles are searched against the card catalog and acquisition files. Titles already held or ordered are discarded and those remaining are keypunched for the computer-based acquisition system.

The automated system relies on receipt of the MARC tapes from LC and selection of items based on classification number. A paper list, a magnetic tape, and punched cards are generated for titles selected.

Costs of the manual system include salaries, keypunching, machine time, LC proofslip subscription and supplies and average $.90 per title. The automated system costs are for development (programming, machine time, keypunching, and supplies) and operations (salaries, machine time, MARC tape subscription, and supplies) and average $1.25 per title. Although the costs of the automated system are higher, there is the possibility of sharing the MARC tape subscription costs with other libraries.

260.  Miller, Ruth H. and Niemeier, Martha W. "Vendor Performance: A Study of Two Libraries." *Library Resources and Technical Services* 31 (January/ March, 1987): 60–68.

Reports on a study of vendor performance done at the University of Evansville and the University of Southern Indiana. Four vendors were involved and both automated and manual acquisitions systems were used. Vendor fulfillment, delivery time, and cost were the primary concerns of the study, while other service elements were investigated as well, e.g., communication, surcharges, reports. Comparative data collected enabled administrators to identify certain vendor characteristics, resulting in the making of better management choices and the enhancement of financial control.

261.  Nisonger, Thomas E. "Cost Analysis of the LIBRIS II Automated Acquisitions System at the University of Texas at Dallas Library." *Library Acquisitions: Practice & Theory* 11 (1987): 229–238.

Analyzes the costs of using the LIBRIS automated acquisitions system at the University of Texas at Dallas Library over a period of three fiscal years from 1982 through 1985. Expenditures are tabulated for the monthly fee, equipment rental, unit charges, communication, and supplies, while the division between fixed and variable costs is calculated. Average cost and time per order is determined using the top down method i.e., by dividing the total cost by the quantity of output. Average cost per order was $3.13 while average time per order was 6.25 minutes for the three year period. Ordering additional material was hypothetically less costly because, in theory, the incremental cost is always less than the average cost per title due to economies of scale.

262. Rovelstad, H. "Economics of the Universal Serials and Book Exchange (USBE)." *Interlending Review* 7 (July 1979): 98–101.

Gives cost per item from 1968–1977. Also includes preliminary figures for receiving items and maintaining the collection. No methodology is given.

263. Rovelstad, H. "Economics of the Universal Serials and Book Exchange (USBE)." In *Studies in the International Exchange of Publications,* edited by Peter Genzel, pp. 110–118. IFLA Publications, 18. New York: K.G. Saur, 1981.

The general operating structure, governance and operations of the Universal Serials and Book Exchange are described.

Cost and item studies yield data on average expenditure per item by relating publications processed for shipping to total annual expenses for 1970 through 1979. For 1977, time and cost per item distributed are provided for administration and overhead; receiving; reviewing, shelving and collection maintenance; processing of requests; and shipping. Those costs are broken down by salaries, fringes, housing and equipment, publicity and board expenses, and other. Further breakdowns of receiving and collection maintenance costs are by numbers of items discarded on receipt, discarded after checking shelves, discarded from shelves, supplied to libraries, and shelved but not yet distributed.

264. Steinbrenner, Julie. "Cost-Effectiveness of Book Rental Plans." *Ohio Library Association Bulletin* 49 (April 1979): 5–6.

—Discussion. 50 (April 1980): 28.

Enumerates advantages of book rental plans and compares costs to those of purchasing the same items.

The average cost of books received through a rental plan is $6.58 and of books purchased is $5.70. Exercise of the purchase option for rental books results in an additional $2.52 cost per book.

The discussion states that rental plans can save time by eliminating some selection, acquisition and weeding.

265. Sumier, Claudia; Barone, Kristine; Goetz, Art. "Getting Books Faster and Cheaper: A Jobber Acquisitions Study." *Public Libraries* 19 (Winter 1980): 103–105.

Determines the costs of acquiring processed materials directly from a jobber rather than from a processing center.

Components of each jobber's costs are: maximum discount, minimum processing fee, and minimum shipping costs. The two jobbers compared are almost equal in these respects; so the questions to be resolved are how well each jobber will meet the terms specified and what turnaround time will be. Because each jobber has some unique features, the members of the processing center develop a study to compare end results of jobber acquisitions.

Data are gathered for the number of books received by category (e.g., adult non-fiction, juvenile fiction, paperbacks), discount rate by category and the number of weeks between order and receipt of materials. An important part of the process is tracking jobber responses to problems. In addition, one library tests an online ordering system.

266. Tatterton, E.; King, K.; and Allardyce, A. "Costing Analysis of the Gift and Exchange of the British Library Lending Division (based on an internal report by R. Steemson)." In *Studies in the International Exchange of Publications,* edited by Peter Genzel, pp. 75–92 IFLA Publications, 18. New York, K.G. Saur, 1981.

Main stages of each operation are flowcharted and block diagrams constructed. Tables of the operations are made and diary forms issued to staff. Data on overhead and administration or management are not collected.

Tasks monitored are listed, time spent on each given and output recorded. Unit costs are extracted on costs of adding and processing books and periodicals coming through the gift and exchange unit.

267. Tyson, Blake. "Too Many, Too Often?" *New Library World* 80 (August 1979): 145–146.

Addresses the effectiveness of purchasing fewer multiple copies. Data needed are cost and use of each volume to establish a cost-effectiveness ratio or CER. Cost multiplied times months since acquisition divided by number of loans recorded yields the CER.

These CER values can be used to justify the purchase of additional copies. The CER value, in pounds, is 50–75 for second copies, 30 for third copies, 20 for fourth copies and 10 for fifty copies.

268. Yu, Priscilla C. "Cost Analysis: Domestic Serials Exchanges." *Serials Review* 8 (Fall 1982): 79–82.

Examines the economics of the University of Illinois' (IU) domestic exchange program. The study looks only at actual subscription costs of serials received and sent out on exchange over a one-year period. Overhead costs are not included. A ten percent sample is systematically selected from the 478 exchange units. The card for each library lists the titles supplied by UI and those received from the library.

Current subscription prices are obtained from *Ulrich's International Periodical Directory* or the piece itself. Slightly over half of the titles received have prices and total $822. Prices cannot be found for one-fourth; and one-fifth are available free.

For those titles sent out by UI, one-third can be priced and are valued at $764. The others are issued by campus departments and are available to the UI Library at no charge.

Tables compare the titles sent and received by broad subject area for number, total cost and average prices. Further study of the social sciences and humanities areas is desirable because of the cost differences between titles sent and titles received on exchange. General benefits of obtaining exchange materials are discussed.

269. Astle, Deana L. "With Sci/Tech Journals, Hidden Costs Cost A Lot." *Library Acquisitions: Practice & Theory* 12 (1988): 163–167.

Addresses the quality problem in journal content. Urges librarians to establish dialogues with publishers to encourage them to support more rigorous editing policies. Librarians also may develop ways to determine impact factors of the journals in library collections. Points to work done in this regard at LSU where citation analysis data are added to cost information on serials.

## SERIALS

270. Blackwell's Periodicals Conference, 2nd. Trinity College, Oxford, 1977. *Economics of Serials Management: Proceedings of the 2nd Blackwell's Periodicals Conference held at Trinity College, Oxford, 23–24 March 1977,* edited by David P. Woodworth. Loughborough: Serials Group, School of Librarianship, Technical College; distributed by Blackwell's Periodical Division, Oxford, 1977.

Journal publishing and distributing are the focus of the first four papers. The library's use of serials and budgeting for serials are covered next. Includes no real cost data; rather, presents general principles for serials use.

271. Bourne, Charles P. [and] Gregor, Dorothy. *Methodology and Background Information to Assist the Planning of Serial Cancellations and Cooperative Serials Collection in the Health Sciences.* Berkeley: Institute of Library Research, University of California, 1975.

Provides details on ten factors to consider in evaluating serial subscriptions on a title-by-title basis. Those factors are subscription costs, subscriptions available elsewhere, extent of coverage by abstracting and indexing services, frequency of citation, extent of recorded library use, frequency of publication, binding and storage costs, availability in microform, relevance to institutional objectives, and ranking or evaluation by the library constituency.

The study confines data collection to the first five areas. The methodology begins with identifying serial titles for study. Possible groups are subject categories, subscriptions of a particular branch or campus library, titles covered by a designated abstracting or indexing or SDI publication, or titles published in particular countries or languages.

Guidelines for cancellation of titles may be based on decision rules such as the following: cancel subscriptions in excess of two if there is less than one circulation per year, cancel subscriptions in excess of one if there are less than two circulations per year, cancel all titles not covered by at least one abstracting or indexing service. There are examples of cuts that could be made if these rules are applied.

272. Cayless, C.F. and Merritt, C.G. "The Keeping Cost of Periodicals." *Australian Academic Research Libraries* 8 (December 1977): 178–185.

Presents a method for determining the keeping cost of an individual title. Keeping costs are variable (continuing) and fixed (one time).

Work sampling techniques are used to obtain standard times for activities of acquiring and maintaining a serial title. Times are related to frequency to yield an annual total. Activities are divided into five areas: acquisitions and cataloging, accounting, check-in, reading room, and overhead. Problems associated with these are discussed.

The method involves activity sampling to ascertain unit times, derivation of fixed costs (overhead, maintenance, and cataloging) and combining these with salary rates and numbers of items to yield the keeping cost.

273. Chudamani, K.S. and Shalini, R. "Journal Acquisition—Cost Effectiveness of Models." *Information Processing and Management* 19 (1983): 307–311.

The development of models can be characterized by: unit of effectiveness, method of ranking, threshold point, ranked list, and graph. Each of these is described briefly. Three models for a journal selection program are compared: the Brooks model, a precision ranking model, and a cost-effectiveness model. Data required for the study are productivity of journal (relevant items), journal cost, journal size (total items per year), and photocopy cost. Examines the models by analyzing the cost versus the threshold point, the percentage of literature available versus cost, journal productivity versus cost, and nuclear zone or journals in common on ranked lists generated by each model. Concludes that the cost effectiveness model offers the best cost effectiveness measure of the three models.

274. Editors of JAL. "Paying the Piper: ARL Libraries Respond to Skyrocketing Journal Subscription Prices." *Journals of Academic Librarianship* 14 (March 1988): 4–9.

Reports on survey sent to ARL library directors on effects of rising journal costs. Responses reveal facts about faculty reactions, campus involvement, retrenchment strategies, long range considerations, service implications, and publisher relations.

275. Fayollat, James. "On-Line Serials Control System in a large Biomedical Library, Part III: Comparison of On-Line and Batch Operations and Cost Analysis." *Journal of the American Society for Information Science* 24 (March/April 1973): 80–86.

Cost data for operating the batch system cover personnel, supplies and computer time. Benefits accrue in the area of interlibrary loan, reference services, claiming and bindery operations. Projection of personnel and equipment costs for online operation of the system show an overall increase in computer charges, equipment and supplies and a decrease in personnel costs.

276. Galejs, John E. "Economics of Serials Exchanges." *Library Resources & Technical Services* 16 (Fall 1972): 511–520.

The cost of a serials exchange is based on materials, personnel, office space, supplies and equipment. These costs must be weighed against the cost of processing individual orders and payments if all or some of the materials acquired by exchange are purchased. Currency conversion, time, and goals and values must also be taken into account.

Costs of the exchange operation at the Iowa State University Library are for materials furnished, personnel, shipping and distribution, and perishable supplies. These costs are compared to the value of serials received. Monetary values are determined by locating prices from bibliographic tools and estimation. Other values and benefits considered include out-of-print materials, single back issues of serials, and the quality and variety of titles received in this manner.

277. Goehlert, Robert. "Journal Use per Monetary Unit: A Reanalysis of Use Data." *Library Acquisitions: Practice and Theory* 3 (1979): 91–98.

Data from a previous use study of political science journals are analyzed. Costs include the subscriptions; ordering, receiving, processing, accounting and shelving; and binding preparation and binding. Storage costs are excluded. Estimated and actual costs are used to calculate the total cost. The journals requested most in the previous use study are ranked according to costs of journals, per request, per user, and per page. Comparisons of journals are made using these data.

The type of cost analysis performed (e.g., per page, per use) affects the ranking of any specific journal. The data can be useful in deciding whether to cancel a subscription, order an additional copy or to obtain articles on interlibrary loan.

278. Hamaker, Charles. "Serials Costs and the Carrying Ability of Serials Budgets 1987." *Serials Librarian* 13 (October/November, 1987): 129–134.

Reports on findings from a number of academic libraries that 10–20% of serials titles are accounting for 50–70% of expenditures. For instance, three publishers—Elsevier, Springer and Pergamon—were found to represent 2.5% of Louisiana State University's serials titles and 19% of current subscription costs. The marketing strategy employed by publishers who attempt to account for a large proportion of serials budgets is described, and methods of coping with it through closer scrutiny and regular review are suggested.

279. Hentschke, Guilbert C. and Kehoe, Ellen. "Serial Acquisition as a Capital Budgeting Problem." *Journal of the American Society for Information Science* 31 (September 1980): 357–362.

Uses operations research to create a model for the decision to purchase periodicals on a one-year versus three-year subscription basis. Obvious factors affecting the decision are average price per title for one or three years, renewal handling costs, and multiple-year rates. Other considerations are price changes, use of (replacement) online services, and change in journals needed. These factors plus the capital costs are built into a model with three alternatives: continue to pur⸱ se periodicals as one-year subscriptions; purchase all periodicals as three-year subscriptions beginning immediately; or convert to a three-year subscription policy gradually over three years.

Testing of the model is done using 20 periodicals from business and management science. The findings suggest that under all conditions savings would result in moving from a one-year purchasing policy to buying all three-year subscriptions at once. If a library can negotiate a budget to allow this course of action, more resources expended immediately will result in spending less in the long run.

Caveats include the subject area of the sample, no three-year subscription rate for all periodicals, a lack of capital available immediately and an inability to cancel a subscription after one year (under a three-year policy). Staffing levels mean that implementation cannot be done immediately but resembles the phased approach.

280. Houghton, B. and Prosser, C. "Rationalization of Serial Holdings in Special Libraries." *Aslib Proceedings* 26 (June 1974): 226–235.

—Line, M.B. [Letter in reply to B. Houghton and C. Prosser]. 26 (November 1974): 447-448.

Applies a modification of Brookes technique of ranking journals in a specific field by number of relevant articles to determine a cutoff point for cancelling subscriptions.

The modified technique includes calculating average cost of a journal subscription plus average cost of selection, acquisition, processing and maintenance of one journal for one year. These costs are compared to the average cost of purchasing a photocopy, including staff costs.

An alternative method to arrive at the cutoff point is examined. This involves arriving at a cost per use figure. The subscription price plus handling cost is divided by the number of recorded uses. It is seen that some titles are less costly per use than indicated by the Brooke's formula. Other drawbacks to the Brooke's technique include inconvenience caused by delay, provision of minority interest journals, varying patterns of journals use, and variability of subscription costs.

A technique involving the relationship between the total use of a journal collection and the total cost of journals is developed. It is based on: rank in descending order of use and total use data; annual subscription costs; and plotting cumulative cost (horizontally) and cumulative use (vertically). The point of diminishing returns is 60–70 percent of total journal costs and 90 percent of use. This technique offers these advantages: average cost of journals is irrelevant, average processing cost is irrelevant, and data collection problems are minimized.

281. Koenig, Michael E.D. and others. "SCOPE: A Cost Analysis of an Automated Serials Record System." *Journal of Library Automation* 4 (September 1971): 129–140.

Approaches analysis of costs as an investment decision. Cost analysis is based on the "net present value method." Cash flows, future and expected, are converted to a present value; and alternative uses of the resources are examined. Some adjustment is necessary because of inflation.

Cost analysis of an automated serials control system covers set-up costs (programming, conversion, personnel, and computer time) and yearly running costs (maintenance, computer time, and machine conversion). Those are subtracted from operational savings and increased efficiency to determine savings.

282. Maass, Eleanor A. "Low-Cost Automation of Periodicals Information in a College Library" In *Cost Reduction for Special Libraries and Information Centers,* edited by Frank Slater, pp. 120–126. New York: American Society for Information Science, 1973.

A batch system based on punched cards is used to create a current subscription list of 2200 periodical titles. The FORTRAN program can also generate printouts by subject or fund.

Data included for each periodical are title, subject, fund, annual cost, format (film or bound), volumes bound per year, and other miscellaneous codes. The printouts generated are used for review of subscriptions by academic departments, weeding and discarding of gift subscriptions, and a list of titles retained or microfilm. A duplicate deck of punched cards is used to generate monthly binding lists.

Check-in and holdings functions are considered but not developed because of the cost and inconvenience of the former and a regional project for the latter.

Costs for file conversion and maintenance are included.

283. Matthews, Mary and Sherman, Steve B. "How to Computerize Your Serials and Periodicals When you Don't Know How." *Wilson Library Bulletin* 44 (April 1970): 361–364.

A case study in developing a computerized serials list.

Fixed length records are designed, information transferred from Kardex to worksheets, and data keypunched. Work with the computer center to develop software to store, sort and print the data is undertaken. Printouts are used to produce multiple copies of the list by title and a reference list arranged by call number.

The costs and time summary includes actual dollar and hour expenditures by the library plus hidden costs and time absorbed by the computing center and duplication service.

284. Miller, Heather S. "Keeping the Lid On: Approaches to the Control of Costs in Reference Book Purchasing in a Academic Library." *Reference Librarian* 15 (Fall 1986): 281–302.

After citing recent statistical findings that indicate that the serials reference book may pose the most severe cost problem for the reference book budget, the article reports on a project at the State University of New York, Albany Library to list all standing orders and chart their costs and price increases. Having this information in manipulable form using a PC has enabled bibliographers as well as acquisitions personnel to keep more careful watch over this portion of the materials budget.

285. Palmour, Vernon C.; Bellassai, Marcia C.; [and] Wiederkehr, Robert R.V. *Cost of Owning, Borrowing, and Disposing of Periodical Publications.* Arlington, Va.: Center for Naval Analyses, Public Research Institute, 1977.

Presents a model to determine whether a library should acquire or borrow specific journals. Bases the decision on frequency of use, cost of borrowing and cost of owning.

Costs of owning include ordering and cataloging a new title or review, renewal, check-in, claiming, shelving, training and supervision, binding preparation and binding as well as subscription fees. Borrowing costs are those incurred for an interlibrary loan transaction: staff time for verification, location and handling plus postage and any charges levied by the lender.

The formula comprising the model is explained in the appendices as is the methodology to be followed.

286. Presley, Roger L. "The Rising Cost of Serials and Effective Collection Management." *Serials Librarian* 13 (October/November 1987): 155–158.

Describes the presentations of Ann C. Weller, Janet A. Dalquist, and Deborah Morrow at a workshop on serials costs and deselection. Weller's ten deselection considerations are listed, and Dalquist and Morrow's experience with a journal expenditure reduction of 43% is recounted and conclusions are drawn.

287.   Reed, J.R. "Cost Comparison of Periodicals in Hard Copy and on Microform." *Microform Review* 5 (July 1976): 185–192.

Replacing current periodicals with microform is examined. Analyzes: paper and microform subscription costs; maintenance costs (binding and replacement); equipment costs (cabinets, readers, and maintenance); environmental costs (air conditioning and humidity control); storage costs (building space per square feet); and service costs (circulation, reshelving or refiling, and user assistance). Determining accurate comparisons depends on number of titles and associated costs.

288.   Riddick, John. "Manual versus Automated Check-in: A Comparison Study of Two Academic Libraries." *Serials Review* 6 (October/December 1980): 49–51.

Studies of check-in operations in two libraries—one doing manual receipt and the other using the OCLC serials check-in system—are conducted over four months. Approximately 25% of the total issues received annually are handled in each location. The check-in process includes these functions: preparation of the issue for checking in, labeling, checking in the issue, and physical processing of the issue. The form for recording data asks for the date, times for beginning and ending each function, total minutes spent on the function and total pieces processed.

Tables compare the percentage of time spent, average processing time per issue, and check-in costs per issue. The automated system takes longer and is more expensive. Possible reasons include slower response time in the mornings and service charges per issue.

289.   Roberts, Constance F.; Vidor, Ann B.; and Bailey, Dorothy C. "Time and Cost Analysis of Title Changes in Serials." *Serials Librarian"* (December, 1986/January, 1987): 137–142.

Analyzes all periodical title changes over a two month period, calculating processing time and resulting labor costs at Georgia Tech Library in an attempt to answer the question "What does a single such title change mean in terms of time and expense for a middle sized research library?" The findings indicate an average of 1.375 hours and $14.14 per typical title change. A complex title change obviously increases both the labor costs and time. Steps in cataloging and processing a title change are enumerated. Georgia Tech spends approximately 160 hours and $1,640 a year in processing these changes, figures somewhat less costly than originally perceived.

290.   Stevens, Jana K.; Kelly, Jade G.; and Irons, Richard G. "Cost-effectiveness of Soviet Serial Exchanges." *Library Resources & Technical Services* 26 (April 1982): 151–155.

Twenty-six Soviet institutions and 70 Soviet serial publications are compared with the publications provided on exchange. Prices can be determined for less than 40 of the Soviet titles. The library determines that they have a monetary disadvantage of over $1800 for serials alone. The overhead and postage costs for Soviet exchanges are relatively small and discontinuance cannot be justified on those bases. The concern is the discrepancy between value received for value given and what to do about it. A policy of obtaining on exchange only those items not available through journal trade channels will result in an even more unfavorable balance.

Close watch needs to be kept on exchange balances and there is a need to keep abreast of vendor offerings. The question of cost is important when items are available outside of exchange agreements. Individual libraries will have to deal with how to maintain a balance in their exchanges.

291. Williams, Gordon; Bryant, Edward C.; Wiedekehr, Robert R.V.; Palmour, Vernon E.; Siehler, Cynthia J. *Library Cost Models: Owning Versus Borrowing Serial Publications.* Washington, D.C.: Westat Research Inc. for NSF, Office of Science Information Service, 1968.

Provides mathematical methods for libraries to use in examining serials costs. The frequency of use of serial titles and the cost of providing those titles are compared to the expenses of obtaining an interlibrary loan or photocopy of the articles needed. Cost alone is not the determining factor however—access time is also an important consideration.

The models are developed using data from a survey of our libraries. Principal cost factors in either owning or borrowing serial titles are identified and operations analyzed for data collection possibilities. The average costs per title of performing 11 serials functions is determined. The functions supporting serial subscriptions are acquisition (excluding subscriptions), subscriptions, cataloging, check-in, claiming, binding preparation, binding, marking administration, training and other.

Costs are charted for no overhead and for 50 percent overhead. Interlibrary borrowing and binding costs are also charted in this way. The cost models presented are based on owning costs: initial selection, ordering, and cataloging; recurring costs of subscription, check-in, claiming, binding and marking; storage or maintenance; disposition or weeding; and internal use and associated reshelving and shelf maintenance. Annual demands per title are dependent in part on back issues held.

Cost comparisons are determined for titles currently being received and for new titles. Options for current titles include discontinuing and discarding back issues, discontinuing and keeping back issues or continuing the subscription. Decisions about new subscriptions may be based on whether a library can borrow or buy back issues if available.

The appendices include a breakdown of the costs associated with owning a serial title, sample data collection forms, and the costs models themselves.

292. Yavarkovsky, Jerome. "On Account: Auditing Acquisitions." *Bottom Line* Charter Issue (1986): 34–35.

Describes the features of audit control as they may be applied to acquisitions processing, document control, responsible vendor performance, and proper authorization.

GENERAL TECHNICAL SERVICES

293. Association of Research Libraries. Systems and Procedures Exchange Center. *Indirect Cost Rates in Research Libraries*. SPEC Kit 65. Washington, DC: ARL, 1980.

Indirect cost categories for federal contracts and grants which are typically recovered by institutions include library costs. These have been determined on the basis of an unweighted headcount of students, professional employees (faculty and other full-time employees) and other users.

Data on materials costs, salaries, and types of users are important in determining methods for allocating library costs.

This kit contains indirect cost studies or calculations from ARL libraries plus data from the National Association of College and University Business Officers.

Data collections forms and survey instruments are included in some of the studies.

294. Ayres, F.H. (Frederick Henry)... [et al.] *USBC (Universal Standard Book Code): Its Use for Union File Creation: A Feasibility Study for a National Database*. London, [England]: British Library, Bibliographic Services Division, 1984.

Provides a methodology for merging machine readable files and detection of duplicate records. Tapes of over 600,000 bibliographic records from eight databases are used.

Preparatory work encompasses tape conversion, machine comparison of records, USBC specifications and runs. The production phase deals with input of tapes, duplicate extraction by generating a USBC derived from the record which is a unique record identifier, and merging of unique records into one database. Duplicates are manually analyzed after machine sorting. The tapes are also checked for duplicates using the ISBN and merged into a second database. The duplicates files are then compared. Costs for coding, sorting, cleaning, and merging are given per 1000 records.

The objectives of the study are to: determine whether the USBC can be used to create a merged retrospective database; estimate the cost of merging retrospective files; identify characteristics of retrospective files which may reduce the effectiveness of the merge process; and provide a detailed analysis of the overlap between retrospective files..

Problems occurring during the study: missing pagination from tag 300, need for defining "duplicate," and series information scattered under six tags.

Economic viability of a national database can be achieved if holdings or location information is kept in a separate file and access to search keys is free while display of the bibliographic record incurs a charge.

Appendices give statistics for record processing at different stages, duplicates, overlap, precision of USBC, occurrence of ISBNs, comparative performances of USBC and ISBN, and storage requirements.

295. Babel, Deborah B. "Archival Tape Processing: Considerations for a Network." *Technical Services Quarterly* 4 (Fall 1986): 11–18.

Areas of decisions for tape processing include: archive tape extraction, removing duplicates, merging holdings, *AACR 2* upgrade (authority control for names and series), and production of bar codes. Considerations for shared or networked systems are lack of *AACR 2* upgrade software and consolidation of institutional tapes. Archival tape processing must advance to meet requirements.

An appendix gives costs of tape extraction by OCLC and SOLINET, local system processing, and bar code production.

296. Bommer, Michael, and Ford, Bernard. "A Cost-Benefit Analysis for Determining the Value of an Electronic Security System." *College & Research Libraries* 35 (July 1974): 270–279.

—Comment by F.H. Ayres [letter], with rejoinder. 36 (March 1975): 153–154.

Two methods for estimating item losses using a sample from the shelflist are presented. Assuming an electronic security system is 90 percent effective, a formula is used to show the benefits gained. The break-even analysis determines when the system will pay for itself.

297. Byrnes, Margaret M. and Elkington, Nancy E. "Continuing Preservation Microfilming Costs at the University of Michigan Library." *Microform Review* 16 (Winter 1987): 37–39.

Reports on streamlining efforts taken in the brittle book replacement program at the University of Michigan Library. Among the procedures modified were those dealing with selectors' review, collation, targeting, bibliographic inspection, circulation paperwork, and transfers and withdrawals. Potential additional cost savings measures are discussed as well.

298. "Cost of Weeding a Library Collection." *Library Journal* 91 (January 15, 1966): 194.

Costs of physically preserving a volume—including deacidifying, providing catalog control and low temperature housing plus maintenance are stated.

Costing the weeding process involves looking at salaries and examination rate to discover the cost per volume discarded.

Excerpted from an Association of Research Libraries report, "The Preservation of Deteriorating Materials."

299. Gertz, Janet. "The University of Michigan Brittle Book Microfilming Program: A Cost Study." *Microform Review* 16 (Winter 1987): 32–36.

Describes operations of program whereby brittle books judged worthy of retention could be systematically replaced. The nine steps of the procedure were identification and retrieval of eligible titles; bibliographic searching; selector's review; noting in RILN the date of the decision to film; collation and completion of the book for filming; target preparation; microfilming; film inspection; and cataloging of a microfilm and upgrading of RILN record. A costs study, based on a sample of fifty titles, was prepared on the nine step process which showed the average cost of evaluating, filming, and cataloging a brittle book was $35.71, two-thirds of which derives from the filming process itself. The difference between locally produced film and commercial replacements was found to be minimal.

300. Haka, Clifford H. and Stevens, Nancy. *A Guidebook for Shelf Inventory Procedures in Academic Libraries.* Occasional Paper number 10. Washington, DC: Association of Research Libraries, Office of Management Studies, 1985.

Presents narratives and flowcharts for in-stack and out-of-stack inventories. The section on "Conducting a Pilot Inventory" includes brief discussions of how to project personnel costs and how to determine cost-benefits.

Conducting the inventory encompasses developing procedures for the inventory itself—which means dealing with misshelved books, processing discrepancies and items missing from the shelves or collection—as well as record keeping for statistical purposes.

There are sample forms for recording the progress of an inventory by class number ranges for both Dewey and Library of Congress classification schemes.

Appendices include the questionnaire for a "Survey of Academic Research Libraries Regarding Inventory Practices (1980)" and a summary of the survey results. There is a short bibliography.

301. Haka, Clifford H. and Ursery, Nancy. "Inventory Costs: A Case Study." *College & Research Libraries* 46 (March 1985): 169–172.
—Discussion. 46 (September 1985): 435.

The process of conducting an inventory is described: reading the stacks, processing cards with no books, processing books with no cards, checking the public catalog, and searching the stacks.

Average time spent per shelflist drawer is divided and a salary cost per drawer is determined.

Costs for both the Dewey and Library of Congress classified sections are given.

302. Johnson, Steven D. "Rush Processing." *Journal of Academic Librarianship* 11 (September 1985): 214–218.

Examines, among other issues, the costs involved in the rapid provision of books that are urgently needed. Describes a rush study done in 1984 at Clemson University Library which suggests the need to keep rush orders to less than 5% of the total in order to control costs.

303. Lawrence, Gary S. "Cost Model for Storage and Weeding Programs." *College & Research Libraries* 42 (March 1981): 139–147.

Discusses the trade-offs in choosing to retain, store, or weed an item. Gives an economic model for determining the cost of storing or discarding an item.

Factors affecting the model, a simplification of Palmour's cost model, are the discount rate and planning period, costs of campus retention or relegation to storage, and costs of weeding or removal from the collection.

There are crossover or break-even points for various storage and disposal options. Areas of potential difficulty are accuracy of cost estimates, acceptability of assumptions and capacity to apply the results.

304. Leimkuhler, Ferdinand F. *Mathematical Models for Library Systems Analysis*. Lafayette, Indiana: School of Industrial Engineering, Purdue University, 1967.

A general discussion of mathematical models that have applicability in libraries.

The marginal analysis or cost minimization model is especially useful. With this model, one identifies the various cost components which are dependent on the activity level of one or more controllable factors which tend to increase costs in some cases and decrease them in others.

Statistical inference allows one to make reliable statements about the content and behavior of large book collections on the basis of relatively small samples.

An example of a library problem studied is efficient storage of library collections. Dividing the collection by size of an item is studied and especially rating assigned to alternatives. Usage models must also be considered as a part of any storage plan.

Another area for study is the application of computer-aided, microanalytic technique of information retrieval to book collections and its relationship to file subdivisions.

305. Martyn, J. and Vickery, B.C. "Complexity of the Modeling of Information Systems." *Journal of Documentation* 26 (September 1970): 204–220.

The roles of user needs, alternative service modes and costing levels are examined as part of the decision making process in designing an information system.

Includes a cost model for the production of an accession list.

306. McClung, Patricia A. "Costs Associated with Preservation Microfilming: Results of the Research Libraries Group Study." *Library Resources & Technical Services* 30 (October 1986): 363–374.

Reports the results of a cost study of the steps in preservation microfilming. Seven institutions gather data on the time and costs for completing each of 12 steps for 50 titles at two different times. The 12 steps are: identification of titles; retrieval of materials; preparation of circulation records; searching for existing microforms; curatorial review to select titles for filming; recording intent to film in the RLIN database; physical preparation of items for filming; preparation of targets; filming; inspection of films; cataloging the microform editions; and storing the master negatives.

Only labor costs are calculated, except for steps 9 and 12, where supplied are included. The average cost at each institution ranges from $25.81 to $71.80 per title. The median cost is $48.20. Steps 1–3 account for less than a $1.00 median cost per title. The median cost for curatorial review (step 5) is $0.41 while the physical preparation (steps 7–8) takes 36.6 minutes and costs $5.28 (median time and cost). Filming costs range from $0.18 per frame to $0.34 for producing three generations of film; and median costs for inspection is $1.44 and averages seven minutes per title. Cataloging and queuing times combined are from 23 to 66 minutes per title and the median cost is $5.60. Costs for labor and supplies used in labeling and shipping is $0.15 and takes 1.75 minutes per title.

Tables present the low, high, and median time and cost data for each of the 12 steps. Variations in time and cost depends on the nature of the materials themselves; labor costs at a given institution; and practices followed for cataloging, catalog production, and filming. Procedures and standards used are agreed to by all participants. Revision of project guidelines and streamlining of procedures is done as appropriate.

For similar projects, one can assume that filming costs will make up 45% to 78% of the total costs. An appendix provides a work sheet for estimating costs.

307.  Overmier, Judith and Ihrig, Elizabeth. "Eighteenth-Century Short-Title Catalogue: A Medical Model of the Costs of Participation by Specialized Collections." *College & Research Libraries* 43 (November 1982): 445–449.

Reviews the history and purpose of the ESTC project. Identifies and surveys over 100 medical libraries about their participation. Only 45 percent of those with medical rare book collections are contributing. Nonparticipation is attributed in part to a lack of knowledge about the project. Other factors are the costs to libraries for staff time and photocopying.

The authors conduct a study at their library to determine costs and to encourage others to participate. Time spent on eight steps in the process is recorded and averages 2.5 minutes per title. Cost per title is $0.41 using professional librarians' time. Some steps can be done by paraprofessional or student help and thus reduce costs. Photocopying of cards ($25.70) and title pages ($128.50) amounts to $154.20 for 1285 titles. Times from a Pennsylvania State University test are included for comparison purposes.

308.  Poole, Frazer G. "Preservation Costs and Standards." *Special Libraries* 59 (1968): 614–19.

Discusses standards for preservation in the areas of preserving the original, binding, microform and environmental standard. Sample costs of preservation in four shops or locations, including the Library of Congress, are presented for: deacidification, repair, restoration, and lamination. Cost of microfilming done at the Library of Congress in 1966–67 plus those for repair and binding of rare books are also given. Cost data were taken from actual price lists and from reports by LC.

309.  Ratcliffe, F.W. "Manchester University Library Bindery: A Study of Library Efficiency and Management." *Libri* 20 (1970): 77–88.

Compares cost of an in-library bindery with commercial services. External binding costs are extracted from price lists for both book and periodical bindings in different size ranges. Internal costs are calculated from statistics of items bound, number of staff and salaries expended.

Extra charges for thick books and pressmarking are not included in the comparisons. Additional services of the library bindery include pamphlet binding, repairs and refurbishing, edgebinding and catalog card cutting and punching. These services are not available from the commercial binderies.

Costs of equipment in the library bindery are given but neither those nor overhead costs are used for comparisons.

310.  Russell, Ann. "If You Need to Ask What It Costs." In *The Library Preservation Program: Models, Priorities, Possibilities: Proceedings from a Confer-*

*ence held in Washington, D.C., April 29, 1983,* edited by Jan Merrill-Oldham and Merrily Smith, pp. 84–87. Chicago: ALA, 1985.

There are no simple answers to the question of restoration costs. The full treatment of a book, including washing and deacidification of every folio and complete rebinding, is likely to cost in excess of $500. Routine cleaning, deacidification and minimal mending may be less than $5 per document. If items are extensively torn or need tape removal or stain reduction, the cost may be over $100 per item. Costs are based on the number of hours of labor at a standard shop rate. That rate covers the direct cost of the conservator's time and benefits. Additionally it covers the indirect cost of activities such as making paste or deacidification solution and cleaning up. Overhead, supervision and training are other indirect costs that must be recovered. All these add up to approximately $33 per hour.

311. Smith, Richard D. "Mass Deacidification Cost Comparisons." *College & Research Libraries News* 46 (March 1985): 122-123.

Compares the costs at the Library of Congress, the Public Archives of Canada, and at Princeton University for mass deacidification.

Four types of cost per book are identified: operational cost, capital cost, capital cost adjusted for inflation, and cost of deacidification.

Total costs range from $2.46 to $15.85 per item.

312. Thompson, Donald D. "Comparing Costs: An Examination of the Real and Hidden Costs of Different Methods of Storage." *Bulletin of the American Society of Information Science* 7 (October 1980): 14–15.

Thompson discusses the costs of microforms, weeding, and remote storage as alternatives. Hidden costs of weeding include providing a previously weeded item to a user or an inability to borrow or purchase such an item.

High-density, low cost storage involves not only construction costs but selection of materials, communications, delivery of materials and operation of the facility.

Because commercially produced microforms are not available for most materials, local filming is necessary. Again selection of items for this treatment is part of the cost. Readers and reader/printers must also be available. Gives comparative selection, implementation and per circulation costs for each of the three alternatives.

313. Weiss, Dudley A. "Need for Increased Funds for Library Binding." *Library Scene* 2 (Winter 1973): 8–10.

Compares the cost of binding, rebinding and the cost of living index in 1957/58 and in 1967/69 with costs in 1971. Although total library binding sales increased substantially, the percentage of the total library budgets allocated to binding declined. The bindery budgets in college and university libraries declined from 9% in 1968 to 3.5% in 1971 and 1972. The percentage of book budgets allocated to binding was about 8 1/2% for college and university libraries and 5 1/2% for public libraries. Seventy (70) percent of college libraries and 43% of public libraries responding to a 1972 survey by the Library Binding Institute would have allocated more funds to binding had the money been available. Only 14% of college libraries had applied for matching LSCA funds for binding periodicals. Three percent applied for funds for rebinding.

The average book, at a price of $15, if it lasts for 30 circulations, cost 50 cents per use. Rebinding extends the life to another 100 circulations, and is less expensive than replacing the item.

# Index

# Index to Bibliography

The following index to the name of authors whose works are listed in the annotated bibliography (pp. 183–278) is keyed to the number of each item.